news media and foreign relations:
a multifaceted perspective

The Ablex
Communication, Culture, & Information Series
Eileen Mahoney, The George Washington University,
Series Editor

news media and foreign relations:
a multifaceted perspective

edited by
Abbas Malek
Howard University

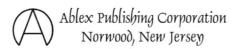

Ablex Publishing Corporation
Norwood, New Jersey

Printed in the United States of America

Library of Congress Cataloging-in-Publication Data

News media and foreign relations : a multifaceted perspective / Abbas
    Malek, editor.
        p.   cm. — (Communication, culture & information studies)
        Includes bibliographical references and index.
        ISBN 1-56750-272-5 (cloth). — ISBN 1-56750-273-3 (paper)
        1. Mass media—Political aspects. 2. Press and politics.
    3. International relations. I. Malek, Abbas. II. Series: Ablex
    communication, culture & information series.
    P95.8.N48   1996
    302.23—dc20   96-32254
                                                                        CIP

Ablex Publishing Corporation
355 Chestnut Street
Norwood, New Jersey 07648

to Cyrus Ram

Contents

acknowledgments

I would like to acknowledge and thank two important teachers, mentors, advisors, and friends, Professors Hamid Mowlana and Majid Teheranian. Dr. Mowlana introduced me to the International Communication Program at The American University while visiting us in Iran in the late 1970s. He was my advisor during my Ph.D. Program, chaired my dissertation committee, and mentored me throughout. He has been a good friend and has made valuable contributions to my professional development. Dr. Teheranian was my teacher and boss during my Masters program in Iran while, at the same time, I was working for him at Iran Communication and Development Institute. He was responsible for my coming to the U.S. and doing my Ph.D. I consider these two professors the two most important individuals in my academic life and want to thank them sincerely for all they have taught me.

As the editor, I would like to thank all the contributors to this volume and express my appreciation for their effort in meeting the deadline for the project.

My special thanks go to Dr. Florence Setzer for her continued reading of almost all my writings with strong critical views for many years. I would also like to thank Tina Patterson, my research assistant for several years, who assisted me in developing the proposal for this project. She worked on several research projects including the very last chapter in this volume.

Editors and the staff at Ablex, especially Kim Burgos and Anne Trowbridge, who worked hard on this project, deserve a very special and sincere thank you for their good work.

—*Abbas Malek*
Washington, DC
Fall 1996

about the editor

Abbas Malek, is an associate professor at the Department of Radio, Television, and Film, School of Communications, Howard University, Washington, DC. He is president of International Communication Section of IAMCR. Dr. Malek teaching and writings are in the area of telecommunication management, international/ crosscultural communication, and news media and foreign policy. Among his most recent publications are: "Islam and the West: Cultural Encounter," in *The U.S. Media and the Middle East: Image and Perception,* 1995; "Mass Media in Iran" in *Mass Media in the Middle East,* 1994; "Over Covered… Under Reported: Mandela's Visit to the United States" in *African American Communications: An Anthology in Traditional and Contemporary Studies.*

introduction

Abbas Malek

In the late 1970s and early 1980s the United States encountered several major foreign policy challenges—the Iranian Revolution—followed by the hostage crisis and the Soviets' invasion of Afghanistan. Although the Soviets' invasion of Afghanistan in 1979 was perceived as an important international crisis, the revolution in Iran and the American hostages remaining in captivity for 444 days became a major foreign policy issue facing U.S. government. At the same time, the degree to which the American media became involved in a foreign policy issue probably was unprecedented in recent history of the U.S., including during the Vietnam War.

At the time, I was a doctoral student at The School of International Service at The American University in Washington, DC. As a foreign student from Iran studying international communication in the nation's capital, I could not ask for a better chance to observe and study the role that media play in American democracy.

Having worked for and studied the media in an authoritarian society, Iran, in which throughout the history all social institutions including the media are restricted in their performance by the government, initially I was extremely impressed by the degree of freedom that American media could exercise in their coverage of American politics. Such an impression, however, withered away rather quickly after I learned more and began to examine closely the relationship between the media and government in American democracy, specifically on foreign policy issues.

As a matter of fact, my interest in the subject developed so deeply that I began a systematic study of this subject in the early stages of my doctoral work. My first study was to see whether there was a difference between the way that the free American and controlled Iranian media were covering an issue that concerned both countries, the hostage crisis. For a simple research paper for a class project a classmate, Judy Weddle, and I examined the content of two elite newspapers, one in the U.S.—*The New York Times*—and one in Iran—*Kayhan.* We discovered that the coverage in both newspapers was similar to their respective governments' official policy on the issue. From the Iranian point of view, the hostages were there for a very legitimate reason. The Iranians wanted to pressure the American government to turn over the Shah, who was in the U.S. at the time. They also wanted a guarantee against U.S. interference in the Iranian affairs of the sort that had occurred for several decades under the Shah. Another reason for hostages not being released, according to the Iranian press, was the demand for recognition of the legitimacy of the Islamic regime in Iran. From the American point of view, the first priority naturally was unconditional release of all the hostages; then came other concerns.

The findings on the Iranian press did not surprise me, knowing the traditional practices of the press in that society. However, for me it was quite interesting to note how, when it came to a critical foreign policy issue such as the hostage crisis, even an elite American paper ignored many other aspects of the issue and pursued the official governmental line. Maybe that behavior illustrates what Mowlana in this volume calls the "foreign policy culture" of the media.

The findings of this very limited study made me truly interested in the relationship between the media and government and how these two institutions act and interact in American democracy. This subject later became my major research interest. I did my dissertation on this subject, and I published several articles and presented several papers in different conferences based on these findings. As a matter of fact, the last chapter in this book is a continuation of that research.

My studies of the news media and foreign policy have convinced me that the subject matter is one of the least systematically explored areas in the field of international relations and international communication. I decided, therefore, to design a course exclusively on news media and foreign policy while I was still a Ph.D. student. The course was approved, and I have been teaching it at The American University every semester since then.

The longer I teach, research, and write about news media and foreign policy, the more I realize how important this subject is, and how scarce the resources are. This book is an attempt to add to a limited existing literature on the subject matter.

As the list of contributors to this book demonstrates, the study of news media and foreign relations does not belong to any one discipline. Studying this subject, like many other subjects in international communication and other areas of communication, requires a multi-disciplinary approach that goes beyond any one discipline. And that is why I decided to invite scholars with diverse backgrounds to contribute to this book.

The existing limited literature on the media and foreign policy is very scattered at its best. As a matter of fact, a big part of the literature is produced by scholars and professionals outside of the field of media and/or foreign policy. At the same time, a close review of the literature reveals that no theoretical framework exists to provide a focus to these studies. These points are well demonstrated in the first chapter by Malek and Wiegand. As a matter of fact, one of the purposes of the first chapter in this book is to demonstrate the state of confusion in the study of the relationship between the media and foreign policy decision-making.

The book is divided into two sections: theoretical and empirical. The purpose of the first section of the book is to lay the foundation for analysis of the role of the media in foreign relations, and the purpose of the second part is, through empirical studies, to demonstrate some of these relationships in a variety of cases. It is not the claim of this book, nor was it its intention, to be an exhaustive source, if that is possible at all.

The purpose was to present focused and diverse theoretical and empirical studies on the role that media play in foreign relations.

In the first chapter, Malek and Wiegand demonstrate the chaotic state of scholarly work and the level of disagreement among writers in the field. The next two chapters are an attempt to produce a theoretical framework for analysis. In chapter two Professor Mowlana suggests that "the study of the media and foreign policy should take into account the multifaced nature of the phenomenon by focusing on" several dimensions: "1) the culture of foreign policy, 2) the decision-making process, 3) public opinion and interest groups, 4) modern communication technology, 5) security, peace and war, 6) economic and trade as foreign policy, and 7) culture and information as foreign policy." Professor Ebo in chapter three examines the dynamic between media diplomacy and foreign policy in the context of national identity, international image and global political power. He argues that, although the primary goal of foreign policy remains the promotion of national interests in the international arena, the strategies have changed. The ability of a nation to use the media to construct an international image is the major focus of the chapter, and the shift from military power to "information power" forms the major thesis of his chapter.

Chapters four demonstrates the use, and to some extent the abuse, of modern media technologies in the conduct of foreign relations. Professor Venturelli argues that "information liberalization applied through the emerging framework of the 'global information highway' is one of the most important forces for advancing the political aims of liberal internationalism which predominantly favor the reconstitution of the world system on the basis of the large-scale proprietary interests." She warns us of the urgency of "assessing the regulatory framework of the information age, which will fix the structures of public communications for the next century."

The section closes with Professor Rivenburgh's chapter, in which she argues that "the study of social identification offers a largely unexplored framework for analyzing media within the foreign policy process. The general logic to this recommendation comes from the view that the analysis of foreign policy is essentially the study of social or intergroup behavior—in this case the relations among nation-states."

The second section of the book opens with a general discussion of the relationship among three institutions in the American political system: the President, Congress, and the media. Professor Bonafede, a long term scholar and practitioner of media, in this chapter discusses how the separate institutions share power in the conduct of American foreign policy. He also demonstrates that how "the emergence of advanced mass communications technology following World War II, with its emphasis on imagery and symbolism... compelled foreign policy decision-makers to be skilled communicators and to establish a symbiotic relationship with an increasingly pervasive news media." In chapter seven Professor Barton provides us with a specific historical analysis of how policy-makers interpret the portrayals of public opinion by the media and use them "to construct an internal rhetoric within the policy-making culture to persuade colleagues about a policy direction, and a corresponding externally directed communications strategy that serves as public relations for the policy." In chapter eight Professor Hackett takes another look at the coverage of the Persian Gulf War by the media in the Canadian and American cases. He assesses the relationship between the press and foreign policy by examining "how the press treats opposition to the State's foreign policy." Professor Cassara in Chapter nine examines one specific foreign policy issue— human rights in Central and South America—during the Carter Administration. In this chapter she explores "the connection between the Carter human rights policy and newspaper coverage of Central and South America." The study is set "to examine one aspect of the interaction of presidential foreign policy initiatives and American press coverage of foreign news." In chapter ten Professor Carrier discusses the "the danger and merits of the global news systems." She presents two schools of thought on the effects of globalization and domestification of global news services and the implications of each system for the national and foreign policy of a nation. Professor Grosswiler, in chapter eleven presents a study of prominent U.S. newspapers editorial coverage of the remaining Communist states in the Post-Cold War era. "Now that the Cold War has ended, the loss of this ideology, its symbols and images may affect the relationship of the media and government in the foreign policy process," he hypothesizes. Then he argues that "the media help shape the way that the public perceives political issues, whether those media symbols are real or imagined." Professor Zaffiro in chapter twelve "investigates [the] relationship between news media and foreign policy in the Republic of Botswana, a France-sized, Southern African democracy of 1.4 million people." Professor Zaffiro demonstrates the difference between the analysis of the relationship between the news media and government in an African country and a Western nation. And in the last chapter, Malek closes the book with a discussion of how, in contrast to the popular belief, the media (here *The New York Times*) have not learned from the past. He details and compares the coverage by the *NYT* of the Iranian revolution and, later on, of the Iran–Iraq war, concluding that "the press, to a great extent, merely reflects the U.S. government's policy toward a particular international issue or event." And if such a finding can be generalized, then one may question the theoretical foundations of belief concerning American media as they relate to the relationship between media and government.

part I

theoretical perspectives

chapter 1

news media and foreign policy: an integrated review

Abbas Malek
Howard University

Krista E. Wiegand
The American University

—These capabilities of modern media to be immediate, sensational, and persuasive
are unsettling the conduct of foreign affairs.
—James F. Hoge, Jr., 1994, p. 136

—A daily assembly line of proposals, tips, press releases, documents, and
interviews rolls out of the White House and the various federal departments.
In a matter of hours, the networks, wire services, and major dailies are
telling the public what the government wants them to hear.
—Michael Parenti, 1986, p. 229

—We can put aside myths that the press in reporting foreign policy is either a
left-wing (or right wing), pushy, opinion-molding, policy destroying political
participant, or a patsy, malleable, myopic sponge under the sway of
crafty public officials.
—Nicholas Berry, 1990, p. xiv

Are the media truly influential enough to sway not only public opinion, but foreign policy itself? Or is it the government that not only manipulates, but controls the media's every statement about foreign policy? Perhaps the media and the government coordinate their manipulation of public opinion of foreign policy. It is even possible that neither the media nor the government purposely intend to sway each other; rather, the system is controlled by chance.

Regardless of the possible framework into which the current relationship of the media and the foreign policy establishment fits, the relationship itself has always been rough. Only in the last few decades has this complex relationship gained real notice among scholars, foreign policymakers, journalists, and the public. Until the late 1960s, in fact, the media's relationship with foreign policy was limited in many ways. Thus, research about this relationship was close to nonexistent. Rather, existing research focused primarily on the role of the media in domestic affairs.

INFLUENCING POLICY: DOMESTIC VERSUS FOREIGN

There is a distinct difference between the media's involvement in domestic policy and their role in the foreign policy process. Too many scholars and journalists have made faulty assumptions about the media's role in the foreign policy process based on studies of the media's reporting of domestic policy. According to several scholars who are aware of the distinction, there are a number of reasons why studies of the media's involvement in domestic policy have little relevance to the foreign policy realm.

Graber pointed out that political pressure on the media is greater in the realm of foreign affairs than on domestic issues (1989, p. 336). Berry explained that foreign policy issues are much more removed from the minds of the public, and the process in which the media participate is much different in regards to foreign policy. According to Paletz and Entman, domestic issues are simply better understood by the public than foreign issues. Additionally, Paletz and Entman claimed that the media seem to allow themselves to be manipulated by powerful government elites whose interest is to further manipulate public opinion (1981, p. 231).

AN EVOLUTION IN THOUGHT

Until Lippmann wrote about the media's influence on public opinion in 1922, the relationship between the media and the foreign policy process was barely researched. Many possible reasons existed, including: a lack of access to information about foreign policy by the media, a lack of public interest in foreign affairs, a less developed state of media technology, a lack of media expertise in foreign affairs, and the fact that during this period the media were not a well developed social institution as far as the field of international affairs was concerned.

Early research about relationship between the media and foreign policy focused primarily on two related issues—the influence of the media on public opinion and the role of the media in foreign policy decision making. In 1922, long before the electronic revolution in communication, Lippmann wrote about the apprehension concerning the impact of the media's coverage of foreign affairs on public perception, stating that the pictures formed in the public's minds by the media were the leading source from which public opinion was formed. The media's influence on public opinion in regards to foreign policy issues has been one of the main concerns of scholars in the field through the century.

Other early scholars in the field believed that the media wielded great influence in the foreign policy-making process. Douglass and Bomer (1932) viewed the media as a "key factor in international relations" (Qtd. in Chang, 1993, p. 24). Stowe (1936) noted that the media played a crucial role in every international conflict, and Coggeshall (1934) indicated that the media have strong diplomatic influence (Chang, 1993, p. 24).

Cohen's pathbreaking study *The Press and Foreign Policy* (1963), which concluded early-on that the media defined and performed their job by themselves, put into perspective the relevance of the media-government relationship. Representing scholars of a new era, Cohen observed reporters as having two simultaneous roles, among others—that of informing the public and explaining foreign policy, and that of participating in the foreign policy process by questioning and criticizing the government decision makers.

Today, scholars of diverse points of view are more concerned about the media's foreign policy role not only because the media themselves have changed over the decades, but also because, according to some scholars, the foreign policy establishment has changed as well. As Judis wrote, "American foreign policy, once the realm of the gods, has become the domain of mere influence peddlers" (1992, p. 55). Herman and Chomsky (1988) agreed, claiming that the elite of the United States are now more consistently reluctant to face the public on the issue of foreign policy conflicts, thus depending on the media to play this role.

THREE PERSPECTIVES OF MEDIA INFLUENCE: ACTIVE, PASSIVE, NEUTRAL

At one end of the spectrum are scholars who believe that the media play a highly active role in influencing decisions made in the foreign policy arena, viewing the media as "a watchdog, an independent observer, an active participant, or a catalyst" (e.g. Cohen, 1963). This opinion is supported by journalists, themselves, as well as scholars whose approach is practical and focuses on mass communication more than foreign policy and political science (Siebert, Peterson, & Schramm, 1956). Moyers (1969) viewed the media as having "the privilege of trying to find out all it can about what is going on" in the government (p. 36). This notion of an all-powerful, authoritative media enthralls journalists and supporters of the news media (Chang, 1993, p. 7).

At the other end of the spectrum are scholars in the same field who view the media as "no more than a pawn in the political game played by the powerful political authority and establishment in Washington" (Chang, 1993, p. 7). Proponents of this view believe that the media, structurally, serve as an instrument in the actual implementation of foreign policy. Nimmo & Combs (1980) viewed the notion of an adversarial media as a "political myth." Rather, the media tend to support the elite class and already existing political initiatives, as discussed by Altschull (1984) Gitlin (1980), Hallin (1987), and Tuchman (1974), all of whom lean toward the notion that the news media only validate the government's decisions by deferring to authority. Some writers have taken this view one step further by asserting that the media act as part of a "propaganda model" (Herman & Chomsky, 1988).

Naturally, there does lie a middle ground. Scholars differ widely in their backgrounds and opinions, but most tend to fall between the two extremes. Whether these approaches should and can be integrated into a formative approach is a question of whether such integration would limit the ability of the field to continue introducing ever changing concepts, challenging the elites.

Scholars who fall into this middle category include Hero (1959), Cohen (1963), Allison (1971), Davision (1974), Batscha (1975), Kern, Levering, & Levering (1983), Ciofi-Revilla, Merritt, & Zinnes (1987), Herman and Chomsky (1988), Berry (1990), and Serfaty (1990). These writers, to one degree or another, argue that neither the media nor the government are as manipulative as extreme positions suggest, nor do they work together to manipulate public opinion. In addition, other scholars, journalists, and representatives of the foreign policy establishment have presented other points of view that do not fit neatly into these categories.

GOVERNMENT MANIPULATION OF THE MEDIA

Those who believe that the government manipulates the media question whether the foreign policy establishment's strong influence on the media limits diversity of opinions about controversial foreign policy issues (Brown and Vincent, 1995). Regardless of the answer, several scholars in the field have claimed that the government, and specifically the Executive Branch, manipulates the media so that its own policy agendas are protected and portrayed positively to the public (see Sigal, 1973; Deakin, 1984; Denton and Woodward, 1985; Tebbel and Watts, 1985; Bennett, 1988; Herman and Chomsky, 1988; Hertsgaard, 1988; and Streitmatter, 1988).

The media's "deference to authority" concerning the foreign policy establishment is an issue raised by other scholars as well. Trattner wrote that the government influences "how, even whether, a story is written" (1982, p. 104), especially because the media tend to depend greatly on official government news sources (Nimmo, 1978). Rourke argued that only the government is capable of gratifying "the hunger of the communications media for news about public affairs" (1961, pp. 197–198). Perhaps the most extreme viewpoint is represented by Herman and Chomsky, who described their "propaganda model" as a system in which news is filtered through money and power, meeting the interests of the elite and not of the public (1988).

In effect, the "elite domination of the media and marginalization of dissidents" (Herman & Chomsky, 1988, p. 2) occurs in such a way that the media, as other scholars have noted, become unaware of the self-screening which they are conducting, convincing themselves of their supposed objectivity. The media's "societal role" becomes one of defending the economic, political, and social goals of the dominating elite, whose private interests dominate the agenda. The media are not adversarial, but instead they lack real interest in challenging the elite class, according to Herman and Chomsky (1988). Yet, of course, debate and dissent are encouraged to some degree, they noted, as long as the elites are not destroyed.

Herman and Chomsky viewed the media's societal role as both presenting a "tolerably realistic portrayal of the world," and simultaneously meeting the requirements and interests of those who dominate the media—the corporate world and the government (1988, p. 303). The news media are perhaps most effective, they claimed, at providing information supported by the system through the function of propaganda by "reliance on market forces, internalized assumptions, and self-censorship, and without significant overt coercion" (1988, p. 306).

Herman and Chomsky also noted that,

> [t]he mass media are not a solid monolith on all issues. Where the powerful are in disagreement, there will be a certain diversity of tactical judgments on how to attain generally shared aims, reflected in media debate. But views that challenge fundamental premises or suggest that the observed modes of exercise of state power are based on systemic factors will be excluded from the mass media even when elite controversy over tactics rages fiercely (1988, p. xii).

Additionally, Herman and Chomsky asserted that, overall, the media support the elites, and when, indeed, there exist facts which undermine the elites, such facts are usually found buried in the back pages of the newspaper. They concluded that, although it is not as evident as in many other nations, suppression of facts is a regular practice of the news media in America.

Gans (1979) discussed the media's reluctance to oppose the government as a watchdog, arguing that the media's support of the elite resulted from the fact that journalists, who are mostly middle-class citizens, share similar societal values as those with power. The result of this similarity is journalists' tendency to support the elite, especially favoring those with the most power, the foreign policy establishment. Herman asserted that the media "serve mainly as a supportive arm of the state and dominant elites, focusing heavily on what is serviceable to them, and debating and exposing within accepted frames of reference" (1993, p. 25). He even ventured to state that the dominant media are actually members of the elite establishment.

Since the owners of the media are part of the elite, according to Herman, they must maintain support of the status quo based on their "extensive social and business connections to other business and government leaders" (1993, p. 26), especially since the media depend on the government for licenses and contracts, and on business for advertising. Although this point could be made across the board relative to all media involvement in policy, it is especially true concerning foreign policy, since the foreign policy establishment represents the most elite group within the government.

Dorman and Fahrang (1987) questioned "the press' inability or unwillingness to exercise judgment independent of that of official Washington" based on economic, commercial, and structural factors which cause distortion of reporting about international affairs. Why would the media conform to official Washington policy? The answer, some scholars have indicated, is that a shared ideology exists, and in some cases there is a lack of any other position publicly advanced, creating a situation in which the media know of no alternative position.

The U.S. Press and Iran, written by Dorman and Fahrang, asks why, indeed, the media strongly support the elite class in a number of foreign policy issues. Dorman and Fahrang concluded that there are real ideological reasons why the media do not oppose the status quo, based on "ideological lens ground by official Washington" (Qtd. in Bennett, 1992, p. 771). Among the ideological hurdles that "American journalists have to overcome before coverage of foreign affairs will improve is their belief that they are nonideological... precisely because journalists believe they are above and beyond ideology they are most susceptible to its effects" (Qtd. in Bennett, 1992, p. 772). Wicker (1979) professed that the media system rarely could turn against the establishment because "it mirrors rather well the character of the American community," (p. 19) implying that the commitment to patriotism and to the nation which the government represents is perhaps stronger than some wish to believe.

MEDIA DEPENDENCE: THE FOURTH BRANCH OF GOVERNMENT

As one critic noted vehemently, "Unfortunately, the version of events served up by our media elite is a steady diet of tendentious news stories carefully designed to serve the political purposes of American liberalism" (Rusher, 1988, p. 32). Rusher concluded that the media had become a fourth branch of the government, and several scholars agree. Others strongly disagree. Zeidenstein, like many scholars who take this stance, stated simply, "the White House can influence—if not completely control—the content, timing, and methods of publicizing the news" (1984, p. 391).

Allison (1971) did not hold the media responsible for being influenced the way they are by foreign policy decision-makers. His classic model of decision-making in foreign policy discussed how decisions were made by an inner circle of elite decision- makers who look at the whole picture. The media represent the outer circle, with limited ability to obtain classified and restricted information, leaving them at a distinct disadvantage, without the capacity to challenge policies as much as their watchdog role inhibits. Reston stated that "it may be true that the influence of the press is so great," but regarding its influence on foreign policy, this notion is "out of date and wildly inaccurate" (1967, p. 45), which Chang (1993) claimed the current literature seems to support. As Allison (1971) asserted, only a handful of policy-makers truly have the access and ability to form policy in the foreign arena, and the media are quite limited in their roles.

Graber wrote that the "bulk of foreign affairs news for the American media actually originates in Washington from various beats in the executive branch" (1989, p. 341). According to Becker, the media are "dependent on governmental sources to provide focus for and information about world events" (1977, p. 364). Tuchman (1974) pointed out as well that the routine of gathering news is parallel to official news primarily because a majority of news stories relate to pre-scheduled government events and issues. Welch wrote that it is inevitable that foreign policy produces "a great deal of the news" (1971, p. 329), noting the domineering characteristic of international issues and events in the media. Thus, perhaps, the media lack any choice of whether they are manipulated if it is the only way to obtain valuable information about the foreign policy process.

THE EXECUTIVE BRANCH AND THE MEDIA

According to Parenti (1986), the government influences the media substantially by providing information and misinformation designed deliberately to present a specific point of view. Parenti argued that the White House specifically controls the media tightly—with correspondents only having access to information from the White House through scheduled meetings, briefings, and press conferences, creating a lack of other options for the media. Additionally, Parenti described the White House as having the capacity to discretely kill media coverage of controversial issues, deny interviews, withhold information, and give misleading information (1986, p. 230).

Such manipulative actions by the Executive Branch, which dominates the foreign policy process, are known by scholars in the field as "spinning a story." According to these same scholars, certain government officials, known as White House "spin doctors" manipulate the media for "political propaganda" and control all access to vital information about foreign policy issues (Jamieson, 1984; Herman, 1993; Brown and Vincent, 1995). *The Media and Foreign Policy*, edited by Serfaty, includes several works by various writers who agreed that the media rely heavily on official news sources and that "spin control" methods are utilized by the government to manage the flow of information to the media. Most of these writers are people who have previously worked for the government and/or the media, and turned to teaching and research (Larson, 1992, p. 159).

A study conducted by Weisman (1984) indicated that, during his first term, President Reagan introduced several different means of dealing with the media simply known as the "art of controlled access," which have influenced the types of information that are passed on to the public. The implication, Weisman wrote, was that such manipulation probably undermined the media's function within the system of checks and balances. Zeidenstein (1984) cited several methods of controlling the media, which included the control of briefings, meetings, and the release of pictures, and the timing of news releases. Additionally, the government manipulates methods of publicizing information or misinformation by planting questions, releasing items to specific newspapers, testing reactions by selective leaks.

Presidential and other governmental influences on the reporting of foreign policy by the media range from leaks of information, deliberate and non-deliberate, to official press conferences, interviews, speeches, news releases, and public briefings. Scholars including Cohen (1963), Graber (1989), Mickelson (1972), Nimmo (1978), Rainey

(1975), Strouse (1975), Wallach (1982), Bennett (1990), Serfaty (1990), and many others have discussed the one-way channel through which the government directly and indirectly informs the media on foreign policy issues. News management, as this phenomenon is called in the literature, is a concept also discussed by Schudson (1978), Zeidenstein (1984), Hohenberg (1968), Linsky (1990), and Chang (1993), among others. Similar to "spinning a story," news management is just as manipulative in the eyes of many scholars.

According to several scholars, journalists are pressured indirectly by the foreign policy establishment to advocate their policies through official leaks and the passing of "secret" information (Hilsman, 1967; Dorman and Fahrang, 1987; Berry, 1990; Chang, 1993). Berry (1990) has pointed out a number of means by which the government evades the media: by leaking specific information, covering facts through secrecy, overwhelming the media with press releases, and officially staged events. Wise (1973) claimed that secrecy is employed by the government in order to control how information is interpreted by the media, and through the media by the people. Grossman and Rourke (1976) considered secrecy by the government as a potent weapon. Paletz and Entman (1980) agreed. The motivation is simple—the government, especially the Executive Branch, often fears that publicity concerning certain delicate foreign policy issues may damage their position (Weisman, 1984).

According to Manheim and Albritton (1984), there was a growing trend in the use of public relations firms by the national government in the early 1980s to improve its image by actively trying to interject items into the agenda-setting framework. A study of the public perception of seven countries indicated that after a public relations firm intervened, perceptions shifted. According to Manheim and Albritton, such intervention represented direct manipulation of the media, which further influenced public opinion.

Paletz and Entman (1980) argued that the President, himself, is capable of producing "news of his own devising, knowing the media will cover him and it. Particularly in foreign affairs, the President's agenda items become the media's priorities…" (p. 417). Geyun (1990) agreed, citing that there is a distinct "power of the President to set the agenda" (p. 32) in the case of news. Ostman and Babcock (1983) claimed further that the President's role "includes the strong possibility that he sets the agenda for the press" (p. 114).

Grossman and Kumar (1981) explained that the relationship between the President and the media is probably best described as one of cooperation. Locander believed that when certain foreign policy issues entice media coverage, "abnormal presidential-press cooperation" occurs (1979, p. 267). Other scholars, including Welch (1971, 1972), Morris (1974), Braestrup (1978), and Larson (1986), have agreed that it is the Executive Branch which strongly influenced the media in foreign policy. Kern, going a step further, asserted that journalists view foreign affairs "through the White House lens" (1981, p. 111).

The President's ultimate ability to form policy in certain cases could be influenced partly by the open-ended access that he has to news media, as some scholars have argued (Rosenbaum et al, 1971, p. 344). This access is cited as the President's "greatest single advantage over his legislative opposition" (Johnson and Walker, 1964, p. 272). Chang (1989) conducted a study of foreign policy pertaining to China during a certain period, and found that the initiative for foreign policy remained in the hands of the President, with the media only reporting what he stated. Grossman and Rourke stated, "the president's ability to determine what news he will exchange for publicity is almost unlimited" (1976, p. 457). Reston declared that the media "may report the news, but the President makes it" (1967, p. 186).

ISSUE COMPLEXITY AND MEDIA PREPAREDNESS

It is not only limited access to information from the government that interferes with the media's capacity to report freely. Foreign policy issues are clearly more complex than domestic policy issues and are more difficult with which to identify. Dorman and Fahrang (1987) discussed this phenomenon at length, describing the media's inability to understand the revolutionary movement in Iran in the late 1970s and how this grossly affected the way the media reported the issue. "To the extent that mainstream journalism failed in Iran," they wrote, "it did so for ideological and ethnocentric reasons rather than because of the economics of the industry or because the press was victimized by a manipulative government, as is more commonly argued in such failures" (Dorman and Fahrang, 1987, p. 204).

Dorman and Fahrang claimed that the media were incapable of understanding the political culture in Iran, and thus they had no choice but to support the position of the American government. Such is the case with many foreign policy issues, according to some scholars. These observers did not view the governmental influence on the media as necessarily manipulative, but rather viewed the media as naive and unprepared to tackle certain issues. Malek (1984) agreed, claiming that the media's failure to be more analytical and investigative resulted in poor coverage of Iranian affairs and thus contributed to the surprise of the Iranian revolution in the West. He also found that newspaper editorials and official government positions on Iranian internal and external affairs were very similar, except during the time of the revolution. During that time, the media became skeptical and their opinions eventually formed the basis for a shift in foreign policy (Malek, 1988).

Welch conducted a study of media coverage of Indochina from 1950 to 1956 and found that the "press response mirrored administration perceptions of the struggle" (1972, p. 225). She found that the American media were incapable of perceiving the Indochina case any differently than did the administration because the media did not have an independent frame of reference. The problem with this mirroring is that the only information given to the public by the media represents the position of the government. Most people do not experience direct contact with foreign events which call for foreign policy, thus forcing the public to depend solely on the media for information and opinion and these, in most cases, are official government positions (Welch, 1972).

In covering the developing world specifically, according to Dorman (1986), the media have tended to take a "parachute journalism" approach in which they only react to events immediately when they have occurred. Journalists' lack of familiarity with the countries and cultures they cover has made media coverage of foreign issues general and reliant on self-interested, official government sources, not only in the U.S. but also in the host country. Therefore, journalists have not necessarily reported about the reality of the country, but rather the perception of the American and foreign governments in power. Dorman recommended that to prevent such reactionary reporting, the media should be better prepared to anticipate foreign events, so they would not have to rely so heavily on official government sources (1986).

Serfaty and supporting writers (1990) have explained that the media have become so internationalized they represent transnational actors and forces. Yet Serfaty was not very critical of the media's lack of cultural relevance. "Information that was once the sole province of governments," he wrote, "is now routinely scrutinized in real time— or its functional equivalent, the same-day news—by cadres of trained and independent professionals" (Serfaty, 1990, p. 1). The media may exert pressure on policy-makers in terms of time constraints, but this is far from setting the substance and shape of foreign policy. Serfaty concluded that the media had alleviated indifference toward world events with increasing and more competent coverage, that foreign coverage in news was improving, and that there remained a generally free channel of information between the government and the media.

According to Graber (1989) though, there is not at all a free flow of information in regards to foreign issues. Rather, the foreign correspondent is the gatekeeper of information about foreign events and issues involving American foreign policy. Due to cost constraints, only a small number of newspapers and networks have maintained foreign offices, and thus a large percentage of foreign affairs coverage has to come from a very limited number of sources. Additionally, the foreign correspondent has more discretion to interpret foreign issues and policy since the public audience is primarily uninformed and often uninterested in foreign affairs. Therefore, the media have maintained an important role as a filter for what is important and unimportant in international affairs coverage (Graber, 1989). Hoge agreed that "[t]he news media may influence but mostly follow the politicians' agenda" (1994, p. 144), limiting their own perceptions. Yet, he also noted that policy-makers must adjust to the powerful capacities of the media, since "[i]n the absence of persuasive government strategy, the media will be catalytic" (Hoge, 1994, p. 138). Several writers have agreed with Hoge, claiming that the media are just as powerful, if not more influential in the foreign policy arena, than the government.

Scholars' assessments of the media's influence on the foreign policy process have differed widely across the board, ranging from the media acting as an "important information source" (See Arno and Dissanayake, 1984; Bennett et al, 1985; and Just and Crigler, 1989) to the media wielding power in informing citizens of foreign policy and playing a key role in agenda setting (See Hopple, 1982; Bennett and Edelman, 1985; Larson, 1986; and Kieh, 1990).

Perhaps these opinions derive from the distrust many scholars have had of the government's influence on the media and the idea that the media "should not make peace with the government" (Modern Media Institute, 1983, p. 26). The notion of an adversarial media tends to appeal to those in the media who fear that a close, supporting relationship of the media and the government will not benefit the nation in the long term (See Serfaty, 1990, Dennis and Merrill, 1991, pp. 26–30). On the other hand, Bray wrote in *Foreign Policy* that the government and the press needed to forge a closer relationship in order to better serve the interests of the country (1976).

Reston noted in 1966 that it was "typical of how journalists view their role in the arena of foreign policy making," and that they "believe, contrary to the empirical evidence, that the news media engage in the making of American foreign policy" (Qtd. in Chang, 1993, p. 1), (See Kaiser, 1977; Koppel, 1985). Reston's classic *The Artillery of the Press* (1966) dealt specifically with this issue, focusing on how active the media were in the foreign policy process. Reston emphasized the importance of revealing negative issues and criticizing the foreign policy establishment when necessary, on behalf of the people.

Most journalists view their role in the foreign policy process as participatory, regardless of the limited access they may have to government information. Journalists can also withhold information in some cases if they are aware that publicity would indeed damage foreign policy initiatives. Chittick (1970) recognized that journalists seem to understand when national security is involved and when to withhold pertinent information. Gans (1979) stated that the media are not dominated by liberal elites, as most neo-conservatives would argue, but rather that the media actually train themselves to ignore certain story implications at times, not allowing the government to manipulate them (Herman, 1993, p. 24). On the other hand, there are also cases in which, if journalists were not able to recognize how delicate an issue was, the government applied pressure on the media to back off to some degree (Schanberg, 1991).

THE MEDIA AS POLICY-MAKER: DEGREES OF INFLUENCE

Scholarly works point out the diversity of the media's influence in actually setting the foreign policy agenda (See Noelle-Neumann, 1974; Benton and Frazier, 1976; Carlsson, Dahlberg, and Rosengren, 1982; Rikardsson, 1981; and Cook, et al, 1983). Chang (1993) has asserted that the media "have become a power center in their own right."

The news media have, over the years, come to be viewed as the "opinion-makers" (Rivers, 1967), "king-maker" (Robinson, 1974), the "forth branch of the government" (Cater 1959), the "shadow government" (Rivers, 1982), or the "third presence" (Serfaty, 1990)"—all of which recognize and accept the critical power that the media have in the foreign policy process. Braestrup (1978) argued that the press actually distorted the reality of the Tet military offensive in 1968. Likewise, Linsky (1990) wrote that the national media have a large impact on federal policy, whether domestic or foreign policy oriented. Schorr pointed out that journalists were also able to alter foreign policy concerning the Kurdish question following the Persian Gulf War due to the impact of television images of Kurdish refugees (1991).

Even if the media do not attempt to influence the government in the foreign policy-making process, the policy-makers still depend on the media on a daily basis to measure public opinion about their foreign policies. The media represent the strongest link between policy-makers and the public; thus, policy-makers have little choice but to assess the media's publications on a regular basis in order to be able to "build effective political support among the public" (Chang, 1993, p. 27). Additionally, as many scholars have noted (e.g., Cohen, 1957, 1973; Elder, 1960; Davision, 1976; and Kegley and Wittkopf, 1979), foreign policy-makers tend to associate the media's coverage of foreign policy issues with public interest in the issues.

Likewise, the "press contributes to international agreement insofar as it illuminates the issues under negotiation, helps to ensure intra-governmental coordination, links governments with interested publics and provides supplementary communication channels for diplomacy," according to Davision (1974, p. 174). Davision claimed that the media have provided a pool of shared information for the government, but also present positions which have made the atmosphere for negotiations difficult. Cutler indicated that television particularly has placed increased pressure on the Executive Branch and policy-makers, due to reduced response times to foreign events and issues (Cutler, 1984).

Ledeen asserted that press clippings help to determine the daily political agenda and even provide a starting point for the nightly news, although this reliance is potentially harmful for policy formation. Ledeen suggested that steps should be taken to make sure that the role played by the media in foreign policy formation is secondary (1984). On a more conservative note, Lefever contended that "recent developments in the mass press, which both reflect and exacerbate certain flaws in American society, jeopardize the future of the United States as a great and humane power" (1976, p. 209). Foreign policy, he claimed, has been hindered "by the combined impact of Vietnam, revisionist ideology, disillusionment with detente, and weariness with the burdens of global responsibility" (Lefever, 1976, p. 224).

COHEN AND THE "INTERDEPENDENCE" THINKERS

As Cohen pointed out, the media often inform the government, especially Congress, of world events. Cohen's 1963 work, *The Press and Foreign Policy*, which has been cited as the "last major empirical exploration of the relationship between the media and United States foreign policy", presented a "two-step theory", according to which the media influence opinion-makers who influence the government. According to Cohen, the media have "become an integral factor in the process of foreign policy-making in the United States today—a factor so deeply involved and of such central concern that its elimination would radically and fundamentally alter the very character of that process" (1965, p. 196).

What is key about Cohen's position is that although he asserted that "[t]he press in its collective sense is perhaps the single most important voice in the foreign policy field; as informer, interpreter, advocate, critic," he also pointed out that the media represent "a continuous and articulate link between foreign policy officials in the government and those people on the outside who follow world events" (1965, p. 194). Therefore, regardless of the degree of influence flowing from the media to the government, and from the government and media to the public, there always exists a fundamental linkage between these institutions. Since Cohen's analysis in the 1960s, many scholars have realized the immense importance of this fundamental linkage, pointing out that it is not necessarily important to know which institution is stronger, but rather to recognize that they do indeed influence each other.

For scholars who think along these lines, the media and the foreign policy establishment are not independent institutions. Rather, both institutions play varying participatory roles, influencing each other both purposely and unconsciously, in an interdependent mode. According to Paletz and Entman, the media play a contradictory role, influencing and protecting the government at times and the American people at other times. Paletz and Entman indicated that the media simultaneously influence the decision-making process and the actions of the government, protect the powerful from being accountable to the people, reallocate power, minimize the ability of the people to respond to political events, stir discontent among the people, and preserve the status quo of the political, economic, and social system (1981, p. 6).

If anything, Paletz and Entman believed that the "media simultaneously disrupt and defend the status quo" (1981, p. ix). They asserted that through the "foreign news formula" the media tended to favor the positions of the elite of the American government giving the elite special access to the media, and creating an interdependent relationship (1981, p. 230). It is ironic that most journalists refuse to admit they are working with the government and not pursuing an adversarial role as a watchdog institution. For example, Paletz and Entman described the media's contribution to supporting the elite's status quo positions on foreign affairs as occurring "unintentionally, often unconsciously, or even against their will" (1981, p. 233).

Thus, when the media are criticized for their lack of thorough international coverage in the past, they defend themselves by claiming that in general there exists a lack of time, knowledge, labor, and interest. Yet, the reality is that the media tend to report about international issues and events which specifically coincide with the interests of the powerful elite, thus sustaining the status quo (Paletz and Entman, 1981, p. 216).

Although Herman and Chomsky (1988) viewed the government as manipulative of the media, they have also maintained a basic belief that the media serve to mobilize support for the special interests that dominate the state and private activity, even though the assumed role of the media is that they are "independent and committed to discovering and reporting the truth, and that they do not merely reflect the world as powerful groups wish it to be perceived" (p. xi). Such being the case, "the standard view of how the system works is at serious odds with reality" (p. xi), according to Herman and Chomsky (1988).

THE MEDIA'S PURPOSE AND ROLE:
A DILEMMA IN THOUGHT

Entman (1989) explored the ideals and realities of the relationships between the media and government and between the media and society, arguing that while in principle the media should foster democracy, they do not do so in reality. Rather, "[r]estricted by the limited tastes of the audience and reliant upon political elites for most information, journalists participate in an interdependent news system, not a free market of ideas" (Entman, 1989, p. 3). DeYoung agreed, stating that the government needs the media to get its foreign affairs message to the public, and simultaneously the government has linked criticism by the media with lack of patriotism (1985).

According to Manning (1968), "On many of the most serious and most sensitive questions of foreign affairs today, press and government diverge in their purposes and in their obligations" (p. 149). He wrote that it was the fault of both the media and the government, which lacked the ability or interest to scrutinize issues at face value to meet their own concerns. In regards to foreign affairs, there has been a conflict, "far less clear-cut, far more elusive" (p. 150) between the media, the government, and the public. Manning also recommended increased partnership between the government and the media in order to produce a better informed public (1968).

Claiming that the media were in "considerable disarray" (p. 150), Manning questioned the degree of realistic responsibility in which the media act in their reporting of foreign policy. Should the media report the truth, even if doing so seems counter to the nation's foreign policy, or is it the responsibility of the media to support the national interest, regardless of their ethical opinions? Cohen (1965) pointed out that during the 1960s some observers of American foreign affairs "wished that the American press would do a more complete job of foreign affairs reporting" (p. 195). On the other hand, there were also observers who "argued that the movement of delicate issues of foreign policy from the privacy of the Foreign Offices to the front pages of the newspapers" led to decreased political efficacy (p. 195).

In 1966, Reston pointed out that regardless of the medium, journalists shared the common problem of whether it was better to report the truth and embarrass officials, or to protect their country. Batscha believed that the obligation to report the truth, however, was far stronger than that to protect the status quo (1975, p. ix). Scholars have split into distinct schools of thought regarding this complex issue.

O'Heffernan conducted a study which "sought to test the general hypothesis that the U.S. foreign policy makers perceive that the policy process is profoundly affected by the mass media in a number of important and identifiable ways" (1991, p. xii). Contending that Cohen's work was out of date, O'Heffernan based his study on the notion that the globalization of media in recent decades has greatly affected and changed the interaction between the two institutions. His study demonstrated that the media and the foreign policy establishment are interdependent actors, exploiting and benefitting each other. He believed that the media were active players in the policy process and that the government also played a significant role in media coverage by use of the media to publicize its policy intentions (1991, p. 113).

Contrary to the often-held belief that the media and government maintain adversarial roles, Guzzardi has claimed that although the media and government profess to dislike each other, in reality they need each other. The media have "become a tremendous—and often unappreciated—force for legitimizing governmental institutions and free enterprise," Guzzardi asserted (1985, p. 2). Arno pointed out that the media can become actors in conflict situations involving foreign issues, but primarily, "[m]edia, like all social actors are never completely autonomous but are meshed into interdependent relationships with other groups and sectors of society (1984, p. 14). Bethell agreed, stating that the "media and government lean on each other because they need each other to survive and prosper" (1977, p. 33).

MINIMAL DEPENDENCE–MINIMAL MANIPULATION

Berry (1990) also viewed the relationship between the media and foreign policy establishment as interdependent. Yet contrary to O'Heffernan's view, Berry noted that the media are neither participants, nor manipulated by the government; rather, the media play a minimal independent role in foreign policy, and government manipulation of the press is just as minimal. He contended that the media are completely aware of the government's attempts to manipulate them, and they are simultaneously able to successfully defy such manipulation. He sees the media "reporting events the way they see them," indicating that the media are neither powerful in influencing foreign policy, nor managed by the government in a manipulative sense (Berry, 1990, p. x).

Unlike some scholars who have described either the media or the government as manipulative, and others who believed both the media and government manipulate each other, Berry's stance is based on the notion that the media tend to report about issues uncritically in the early stages of the policy process, and only when policy fails do they become more intricately involved. The thrust of Berry's 1990 work, *Foreign Policy and the Press*, was to "challenge some conventional wisdom about the press," claiming that the media were just not capable of evaluating foreign policy at the early stages because it was more important for journalists to gather initial information and listen to government officials (p. xiii).

Berry believed that it was unnecessary for the government to manipulate the media if foreign policy was successful. Only when foreign policy was failing would the media criticize the government, pursuing its watchdog role. "Failure is the sunlight," Berry wrote, "that illuminates foreign policy performance and unleashes a critical press" (1990, p. xiii). His hypothesis was supported by Liebovich's *The Press and the Origins of the Cold War: 1944–1947*, in which Liebovich wrote that the media were fairly passive during these formative years and that they only reacted after foreign policy goals were established, rather than being on the "cutting edge of foreign policy decisions" (Qtd. in Berry, 1990, p. 141). Berry also asserted that "[t]he press' main task is to inform its readers what the government wants foreign governments to do or not to do, how the government intends to bring about that result, and what its early moves are" (1990, p. xiii).

PUBLIC OPINION AND DEMOCRACY

Regardless of the degree to which the media influence public opinion, specifically about foreign policy issues, Cohen summed it best by writing that the media "may not be successful much of the time in telling people what to think, but it is stunningly successful in telling its readers what to think about" (1960, p. 165). As scholars such as McCombs (1981), Demers, Craff, Choi, & Pessin (1989), Eaton (1989), and Yagade and Dozier (1990) have demonstrated, the impact of the media on the people's opinions about foreign policy is quite limited.

Why is this the case, when scholars have shown that the media do indeed influence public opinion about most domestic issues? Foreign policy and what goes on outside the U.S. border are such complex issues for most of the public that there is a general lack of interest or concern. Thus, when the media portray pertinent or not-so-pertinent foreign policy issues to the public, there is no guarantee that the public will even pay attention to what is written, let alone be influenced by such information.

On the other hand, it can be argued that for those who are attentive to foreign policy issues in the media, most, if not all, of the information about such issues is derived from the media (Kegley and Wittkopf, 1979). Brown and Vincent (1995) indicated that the public are especially dependent on the media because of the limited access most of the public has to foreign policy information from other sources. Thus, the media are "instrumental in creating, perpetuating, and modifying images of foreign nations and international leaders" (Merrill, 1991, p. 66). Weiss (1974) indicated that the media are the "leading source of information and ideas" about foreign policy issues and that "the press performs an invaluable and probably irreplaceable function: the sending of messages back and forth among individuals, factions, and agencies...", especially in the case of foreign policy (1974, p. 17). Cohen (1963) claimed that it is the media who draw the political map of the world, not cartographers. As Chang (1993) concluded, the press become "a surrogate observer for the public at large and perform an important function: creation of external reality for the audience" (pp. 26–27).

Since the dawning of the Constitutional right of freedom of the press, the media have actively played a role in furthering democratic goals—informing citizens of government decisions and allowing the citizens to speak through a public forum, stirring debates about government decisions. As Lippmann wrote in 1922, the media represent "an organ of democracy" (p. 229) and Nimmo recognized that the media are "...channels of political communication connecting the citizens and officials..." (1964, p. 210). Goren viewed the media as being able to engage the public by presenting information on issues and helping to formulate national images that reflected in policy making. Yet because of the lack of interest by the public in foreign policy issues, the media have exerted their greatest influence on the policy-making process directly and public opinion indirectly (1980).

According to Cohen, the media have three primary roles in the foreign policy process—*communicating, interpreting,* and *advocacy.* Additionally, the media *initiate* governmental and social reactions to certain issues, although Cohen claimed this does not happen often. The most important role of the media though, according to Cohen, was that the media helped to "create or shape the outlines of foreign policy issues in the minds of the general public, of organized groups, and of government officials more or less remote or removed from these particular issues" (1965, pp. 199–200).

Although Serfaty (1990) wrote that the media greatly influence foreign policy, he did not believe the media "usually determine the foreign policy agenda." He, like Cohen, viewed the media's key role as relaying vital information to and from the public, rather than acting as a key player in the inner workings of the foreign policy making process. It is only when foreign policy debates "spill from the closed circle over into the public domain" that the media's influence increases greatly (Chang, 1993, p. 24; Hilsman, 1967).

Some scholars view the media as having great influence on public opinion, but a different kind of influence than they have over the government. Paletz and Entman pointed out that "the mass media tend to speak in a monolithic voice, to report a narrow perspective, to limit rather than expand public knowledge of alternative possibilities" (1981, p. 215). Thus, they claimed, the news media depict the opinions of the powerful elites who maintain specific international interests.

As Lippmann, the pioneer of public opinion, pointed out, it may not be beneficial to have the media, or the public, as influential or interactive in all government issues. He once wrote, "The notion that public opinion can and will decide all issues is in appearance very democratic. In practice, it undermines and destroys democratic government. For when everyone is supposed to have a judgment about everything, nobody in fact is going to know much about anything.... The only effect of inviting everybody to judge every public question is to confuse everybody about everything..." (Qtd. in Manning, 1968, p. 154).

On the other hand, is it correct to state that the media "mold public opinion of world events?" (Brown and Vincent, 1995, p. 66) (See Galtung and Ruge, 1965; Galtung and Vincent, 1992). Lippmann raised this question long before the dawning of television, writing that because of the strong elitist tradition about the proper roles of the government and the citizens in regards to foreign policy, "the public is seen as stupid, volatile, and best kept in the dark, with policy left in the hands of a superior elite who can better judge the national interest" (1922, pp. 31–32).

Several scholars have noted that "media organizations and personnel, by following their own interests and habits, unintentionally but often markedly influence the political thinking and behavior of the few Americans who possess power and the vast majority who do not" (Paletz and Entman, 1981, p. ix). Brown and Vincent (1995) recently suggested that in order to change such a system, future research in the field should specifically assess the effects of the media's portrayal of foreign policy on public opinion, a recommendation Lippmann made over seven decades ago.

NEWS MEDIA AND FOREIGN POLICY:
LACK OF INTEGRATION

It is difficult to balance the lack of integration of the fields of political science and mass communication research due to the extensive schools of thought portraying the role of the news media in regards to the foreign policy process. Thus, it is imperative to assess the theoretical concepts existing in twentieth century social science literature which focus on the bonding of foreign policy and the news media. As the literature in the field reveals, there is a lack of consensus about this intimate and complex relationship. Bullion clarified this intense debate by stating that "there is a major gap in international mass communication and foreign relations research regarding the role of the press in diplomatic communication" (1982, p. 187), noting that the media are scarcely cited in foreign policy literature. Likewise, the number of media studies focusing specifically on foreign policy is limited as well.

The lack of agreement in the field primarily concerns the extent of power the media have in affecting the foreign policy decision-making process at the national level, and vice versa. Besides speculating on the degree of power of the media and/or government, researchers also debate about the media and/or government's influence on public opinion in regards to foreign policy decisions. Simply stated, the debate focuses on the directions and paths by which information flows and is exchanged between the government, specifically foreign policy decision-makers, the news media, and the public. Schanberg, (1991), McGowan and Shapiro (1973), and several other scholars have claimed that the relationship as a field of inquiry lacks "scholarly integration and a need for longitudinal, systemic, and empirical analysis" (Chang, 1993, p. 3).

Why should scholars be interested in such a debate? James F. Larson pointed out two concurrent transformations which have forced scholars to rethink the relationship between the media and foreign policy process. Larson (1992) cited the crumbling of the Cold War consensus and the rise of global communication as two factors which have changed the way the media interact with foreign policy decision-making. It is likely that these two transformations greatly influenced the issue at hand, and perhaps there are other factors which have influenced the relationship of the media and the foreign policy process in recent decades. Yet, regardless of the factors that have changed the relationship, it is crucial to understand the current lack of consensus that exists in the field and perhaps review why there is such divergence among scholars. Larson noted that the roles portrayed by the media and the government during the Persian Gulf War were reminders that "earlier approaches are inadequate" (1992, p. 160).

According to Bennett, the "new era of political communications" spawned by technological advances in the media across the globe has required participants in the foreign policy process to reassess the current situation. Traditional news management by decision-makers has become more and more difficult, with satellites bouncing images from thousands of miles away in just minutes to a more curious American society. With such changes, the entire relationship between the media and the foreign policy establishment is in desperate need of re-analysis, and the only means by which such improvement can occur is by reviewing the existing literature and assessing the reasons for diversity and lack of integration (1988).

CONCLUSION

Too often, scholarly books and journals simplify ideas about the media's relationship with the foreign policy establishment. Yet, this relationship between two of the most powerful institutions in the United States is so deep and complex that a simplified, narrow, or monolithic view of the media or the foreign policy establishment does not seem to suffice. Rather, as Cohen pointed out, the media "serve many different functions in the foreign policy-making process; and thus it can have many different effects on that process or on the behavior of the other persons and institutions involved with the process" (1965, p. 196).

Larson made a key point by stating, "The contemporary changes in media and foreign policy are transnational—that is, they extend beyond national boundaries—and hold significance for virtually all nations in the world" (1987, p. 5). Thus, the relationship between the media and government needs to be re-thought, for a number of reasons which have been discussed. Larson pointed out that most previous research on this relationship occurred prior to the global information explosion, that foreign policy had previously been considered in isolation from domestic social forces, and that in the past there was a belief that the media and government were adversaries (1987). In short, many scholars are recognizing the immense need to re-evaluate the current relationship, since communication technology has caused changes in the conduct of foreign policy and diplomacy.

Berry went as far as stating that the notion that media were active or passive participants was not valid. Rather, he claimed, "[b]oth schools are partially right, though wrong overall" (Berry, 1990, p. 144). In 1975 Batscha wrote, "Whether the press is conceived as the critic of government, the upholder of the status quo, the fourth branch of government, or the representative of the people is as much, if not more, the result of the actual role conceptions of the participants in the press corps as it is of our philosophical and political traditions that attempt to prescribe what its role should be. This debate has never been settled" (p. 61). Twenty years later, the issue remains undecided.

REFERENCES

Allison, G. T. (1971). *Essence of decision: Explaining the Cuban missle crisis*. Boston: Little, Brown Publishing.

Altschull, J. H.(1984). *Agents of power: The role of the news media in human affairs*. New York: Longman Press.

Arno, A. & Dissanayake, W. (1984). *The news media in national and international conflict*. Boulder, CO: Westview Press.

Batscha, R. M. (1975). *Foreign affairs news and the broadcast journalist*. New York: Praeger Publishers.

Becker, L.B. (1977). Foreign policy and press performance. *Journalism Quarterly, 5*(54), 364–367.

Bennett, W. L. (1988). *News, the politics of illusion*. New York: Longman Press.

Bennett, W. L. (1990, Spring).Toward theory of press-state relations in the United States.*Journal of Communication, 40*(2), 103–125.

Bennett, W. L. (1992, Autumn). Book review. *The U.S. press and Iran: Foreign policy and the journalism of deference* by W. Dorman & M. Farhang. *Journalism Quarterly, 69*(3), 762–764.

Bennett, W. L. & Edelman, M. (1985).Toward a new political narrative. *Journal of Communication, 35*(4), 156–171.

Bennett, W. L., Gressett, L. A., & Halton, W. (1985). Reparing the news: A case study of the news paradigm.*Journal of Communication, 35*(2), 50–68.

Benton, M. & Frazier, P. J. (1976). The agenda-setting function of the mass media at three levels of information holding. *Communication Research*, (3), 261–274.

Berry, N. O. (1990). *Foreign policy and the press: An analysis of the New York Times' coverage of U.S. foreign policy*. New York: Greenwood Press.

Bethell, T. (1977, January). The myth of the adversary press. *Harper's*, 33–40.

Braestrup, P. (1978). *Big story*. New York: Yale University Press.

Bray, C. W. (1976, Fall). The media and foreign policy. *Foreign Policy*, (16), 108–125.

Brown, W. J. & Vincent, R. C. (1995, Spring). Trading arms for hostages? How the government and print media "spin" portrayals of the U.S. policy toward Iran. *Political Communication, 12*(1), 65–79.

Bullion, S. J. (1982). *International perspectives on news*. Carbondale, IL: Southern Illinois University Press.

Carlsson, G., Dahlberg, A., & Rosengren, K. E. (1982) Mass media content, political opinions, and social change: Sweden 1967–1974. In *Mass Communication Review Yearbook, 3*.

Cater, D. (1959). *The fourth branch of the government*. New York: Vintage Books.

Chang, T. (1989, August).The impact of presidential statements on press editorials regarding U.S.–China policy, 1950–1984. *Communication Research, 16*(4), 486–509.

Chang, T. (1993). *The press and China policy: The illusion of Sino-American relations, 1950–1984*. Norwood, New Jersey: Ablex.

Chittick, W. O. (1970). *State department, press, and pressure groups: A role analysis*. New York: Wiley-Interscience.

Cioffi-Revilla, C., Merritt, R. L. & Zinnes, D. A. (1987). *Communication and interaction in global politics*. Beverly Hills, CA: Sage.

Coggeshall, R. (1934). Diplomatic implications in international news. *Journalism Quarterly*, (11).

Cohen, B. C. (1957). *The political process and foreign policy: The making of the Japanese peace settlement*. Princeton, NJ: Princeton University Press.

Cohen, B. C. (1960). The present and the press. *World Politics*, (13).

Cohen, B. C. (1963). *The press and foreign policy*. Princeton, NJ: Princeton University Press.

Cohen, B. C. (1965). *Foreign policy in American government*. (pp. 194–204). Boston: Little, Brown and Company.

Cohen, B. C. (1973). *The public's impact on foreign policy*. Boston: Little, Brown and Company.

Cook, F., Tyler, T., Goetz, E. G., Gorden, M.T., Protess, D., Leff, D. R., & Molotch, H. L. (1983). Media and agenda setting: Effects on the public, interest group leaders, policy makers, and policy. *Public Opinion Quarterly*, (47) 16–35.

Cutler, L. N. (1984, Fall). Foreign policy on deadline. *Foreign Policy, 56,* 113–128.

Davision, W. P. (1974, Spring). News media and international negotiation. *Public Opinion Quarterly*.

Davision, W. P. (1976). Mass communication and diplomacy. In J. N. Rosenau, K. W. Thompson, & G. Boyd (Eds.), *World Politics*. New York: The Free Press.

Deakin, J. (1984). *Straight stuff: The reporters, the White House, and the truth.* New York: William Morrow Press.

Demers, D. P., Craff, D., Choi, Y. H., & Pessin, B. M. (1989). Issue obtrusiveness and the agenda-setting effects of national network news. *Communication Research, 16,* 793–812.

Dennis, E. E. & Merrill, J. C. (Eds.). (1991). *Media debates: Issues in mass communication.* New York: Longman Press.

Denton, R. E., Jr. & Woodward, G. C.(1985). *Political communication in America.* New York: Praeger Press.

DeYoung, K. (1985, January). Understanding U.S. foreign policy: The role of the press. *USA Today*. 66–69.

Dorman, W. A. (1986). Peripheral vision: U.S. journalism and the third world. *World Policy Journal, 3,* 419–445.

Dorman, W. A. & Fahrang, M. (1987). *The U.S. press and Iran: Foreign policy and the journalism of deference.* Berkely, CA: University of California Press.

Douglas, P. F. & Bomer, K. (1932).The press as a factor in international relations. *The Annals of the American Academy of Political and Social Science*.

Eaton, H. (1989). Agenda-setting with bi-weekly data on content of three national media. *Journalism Quarterly*, (66), 942–948.

Elder, R. E. (1960). *The policy machine: The department of state and American foreign policy.* New York: Syracuse University Press.

Entman, R. M. (1989). *Democracy without citizens: Media and the decay of American politics.* New York: Oxford University Press.

Galtung, J. & Ruge, M. (1965).The structure of foreign news. *Journal of Peace Research,* (2), 64–91.

Galtung, J. & Vincent, R. C. (1992). *Global Glasnost: Toward a new international information/ communication order?.* Cresskill, NJ: Hampton Press.

Gans, H. (1979). *Deciding what's news.* New York: Vintage Books.

Geylin, P. (1990). The strategic defense initiative: The president's story, in S. Serfaty. (Ed.), *The media and foreign policy.* New York: St. Martin's Press.

Gitlin, T. (1980). *The whole world is watching: Mass media in the making and unmaking of the new left.* Berkley, CA: University of California Press.

Goren, D. (1980). The news and foreign policy: An examination of the impact of the news media on the making of foreign policy. *Research in Social Movements, Conflicts, and Change, (3),* 119–141.

Graber, D. A. (1989). *Mass media and American politics.* Washington, D.C.: CQ Press.

Grossman, M. B. & Kumar, M. J. (1981). *Portraying the president: The White House and the news media.* Baltimore: Johns Hopkins University Press.

Grossman, M. B. & Rourke, F. E. (1976).The media and the presidency: An exchange analysis. *Political Science Quarterly*, (91).

Guzzardi, W. (1985, August/September) The secret love affair between the press and government. *Public Opinion, (8)*, 2–5.

Hallin, D. C. (1987). Hegemony: The American news media from Vietnam to El Salvador, In D. Paletz, (Ed.), *Political communication research*. Norwood, NJ: Ablex.

Herman, E. S. (1993, Summer). The media's role in United States foreign policy. *Journal of International Affairs, 43*(1), 23–45.

Herman, E. S. & Chomsky, N. (1988). *Manufacturing consent: The political economy of the mass media*. New York: Pantheon Books.

Hero, A. O. (1959). *Mass media and world affairs*. Boston: World Peace Foundation.

Hertsgaard, M.(1988). *On bended knee: The press and the Reagan presidency*. New York: Farrar Straus Giroux Publishing.

Hilsman, R. (1967). *To move a nation*. New York: Doubleday Press.

Hoge, J. F., Jr. (1994, July/August). Media pervasiveness. *Foreign Affairs, 73*(4), 136–144.

Hohenberg, J. (1968). *The news media: A journalist looks at his profession*. New York: Holt, Rinehart & Winston.

Hopple, G. W. (1982). International news coverage in two elite newspapaers. *Journal of Communication, 32*(1), 61–74.

Jamieson, K. H. (1984). *Packaging the presidency: A history and criticism of presidential campaign advertising*. New York: Oxford University Press.

Johnson, D. B. & Walker, J. L. (Eds.). (1964). *The dynamics of the American presidency*. New York: John Wiley & Sons.

Judis, J. B. (1992). *Grand illusion: Critics and champions of the American century*. New York: Farrer, Straus, and Giroux.

Just, M. & Crigler, A. (1989). Learning from the news: Experiments in media, modality, and reporting about star wars. *Political Communication and Persuasion*, (6), 109–128).

Kaiser, R. G. (1977, November 16). Cronkite: Matchmaking in the Mideast. *Washington Post*. p. A20.

Kegley, C. W., Jr., & Wittkopf, E. R. (1979). *American foreign policy: Pattern and process*. New York: St. Martin's Press.

Kern, M. (1981). The invasion of Afghanistan: Domestic vs. foreign stories. In W.C. Adams, (Ed.), *Television coverage of the Middle East*. Norwood, NJ: Ablex Publishing Corporation.

Kern, M., Levering, P. W. & Levering, R. B. (1983). *The Kennedy crisis: The press, the presidency, and foreign policy*. Chapel Hill, NC: The University of North Carolina Press.

Kieh, G. (1990). Propaganda and the United States foreign policy. *Political Communication and Persuasion*, (7), 61–72.

Koppel, T. (1985, April 8). TV Diplomacy in South Africa. *Newsweek*. (p. 14).

Larson, J. F. (1986). Television and U.S. foreign policy: The case of the Iran hostage crisis. *Journal of Communication, 36*(4), 108–130.

Larson, J. F. (1987, March/April). *Global television and foreign policy: Headline news series*. New York: Foreign Policy Association.

Larson, J. F. (1992, Winter). (Books Review). *The media and foreign policy*. S. Serfaty (Ed.), in *Journal of Communication, 42*(1), 159–161.

Ledeen, M. (1984, August/September). Public opinion, press opinion, and foreign policy. *Public Opinion, 7*(4), 5–7.

Lefever, E. W. (1976, Spring). The prestige press, foreign policy, and American survival. *Orbis, 20*.

Liebovich, L. (1988). *The press and the origins of the Cold War: 1944–1947.* New York: Praeger Press.

Linsky, M. (1990). How policymakers deal with the press. In D.A. Graber, (Ed.), *Media Power in Politics.* Washington, D.C.: CQ Press.

Lippmann, W. (1922). *Public opinion.* New York: The Free Press.

Locander, R. (1979). The advesary relationship: A new look at old ideas. *Presidential Studies Quarterly, 9*(3), 226–274.

Malek, A. (1984, August). *International communication and foreign policy: The U.S.–Iran conflict.* Paper presented in XIV General Assembly of the International Association for Mass Communication Research, Prague, Czechoslovakia.

Malek, A. (1988). New York Times' editorial position and the U.S. foreign policy: The case of Iran. *Gazette,* (42), 105–119.

Manheim, J. B. & Albritton, R. B. (1984). Changing national images: International public relations and media agenda setting. *American Political Science Review,* (78), 641–657.

Manning, R. (1968). International news media. In A. S. Hoffman. (Ed.), *International communication and the new diplomacy.* Bloomington, IN: Indiana University Press.

McCombs, M. (1981). The agenda setting function of the mass media. In D. Nimmo and K. R. Sanders (Eds.), *Handbook of political communication.* Beverly Hills, CA: Sage.

McGowan, P. & Shapiro, H. B. (1973). *The comparative study of foreign policy: A survey of scientific findings.* Beverly Hills, CA: Sage.

Merrill, J. C., (Ed.) (1991). *Global journalism* (2nd ed.). New York: Longman Press.

Mickelson, S. (1972). *The electric mirror: Politics in an age of television.* New York: Dodd, Mead.

Modern Media Institute. (1983). *The Advesary Press.* St. Petersburg, FL: Modern Media Institute.

Morris, R. (1974). Henry Kissinger and the media: A separate peace. In M. C. Emery & T. C. Smythe, (Eds.), *Readings in Mass Communication: Concepts and Issues in the Mass Media.* (2nd ed.). Dubuque, IA: Brown.

Moyers, B. D. (1969). The press & government: Who's telling the truth? In W. K. Agee. (Ed.), *Mass media in a free society.* Lawerence, KS: The University Press of Kansas.

Nimmo, D. D. (1964). *Newsgathering in Washington.* New York: Atherton Press.

Nimmo, D. D. (1978). *Political communication and public opinion in America.* Santa Monica, CA: Goodyear Publishing.

Nimmo, D. D. & Combs, J. E. (1980). *Subliminal politics: Myths and mythmakers in America.* Englewood Cliffs, NJ: Prentice Hall.

Noelle-Neumann, E. (1974). The spiral of silence: A theory of public opinion. *Journal of Communication,* (24), 43–51.

O'Heffernan, P. (1991). *Mass media and American foreign policy: Insider perspectives on global journalism and the foreign policy process.* Norwood, NJ: Ablex.

Ostman, R. E. & Babcock, W. A. (1983). Three major newspapers' content and President Kennedy's press conference statements regarding space exploration and technology. *Presidential Studies Quarterly, 13*(1), 111–120.

Paletz, D. L. & Entman, R. M. (1980). Presidents, power, and the press. *Presidential Studies Quarterly, 10*(3), 416–426.

Paletz, D. L. & Entman, R. M.(1981). *Media, power, politics.* New York: The Free Press.

Parenti, M. (1986). *Inventing reality: The politics of the mass media.* New York: St. Martin's Press.

Rainey, G. E. (1975). *Patterns of American foreign policy*. Boston: Allyn and Bacon.

Reston, J. B. (1966). The press, the president, and foreign policy. *Foreign Affairs, 44*(4), 553–573.

Reston, J. B. (1967). *The artillery of the press: Its influence on American foreign policy*. New York: Center for the Study of the Presidency.

Rikardsson, G. (1981). Newspaper opinion and public opinion. In K. E. Rosengren, (Ed.), *Advances in Content Analysis*. Beverly Hills, CA: Sage Publishers.

Rivers, W. L. (1967). *The opinion makers: The Washington press corps*. Boston: Beacon Press.

Rivers, W. L. (1982). *The other government: Power and the Washington media*. New York: Universe Books.

Robinson, J. P. (1974). The press as king-maker: What surveys from last five campaigns show. *Journalism Quarterly, 51*(4), 587–594.

Rosenbaum, W. A., Spanier, J. W. & Buris, W. (1971). *Analyzing American politics: A new perspective*. Belmont, CA: Wadsworth Publishing.

Rourke, F. E. (1961). *Secrecy and publicity: Dilemmas of democracy*. Baltimore: The Johns Hopkins Press.

Rusher, W. A. (1988, March 18) All the news that's fit for Democrats. *National Review, 40*, 32–33.

Schanberg, S. H. (1991, February 12). Reporting from the front shouldn't be unthinkable. *Star Tribune*. (p. 13).

Schorr, D. (1991, July/August). Ten days that shook the White House. *Columbia Journalism Review, 30*(2), 21–23.

Schudson, M. (1978). *Discovering the news: A social history of American newspapers*. New York: Basic Books.

Serfaty, S. (Ed.) (1990). *The media and foreign policy*. New York: St. Martin's Press.

Siebert, F. S., Peterson, T., & Schramm, W. (1956). *Four theories of the press*. Urbana, IL: University of Illinois Press.

Sigal, L. V. (1973). *Reporters and officials: The organization and politics of newsmaking*. Lexington, MA: D.C. Health.

Stowe, L. (1936). The press and international friction. *Journalism Quarterly*, (13).

Streitmatter, R. (1988, Winter). The rise and triumph of the White House photo opportunity. *Journalism Quarterly, 65*(4), 981–985.

Strouse, J. C. (1975). *The mass media, public opinion, and public opinion policy analysis*. Columbus, OH: Bell & Howell.

Tebbel, J. W. & Watts, S. M. (1985). *The press and the presidency: From George Washington to Ronald Reagan*. New York: Oxford University Press.

Trattner, J. H. (1982). Reporting foreign affairs. *Washington Quarterly, 5*(3), 103–111.

Tuchman, G. (1974). *The TV establishment: Programming for power*. Englewood Cliffs, NJ: Prentice Hall.

Wallach, J. P. (1982). I'll give it to you on background: State breakfasts. *Washington Quarterly, 5*(2), 53–66.

Weisman, S.R. (1984, October 14) The president and the press: The art of controlled access. *The New York Times Magazine*. (pp. 34–37).

Weiss, C. H. (1974, Spring). What America's leaders read. *Public Opinion Quarterly, 38*(1), 1–21.

Welch, S. (1971, October 11). Vietnam: How the press went along. *The Nation, 213*(1), 327–329.

Welch, S. (1972). The American press and Indochina, 1950–1956. In R. L. Merritt, (Ed.), *Communication in international politics*. Urbana, IL: University of Illinois Press.

Wicker, T. (1979). *On press*. New York: Berkeley Publishing Corporation.

Wise, D. (1973). *The politics of lying: Government deception, secrecy, and power*. New York: Vintage Books.

Yagade, A. & Dozier, D. M. (1990). The media agenda-setting effect of concrete versus abstract issues. *Journalism Quarterly, 67*(1), 3–10.

Zeidenstein, H. G. (1984). News media perceptions of White House news management. *Presidential Quarterly, 14*(3), 391–398.

chapter 2

the media and foreign policy: a framework of analysis

Hamid Mowlana
American University

A s a whole, the literature on the media and foreign policy tends to be both diverse and dispersed. Most of the studies and research in this area conventionally have dealt with the relationship between the communication media and the process of information gathering and retrieval by policy makers. This conceptual chapter looks at the media and foreign policy from the broader theoretical and methodological perspective of the international flow of information, taking into account the complex intermingling and interdependencies of not only the various actors (including journalists, government officials and the public), but also such factors as technological innovations, structural conditions, and perceptual circumstances.

In describing the dilemma of United States foreign policy, Alexander E. Campbell, professor of emeritus of American History and former director of American Studies at the University of Birmingham in England recently wrote, "the president and his advisors seem to resemble the helpless British cavalry immortalized by Tennyson:

> Cannon to right of them
> Cannon to left of them
> Cannon in front of them
> Volley'd and thunder'd."

Professor Campbell went on to say that "Though the cannons in question today are those of American journalists rather than Russian gunners, a situation in which retreat means humiliation and advance, at best, survival is not one to encourage the making of sensible foreign policy." (Campbell, 1995, p. 54).

Given the complexities of communication and decision-making processes and considering the intricacies of foreign policy formulation, it seems that the study of the media and foreign policy should take into account the multifaceted nature of the phenomenon by focusing on the following dimensions: 1) the culture of foreign policy, 2) the decision-making process, 3) public opinion and interest groups, 4) modern communication technology, 5) security, peace and war, 6) economics and trade as foreign policy, and 7) culture and information as foreign policy.

THE CULTURE OF FOREIGN POLICY

The culture of foreign policy consists of all those historical, linguistic, social and psychological elements that make up the formulation and the execution of principles which are adopted by a state in its ideal form when it deals with other states to develop or protect its perceived national and/or global interests. For a long time, the political-military involvements of the situation and the physical environment of the state were two important dimensions of foreign policy. The importance of geopolitics in foreign policy has been well documented by such historians and political observers as Ibn Khaldun (1967) in the 14th Century, Karl Haushofer and Kurt Trambler (1931) in the 19th Century. However, the concepts of air defense, security, and sovereignty have been particularly newsworthy and have been changed, first with the launching of Sputnik by the former Soviet Union in 1957 and in later years by the tremendous growth and expansion of communication and transportation technologies worldwide. Communication and media strategy have become vital aspects of international relations in general and foreign policy in particular.

In addition, international relations have been profoundly affected by economic factors including the unrestricted movements of capital and labor across national boundaries as well as the globalization of the means of production and distribution by the transnational corporate structures. In short, the culture of foreign policy has acquired a new ecology of action unprecedented in contemporary history. The persistence of habits, attitudes, ideas, customs and to some extent institutional structures, that are incongruous with and stifling to the existing international system constitute a cultural lack in foreign policy especially when the state acquires the stature of world power.

In the United States, this cultural lack was reflected in its educational and foreign service systems and in its vastly provisional media structure. The country's rich material resources, its continental self-sufficiencies and its geographical isolation until World War II were curtains hiding it from world complexities. Until very recently, there were few American foreign service officers, journalists, and business people who could speak a foreign language even tolerably well and fewer still who bothered to intimately learn another nation's culture, religion and history. Until the 1950s there were only a few schools that trained students for international careers in diplomacy and business. Factors contributing to the foreign policy culture of the United States always included such items as the large geographical size of the country and the relatively long distance of most citizens from an international frontier (which contributed to the feeling of isolation), a democratic idealism that always sought to emphasize the uniqueness of

American society and the missionary role to propagate these ideas around the world.

There is also a general belief that although public opinion and citizenry are essential in the support of foreign policy, especially during war and crisis, they nevertheless are incapable of judging and articulating international development and defining what is known as the "national interests" of the country. Thus, while the United States is becoming increasingly dependent on the rest of the world, its citizens have little understanding of its connections between their everyday life and global social and economic processes. The question then arises: How did it come to pass that many United States citizens are so critical of the many social, economic, and political issues at home blaming the congress and its government officials for their existence and yet reluctant to apply the same norms to similar activities, by the same people, concerned with foreign policy? A number of factors seem to shed some light on this question, chief among them United States foreign policy culture, remnants of U.S. isolationist traditions, belief that foreign policy is uniquely different from government policy at home and the mainstream media's long standing habit of reinforcing this tradition. Another answer to this question may be found in the words of George Ball:

> Diplomatic practice has been set back three hundred years. We have, as a people, accepted this retrogression to a personalized diplomacy because it has been congenial with another facet of American life—the habituation to spectacle and the dramatized event as distinct from the process, which results largely from the fact that, as a people, we now watch rather than listen, listen rather than read. When one absorbs the news through television, events become a series of vignettes, and foreign policy a matter of unconnected visual images. (Ball, 1976)

THE DECISION MAKING PROCESS

It is generally agreed that the American media do not play a direct role in the formulation of foreign policy but continue to have a growing influence in its implementation, explanation and articulation. The influence of the American media on United States foreign policy is primarily exerted through congress and through non-governmental interest groups rather than through the mass audience and the public. Congress frequently initiates investigations because of media obligations and directly affect foreign policy through committee actions, authorizations and appropriations. (Cohen, 1963; Almond, 1950)

The media's involvement in the American foreign policy process is best witnessed in the way the government uses it to publicly set the political agenda. Thus, the media are consistently used by the government as a diplomatic forum to help set the tone, pattern and agenda for foreign policy matters. This is a unique characteristic of the American media in that it serves to crystallize public opinion and create a consensus around and among political elites. By sheer emphasis and publicity of various foreign policy actions, the media have the ability to dictate the importance of news, to highlight policy and help bring it to the fore. However, it must be noted that most governmental criticism by the media usually surfaces after the fact. In fact a number of studies conducted over the last four decades show that the American media, auspiciously the elite press and the major media outlets, have consistently supported American foreign policy decisions, at least in their initial stages, without seriously challenging the basic assumptions inherent in these decisions. Examples include U.S–Soviet relations and U.S–China relations since World War Two, the early U.S. involvement in Indochina and the early years of the Vietnam War, the arms race, the cold war, detente, Cuba, Chile and more recently, Iran and Lebanon.

For instance, a study conducted to examine the American press coverage of the Indochina war during 1950–1956 showed that news coverage and the positions of three major newspapers, including the *New York Times*, leaned toward the administration's policies on the issues at that time. Not only were the major assumptions of the government in relation to U.S. security in that part of the world not challenged but the coverage generally represented a consensus and common perceptions between the administration, the congressional committees and the editors and columnists of the media (Welch, 1972).

PUBLIC OPINION AND INTEREST GROUPS

Non-governmental interest groups, which are important communicators in the field of foreign policy, include lobby associations representing various ethnic groups, nearly every form of industry, trade and commercial services, religious and educational institutions. These groups are not only influenced by the press but also use the media to get coverage for their causes. Thus they gain their primary influence by acting as a channel for information transmission to the congress. In this context the media are directly influenced by interest groups and lobby associations who, through their appearances in radio and television and the print media and by providing desired information, exert considerable influence in foreign policy deliberations. For example, it has been found that "network television seems unlikely to allow a foreign government lacking a domestic constituency to effectively challenge the president during times of crisis." (Newsom, 1995) Strong domestic constituency is a prerequisite for the entry in the media even during a crisis, when all other signs point to great presidential power definition.

In the last few years the media, especially television, have succeeded in sharply increasing their policy significance. In many instances they have done this not by promoting "official" government views, but "unofficial" and dissident ones. A series of new methods have played a critical role in amplifying this process which include a hidden coupling between governmental authorities and the media whereby dissident opinion, hitherto "secret" documents, have been made available to the media. Other methods are more conventional and well known: trial balloons—suggesting an idea and then watching the public's reaction—news leak, planted story, and staged events such as hijacking. In this context, the very structure of the media and their desire to cover drama and human interest events are important items that should be studied carefully when the relation of the media to violence and terrorism are considered.

One of the major sources of media influence on foreign policy is the lobbying process, exercised by interest and pressure groups who on behalf of countries, governments and even individuals, attempt to publicize and promote their objectives. The lobbying process, one of the most visible dimensions of the media and foreign policy, is particularly distinguished in the United States by large ethnic groups, predisposed to a nation's cause. Since the lobbies are seeking to shape perceptions of international events, they usually work through the Congress, various governmental departments, the media and academia. Since World War II and especially after the demise of the Soviet Union and the Cold War, special interest groups on behalf of foreign causes have become significant with the emergence and dominance of the U.S. as a world power. In 1994, there were 741 individuals and firms registered under The Foreign Agent's Registration Act who regularly filed copies of their political propaganda with the attorney general in Washington, D.C.

For example, among the ethnic groups, according to David D. Newsom, former ambassador and Under Secretary of the State and currently at the faculty of the University of Virginia, "No group has been more successful...than the American Jewish community in influencing policy." Such groups as the so-called China lobby, the Greek lobby and the Taiwanese lobby not only flood Congress with mail but attempt to utilize the media and in particular television and opinion magazines with their causes. (Newsom, 1995) Newsom gives numerous examples of lobbying and pressure groups and their persuasive power of image-making through the media and the congress. (Newsom, 1996)

MODERN COMMUNICATIONS TECHNOLOGY

On the national level, the interface between foreign policy and communications media in the last several years has increasingly become a subject of study and inquiries. This new emphasis, in large, has been wrought by technological progress in electronic communications and data handling and by a number of major world events ranging from the Islamic Revolution in Iran to the demise of the Soviet Union. Other factors which have helped focus attention on the foreign policy/media issue are the roles played by a particular communication technology such as television in international conflict, the role of the media in agenda-setting and legitimizing events and personalities, the role of the media as an alternative and additional source of international diplomacy and the government/media power shuffle in which the practitioners of government move to the media while some journalists become bureaucrats.

In the United States, the news media generally perform four essential roles that are characteristics of their structural and historical development, especially as they relate to their functions in providing information about, and their tendency to affect the conduct of, national and foreign affairs:

1) As observer of the world situation, the news media perceive that their primary enterprise is that of reporting the most important news and events of the world. Because of this self-image, and because of the advance of satellite and other telecommunication/computer technology, they have been overwhelmed by the very torrent of events and facts and thus overloaded by opinions in a fragmentary nature.

2) They participate in an exchange of information and interpretation with national decision-makers and although they believe in some kind of "neutrality" syndrome, "fair treatment" or simply journalistic "objectivity" they are, indeed, directly or indirectly, involved in subjective social realities and the entire political process.

3) They act as catalysts to non-governmental and interest groups and the general public and, in this case, the news media are extremely vocal about their rights and prerogatives in what may be called the cult of "disclosure." They see themselves as the "Fourth Estate" or the "Fourth Branch of Government"—the protector of democracy—which by exposing "truth" enables the public to form opinions on national and international policies.

4) And paradoxically, they see themselves as profit-makers not only in the marketplace of ideas but, equally if not more, in the marketplace of dollars. In this sense, the American media often see a connection between American ideals, their own commercial self-interest, and the appropriate direction for world communication.

The importance of national and global patterns in the flow of information cannot be denied, especially in view of our heavy reliance on the media for interpretation of international events. The periodic news and commentaries of the world, as reported in the media, are the most common source of information underlying our comprehension of international developments. Imagine the state of international relations or the degree of the public's understanding of international politics without international news communication. Despite the fact that the mass media are universally criticized for being biased and inaccurate, newspapers, wire services, magazines, and broadcast organizations continue to provide most of the information received by individuals in industrialized societies. Government officials and scholars—more than ordinary media consumers—make extensive use of daily reporting by the media. For example, unless the student of international politics is prepared to wait for extended periods of time until government papers and documents are declassified, he has no real alternative but to base his analysis of contemporary international relations on day-to-day reporting of events by the media.

It is in this context that the first major salient items in the entire question of the media and foreign policy must be considered—the quantity and quality of foreign news and the direction and patterns of international flow of news. The myth widely accepted by the public is that the most important news of the world, if not the entire stream of events, is in the column of their daily newspapers or may be found on their television screens. Yet empirical investigation over the last two decades supports the hypothesis that the selection and dissemination of what constitutes "the most important news of the day" is a function of the nation's national culture and political norms and that economic and commercial factors play a decisive role in this process. The silence of the American press at the Bay of Pigs invasion and the extraordinary coverage given to the Iranian and the Lebanese hostage events, the uneven coverage of the 1956 Suez War and the 1982 Falklands conflict by the British press and the management of news during the Persian Gulf War are all well documented. (Mowlana, 1992; Said, 1981)

Today there are a number of factors that contribute to making the mainstream media in the United States supportive of governmental policy and thus vulnerable to "news management" by the government (Herman, 1993, pp. 23–45). As members of the corporate elite establishment, the dominant media tend to rely excessively on government and corporations as major sources of news. I once heard Leslie Gelb, one of the former editors of the *New York Times*, speaking before international non-governmental organizations at the UN, say that the *New York Times* covers centers of power and the paper is interested in getting the persons at the centers of power to speak and write. The economics of the media and the commercial nature of the communication and cultural industry in the United States not only create constraints and limits on international and foreign affairs reporting but also establish a particular linkage of policy perceptions in defining "news" and "information."

SECURITY, PEACE AND WAR

Most of the studies on the media and foreign policy have traditionally dealt with matters of security, conflict, war and revolution. The American entrance as a superpower in world affairs after World War II and the appearance of the Cold War as a central focus of the U.S.–Soviet hegemonies in various parts of the world focused the attention of foreign policy analysts and the media on such areas as the arms race, disarmament and conflict.

During the cold war era certain rules of political outlook and behavior were accepted within the larger community and the mainstream media and opinion-making structures. By engaging in the arms race, it recognized that peace was not, and could not be, the main objective of foreign policy, that the "equality of nations" would have to be discarded, that the doctrine of "non-intervention in the internal affairs of other nations" would have to be discarded altogether.

It is also interesting to note that one could speak not only of U.S. foreign policy with individual nations, but more accurately, U.S. global policy which, in large part, determined the outcome of American foreign relations with each individual country. It is precisely at this juncture of global policy that the role of the media should be examined.

One of the major hypothesis in relations of the media to foreign policy is that in international conflict, the media often side with the perceived national interests of the system of which they are a part, making it difficult to maintain journalistic independence and neutrality in the face of patriotism and national loyalty. Research covering the United States media performance during the United States–Iran conflict and

Afghanistan's invasion by former Soviet troops as well as the Persian Gulf War showed that journalists were emotionally and ideologically compatible with domestic standards which included, among other things, patriotism. Research examining the coverage of Afghanistan by the U.S. media concluded that "television news clearly does not attempt to convey a foreign perspective, but rather responds to the U.S. outlook. What we saw in television coverage of the Afghan crisis is what we were: a nation fearful of American setbacks in the Middle East, and worried that the former Soviet Union would take advantage of the weakness" (Kern, 1981).

Until the eve of the Islamic Revolution in Iran in 1978–1979, the United States media in general, especially the elite newspapers and the major television networks, presented the shah and his regime in the positive light in which the U.S. foreign policy-makers were seeing him. Indeed, for more than two decades, an iron triangle of media-government-academia, through reports, policies, research, and conferences had created such a mood or a frame of mind about the Pahlavi dynasty and the shah's so-called "stability" in the region, that the collapse of the U.S.–supported shah and the demise of U.S. foreign policy influence in that part of the world seemed as embarrassing as it was shocking to all the parties involved.

A study examining the editorial positions of the *New York Times* and the United States policy positions reflected in the *Department of State Bulletin* toward Iran during a decade prior to the Islamic Revolution revealed that the two had very similar and "positive" attitudes about Iran and that there were no significant differences between the two sources between 1968–1978 (Malek, 1988). A statistical survey measuring the amount of coverage given to Iran during the 1972–1978 period as well as the nature of such coverage also underlined the earlier hypothesis that television news rarely strayed from the administration's official line, in either their perceptions or coverage of the Iranian political development (Mowlana, 1984). Equally revealing was the study that examined all contents of the *Middle East Journal, Foreign Affairs,* and *Foreign Policy* from 1970 through the Summer of 1978 to see whether foreign policy experts had noted signs of internal instability in Iran that might not have been picked up by the media. The analysis showed that few, if any of the experts writing for these journals detected the popular anti-Shah and pro-Islamic sentiments building in Iran (Mowlana, 1984).

ECONOMICS AND TRADE AS FOREIGN POLICY

One of the most neglected areas of study of the media and foreign policy is the role of the press, electronic media and the specialized business journals in what is known as economic foreign policy. Almost no attention has been paid to the systematic study of the media in such foreign economic policy areas as the General Agreement on Trade Tariffs (GATT) negotiations, world intellectual property rights, trade negotiations, the division of labor and the entire area of import-export. For example, in the realm of U.S. foreign policy, especially after the collapse of the Soviet Union and the Cold War, economic issues, especially in regard to tariffs and trade, have occupied prominent positions in United States relations with Japan, China, and the European Union. In addition to trade journals and specialized publications, financial newspapers as well as business sections of leading mainstream media have become one of the major sources of the nation's foreign policy positions vis-a-vis the other countries. Indeed, looking over the last two decades, with the expansion of international telecommunications, banking and financial credit networks, the public's direct involvement in foreign affairs have become even more evident and their exposure to American international economic policy has become more pronounced.

In addition, the atrophy of diplomatic and trade relations increases both the traffic and significance of messages carried by the mass media and private citizens. In short, the growth and concomitant centralization of international telecommunications hardware, combined with the expanding role of transnational media, have increased the motivation, for and the possibility of, using these developments as tools of foreign policy. As opportunism of politicians and the commercial considerations of news media help fan the feelings of a significant segment of the public during a given crisis, the media become the instruments through which individuals, organizations, and government officials manipulate public opinion and stir mass emotion.

CULTURE AND INFORMATION AS FOREIGN POLICY

Equally, over the last several decades the media have played a very prominent role in the information and cultural dimensions of foreign policy as cultural industries and communication technologies have become central to international affairs. For example, the role of the U.S. media in exporting the first amendment of the U.S. Constitution to Europe and elsewhere, immediately after World War II and during the Cold War era, cannot be denied. Nor can we ignore the role played by the U.S. mainstream media, especially the press and broadcasting owners, in defending the U.S. position during the international debate on the New World Information and Communication Order during the 1970s. The media's direct involvement in expanding the new culture of "democracy" and "free market" during the post Cold War era are also undeniable (Mowlana, 1993). Yet few attempts have been made so far to document the systematic media involvement and monitoring in the information and cultural dimensions of foreign policy.

During the last two decades, a considerable number of articles, essays, and empirical studies have appeared examining the flow of news and images across national boundaries and the role played by the media in foreign policy of the United States. Thus far, evidence has been gathered in the following areas: the crucial role played by the transnational media in the process of legitimization, the weakness of the media in interpreting the events in light of cultural and religious factors, the importance of prior patterns of information in understanding the current development of the world, the importance of political and economic interests in disseminating news and information, the role of international telecommunication in conflict and crisis reporting and the commercial and political nature of the media.

For example, it has been demonstrated that cultural values and ideological frames of reference reduce the media's ability to serve as an independent source of information for the public and policy-makers alike, particularly in times of international conflict and crises. For decades, the United States media in general was sympathetic to the Shah of Iran because "he was a force for modernization." Yet, "modernization" was not an issue in the United States support of dictatorships in Latin America and elsewhere. In at least several Latin American countries, the United States media tended to oppose those favoring modernization. The most common types of United States media filters included: Communist "threat," East-West conflict, stability of the regimes in power, status of the United States foreign investments and friendship toward the United States. Yet the media showed little interest in advances in health, education, culture, and welfare in foreign countries.

Other factors accounting for the nature of foreign policy and international affairs reporting include the problems of access and the government's advantage in controlling the release of information. Added to these are the censorship in foreign countries, little time to write a fast-breaking story, inadequate research particularly of complicated issues, headline hunting and seeking to emphasize drama in order to get bigger headlines—all these are important structural factors that shape the pattern of foreign affairs reporting.

In the study of the media and foreign policy, the terms "the media" and "mass media" or "news media" should be defined and clarified. For example, whereas personal media may involve a telephone conversation or a letter writing process, personal communication involves the notion of exchange and certainly direct and face-to-face communication. Similarly, the organization of media and mass media, depending upon their structure and distributing limits vary considerably in circulating opinion and ideas about foreign policy. To confine the term mass media to newspaper, magazines, flyers, books and radio is to limit the scope of communication media that are directed toward some differentiated or undifferentiated larger segments of the population. News media such as electronic and computer networks—internet—or organizational media specifically directed to foreign policy subjects such as foreign affairs and foreign policy magazines are examples of specialized media of communications that are considerably different in their impact on foreign policy opinion-making process.

The international political system continues to be dominated by competitive states with foreign policies dedicated primarily to selfish "national interest." At the same time the transnational actors outside the formal nation-state systems such as multinational corporations of all kinds and interest groups have become important factors in global political, economic, and cultural policies. Over the last two decades the growing number of powerful national and transnational media actors in the field of cultural industry have made the conduct of foreign policy more complex. In short, the battlefield of international politics has shifted from geographical and the physical to the cultural and socio-economic levels.

THE EFFECT OF THE MEDIA ON FOREIGN POLICY

In summary, it must be noted that while the media are bound by many institutional, technical and cultural factors in the coverage of foreign affairs and foreign policy, their influence in the foreign policy process is undeniable. Thus, as was observed, the media can and do perform several major functions in the foreign policy process. They have the ability to define situations and to confer legitimacy to an event and personality and this is what is known as the agenda setting function. The media also can act as catalyst and can, indeed, clarify or distort issues. Another function of the media has been to accelerate or impede government policies in foreign affairs—though, as research indicated, this function has been more in the direction of the former than the latter. The media can also serve as knowing or unknowing tools for propaganda in foreign policy formation and execution. Despite all this influence in the foreign policy field, the media cannot change policies, nor can the media dictate policies. The fact that the major media outlets have shared the same perceptions and assumptions about major foreign policy issues with the administrations over the last several decades is in itself highly significant.

The media's role in mobilizing the public on behalf of foreign policy issues has become even more prominent during the last two decades due to the enormous expansion of electronic media and instantaneous exchange of information. Thus, modern media more than ever, have become the major attention-getters of the public on a platter of diverse but often difficult international issues. In short, modern media make all such foreign policy issues visible to the public whose attention span is short and whose interest in most outcomes is not great. The crucial question in the analysis of the media in foreign policy is thus not so much what the media *can* or *should* do, but rather, how the media *do* operate under certain structural conditions and in response to particular political, economic, cultural and technological environmental factors. For example, cultural values and ideological frames of reference reduce the media's ability to serve as independent sources of information, particularly in times of international conflict and national crisis.

Because the reporting of the media is, in many ways, contradictory to that of the traditional pattern of diplomacy, the media in many instances act as an alternative source of information for diplomats when governmental channels are closed off during crisis and conflicts. The classical definition of diplomacy is the application of intelligence and fact to the conduct of official relations between governments' negotiation, reporting, and representation. Diplomatic relations can only be established subsequent to the mutual consent of both parties, and such relations endow the diplomat with certain privileges and immunities from the hosts' civil and criminal jurisdictions. Thus, with the possible breakdown of diplomatic communications, which often characterizes some of the most recent phenomenon in international relations, the media are burdened with a crucial and delicate role in the confrontation among powers. They often become conduits for official exchanges, reluctant publicists for the actors, and valuable sources of information for governments.

On the positive side, the media can function and be activated as mechanisms for peaceful solutions to issues reminding the participants that such channels are available to them. The media can also contribute to the success of negotiations in foreign policy by helping to insure that each side is truly familiar with the other side's position. This can be done by employing the concept of empathy to reduce misunderstanding and distortions through the factual reporting of opposing points of view. Agreements can also be facilitated if each party is willing to acknowledge publicly and in its own media that it understands the position of the other. In addition, in situation of mediation in foreign policy, mass communication can make the mediator's task somewhat easier through the media's ability to confer prestige on the mediators. Perhaps the greatest potential contribution of the media to foreign policy decision-making processes is in the media's ability to influence the *moods* of government, elites and the public.

In summary, some of the most salient points for investigating the role of the media in foreign policy especially in regard to the recent changes in international political systems include (a) the role played by a particular communication technology in the foreign policy process; (b) the role of the elite and transnational media in agenda-setting and legitimizing events and personalities; (c) the role of international broadcasting as both the only and alternative source of news and information; (d) cultural and knowledge gaps among the media personnel and communicators in regard to international issues; (e) national interests, patriotic feelings, and reporting of international and national events, and (f) role perceptions of journalists and news media personnel and their perceptions of their functions in the political decision-making process.

REFERENCES

Almond, G. A. (1950). *The American people and foreign policy.* New York: Harcourt, Brace & Co.

Ball, G. (1976). *Diplomacy for a crowded world: An American foreign policy.* Boston: Little, Brown & Co.

Campbell, A. E. (1995). The dilemma of U.S. foreign policy. *Cosmos: A Journal of Emerging Issues, 5,* 54–59.

Cohen, B. C. (1963). *The Press and foreign policy.* New Jersey: Princeton University Press.

Haushofer, K., & Trambler, K. (1931). *Deutschlands weg an der zeitenwende.* Munich, Germany: H. Hugendubel.

Herman, E. S. (1993). The media's role in U.S. foreign policy. *Journal of International Affairs, 47*(1), 23–45.

Kern, M. (1981). The invasion of Afghanistan: Domestic U.S. foreign stories. In W. A. Adams (Ed.), *Television coverage of the Middle East.* (pp. 121–131). Norwood, NJ: Ablex.

Khaldun, I., & Rahman, A. (1967). *The Muaaddimah: An introduction to history.* (Translated from Arabic by F. Rosenthal & N. J. Dawood, Ed.). London: Routledge and Kegan Paul.

Malek, A. (1988). New York Times' editorial position and the U.S. foreign policy: the case of Iran. *Gazette: International Journal for Mass Communication Studies. 42,* 105–119.

Mowlana, H. (1984). The role of the media in the U.S.-Iranian conflict. In A. Arno & W. Dissanayake (Eds.), *The news media in national and international conflict*, (pp. 71–99). Boulder, CO: Westview Press.

Mowlana, H. (1993). Toward a NWICO for the twenty-first century? *Journal of International Affairs, 47*(1), 59–72.

Mowlana, H., Gerbner, G., & Schiller, H. (1992). *Triumph of the image: The media's war in the Persian Gulf—a global perspective*. Boulder, CO: Westview Press.

Newsom, D. D. (1995). Foreign policy follies and their influence. *Cosmos: A Journal of Emerging Times, 5*, 48–53.

Newsom, D. D. (1996). *The public dimension of foreign policy*. Bloomington, IN: Indiana University Press.

Rosenau, J. (1961). *Public opinion and foreign policy*. New York: Random House.

Said, E. W. (1981). *Covering Islam: How the media and experts determine how we see the rest of the world*. New York: Pantheon Books.

Welch, S. (1972). The American press and Indochina 1950–1956. In R. L. Merritt (Ed.), *Communication in international politics* (pp. 207–231). Urbana, IL: University of Illinois Press.

chapter 3

media diplomacy and foreign policy: toward a theoretical framework*

Bosah Ebo
Rider University

INTRODUCTION

T he nature of international relations changed dramatically after World War II
with the information revolution. The technology of communication linked
people all over the world into a global village. Media became a dominant
source of information for people all over the world and a powerful player in international relations. Foreign policy, usually conducted behind the scenes, became a public
activity in the information age.

While the primary goal of foreign policy remains the promotion of national interests in the international arena, the strategies have changed. Before World War II, military advantage played the dominant role in shaping the national identity and
international image of a nation, consequently its placement on the global political hierarchy. Nations with superior military advantage used that advantage to push for global acceptance of their national identity and political agenda.

But in the information age, "power" is derived as much from the ability of a nation
to use media diplomacy to align its international image with its national identity. The
stature of a nation in the world community and its placement in the global political
hierarchy is now tied to its media diplomacy capability. For a nation to have a sense of
dignity, and for that dignity to lead to some significant stature in the international arena,

* The author thanks Professors Jonathan Mendilow and Frank Rusciano of the Political Science
Department at Rider University in New Jersey for valuable comments on this chapter.

the nation must be able to orchestrate effective media diplomacy. Projecting "power" in contemporary international relations also means the ability to project one's preferred national identity into an international image.

Inherently, nations that have superior communication technology will have more influence over the flow of global information and the construction of their international image. While every nation will be able to construct its national identity internally by controlling domestic media, only nations with global media advantage will have the best chance to shape their international image. Thus, a nation's global "power" now emerges from its potential for effective media diplomacy. Hence, foreign policy must be examined within the role of media diplomacy in constructing a preferred national identity and a complementary international image that influences a nation's global power position.

MEDIA DIPLOMACY AND FOREIGN POLICY

Media diplomacy, broadly defined, is the use of the media to articulate and promote foreign policy. Other definitions exist in the literature. Ramaprasad (1983, p. 70) defined it as "the role the press plays in the diplomatic practice between nations." Specific terms, such as "newspaper diplomacy," "television diplomacy" and "satellite diplomacy" have also been used to describe the concept (Ramaprasad, 1983, p. 70). Media diplomacy assumed importance after World War II because of the revolution in communication technology. Before then, the "old diplomacy" was conducted behind the scenes, with little fanfare and public knowledge. Ramaprasad (1983, p. 69) noted that "Diplomats spoke discreetly to one another about matters of common concern, and just as quietly reached agreements and drew up documents." By contrast, the information age ushered in a "new diplomacy" that is played out in public, with active involvement of the media (Tehranian 1990; Serfaty, 1990; Cohen, 1963).

Traditionally, the placement of nations in the global political hierarchy has been based primarily on military superiority (George, 1991). But in contemporary foreign policy, media diplomacy constitutes a predominant factor that moderates the sense a nation has of itself and the image the rest of the world has of it. If a nation is to create and maintain a favorable international image in the world community now, it must have the ability to project its preferred national identity in the global arena. The stature of nations in the world community and the role nations play in the world community, to a large extent, is dependent on national identity and international image of nations (Skurnik, 1981; Tunstall, 1977). Thus, an important function of foreign policy is to use the media to articulate and promote a preferred national identity and a complementary international image in the world community (O'Heffernan, 1991; Hansen, Fishlow, Pearlberg, & Lewis, 1982). This partly explains why the status deficiency which results from the loss of a nation's favored image in the world community creates a need for that nation to search for alternative means of delineating its national identity and international image (Rusciano and Ebo, 1992). Argentina, Indonesia and Turkey, for instance, serve as examples of nations that were isolated by the international community between 1975 and 1977 because of various crises, and were forced to use professional public relations firms to redefine their national identities and international images (Albritton, Manheim, & Jones, 1983).

The implication that emerges from the relationship between media diplomacy and foreign policy is that while every nation will have power to some extent to shape its national identity internally by exerting control over domestic media, only nations with dominant global media advantage will have the capability to influence their international image (Galtung, 1992; Harris, 1974). The more influence a nation can exert over the international media with the use of media diplomacy, the more advantage it will have in aligning its international image with its preferred national identity (Davison, 1974; Stein, 1970). This also means that those nations will have some influence over their placement in the global political hierarchy (Harris, 1974). On the other hand, nations that have weak media diplomacy, in terms of influencing international media, or rely primarily on external media sources for information will have a foreign policy agenda that is incapable of pushing their preferred national identity or international image (McPhail, 1987; Rosenblum, 1979; Boyd-Barrett, 1980). Hence, the dynamics between media diplomacy and foreign policy must be a significant part of any analysis of contemporary international relations.

MEDIA DIPLOMACY AND NATIONAL IDENTITY

Most analyses of national identities and international images focus on citizens' sense of national consciousness, in terms of such characteristics as economic philosophy, language, religious and ethnic affiliations (Huntington, 1993, p. 22). The dynamic between national consciousness and international image is generally ignored. The assumption is that national consciousness and international image are isolated variables, and that national consciousness is the primary determinant of national identity (Rusciano and Ebo, 1992). But nations generally seek to create and maintain a favorable stature in the community of nations, and that stature often reflects the ability of a nation to project its national identity onto the global arena (Schiller 1976, 1992; Bloom, 1990).

The dominant political orientation in a society influences the relationship between the media and the government, and the characteristics of media diplomacy. Media institutions operate within the social, political and economic parameters of society and, as such, are symbolic reflections of the philosophical tenets of society. In absolutist political systems, governments tend to own media or at least directly control the media institution. It is not unusual for governments to openly use the media to articulate and promote foreign policy in such systems (Peterson, Schramm, & Siebert, 1956; Mickiewicz, 1988). For instance, many African governments are primarily interested in building nationhoods and see media as a legitimate official tool for political governance (Momoh, 1987; Hachten, 1971). They argue that the news media must openly and directly serve the interests of the nation and are legitimate official forums to articulate and promote foreign policy initiatives (Brice, 1992; Domatob, 1987). African governments believe that as young nations trying to build stable and cohesive political structures, adversarial media systems are not conducive to national development.

In libertarian political systems, on the other hand, the relationship between the media and the government has adversarial tendencies. The media are perceived as a watchdog and the fourth estate, and are expected to oversee the activities of the government in the interest of the public. Hence, media diplomacy has a discreet nature, to protect the integrity of the media (Altschull, 1995; Cohen, 1963; Peterson et al., 1956). In the United States and many Western democracies, for instance, constitutional protection gives the media enormous independence and power in publishing stories. Many media practitioners and foreign policy experts believe this power often hampers the ability of Western governments to conduct effective media diplomacy. One of the common examples of this is the argument that the United States lost the Vietnam War because the media freely published negative stories and pictures of the war. The media diplomacy of the United States government could not counteract the horrible images on American television of an eight-year-old Vietnamese girl running naked in a desperate attempt to escape a napalm bomb and a North Vietnamese soldier summarily executed on the street of Saigon. Such images would be suppressed at least internally, in absolutist political systems where the government controls the media.

Indeed, the media diplomacy of the United States government with regards to military conflicts has evolved in the aftermath of the Vietnam War. During the 1983 invasion of Grenada, the United States government instituted a news blackout (Servaes, 1991; Cuthbert, 1985). Correspondents were allowed to enter the country only after it was secured. The media decried the tactic, and the government was forced to introduce the "pool" format. The idea was to maintain a tight rein on information by giving only a select group of reporters access to soldiers and battlefronts. The group would share the information with the rest of the press corps. The format was used for the first time during the invasion of Panama in 1989 (Chomsky, 1990; MacArthur, 1992). The United States government also used the "pool" format during the Gulf War (Kellner, 1992; Apple, 1991). The media diplomacy benefit of the format was obvious during the Gulf War because correspondents were forced to rely heavily on press releases and official government sources for information because of limited access to battlefronts (Kellner, 1992; Apple, 1991).

The relationship between the media and the government becomes collaborative when the potential exists for grave harm to national security. In the late 1950s, for instance, the *New York Times* knew that the United States government was flying high-altitude U-2 spy planes over the Soviet Union but withheld the information. The paper revealed that it was aware of the secret mission only after one of the planes was shot down by the Soviets in 1960. The paper also knew in 1960 that the Central Intelligence Agency was training Cuban exiles in Florida to invade Cuba but withheld the information until the Bay of Pigs fiasco. Ironically, President Kennedy would later remark that he wished the paper had published the information and saved the United States from a colossal mistake (Kern et al., 1983).

The United States media coverage of the events surrounding the bombing of Libya in 1986 is another example of collaborative media diplomacy. The United States media generally accepted the claim by the government that Libya was behind the 1986 West Berlin disco bombing which precipitated the U.S. bomb attack on Libya (Nelson, 1981). Breslau (1987, p. 46) observed that:

> Strangely absent from the subsequent press account of the bombing was any serious inquiry into the nature of the 'evidence' used by the administration to justify its attack. Also left unexplained was the nature of the threat America was 'defending' itself against, and why it was Libyan terrorism—not Syrian or Iranian—that represented the gravest and most immediate 'danger' to the United States and its citizens.

The U.S. media acquiesced by staying away from any serious examination of government evidence, even though much of it actually pointed to Syria. ABC News had prior knowledge that the U.S. was planning the attack on Libya and chose not to publish the information (ABC Nightline Viewpoint, February 6, 1987). As it turned out, the claim from the United States government that Libya was responsible for the disco bombing was a disinformation campaign to justify the attack on Libya (Breslau, 1987, p. 46). In essence, media diplomacy is not only used to promote the prefereed national identity of a nation in the global arena but also to undermine the preferred national identity and international image of enemies. In some extreme cases, governments use correspondents as intelligence agents to collect information. British international news agency Reuters has worked covertly for the British intelligence agency since World War I (Preston et al, 1989, p. xxiv). There have been several cases where the CIA used correspondents as intelligent agents to gather covert information (Loory, 1974; Fletcher, 1981; Preston, Herman, & Schiller, 1989, p. 75).

MEDIA DIPLOMACY AND INTERNATIONAL IMAGE

The respect a nation enjoys in the world community and the role the nation plays in contemporary international relations are influenced by the national identity and international image of the nation. National and international media play an important role in defining the national identity and international image of a nation in the information age. A major variable in the effectiveness of a nation's media diplomacy is its ability to use the major international media to assert its version of national identity and international image. Indeed, the international image of a nation as articulated in the international media is an important assessment of the acceptance or impact of a nation's foreign policy in the global arena. This explains why governments maintain expense accounts for domestic and international public relations. Manheim and Albritton's (1983) study indicates that public relations campaigns directed at the media generally result in positive media coverage for nations.

For years during apartheid, the South African government retained the services of powerful public relations firms in the United States to polish its tarnished image in the world (Windrich, 1989) . Before the Gulf War, the Kuwaiti government hired the high powered public relations firm of Hill and Knowlton to portray Saddam Hussein as a monster, and to induce the reluctant American public to support military action against Iraq. Some countries take it upon themselves to orchestrate their public relations campaigns. The Togolese government, for instance, flies in foreign correspondents, all expenses paid, and fete them to cover national events (Lee and Astrow, 1987).

During the Cold War the United States and Soviet Union engaged in an intense media diplomacy aimed at creating negative international image of each other. When ABC network produced the $40 million controversial mini-series "Amerika" in 1987 which depicted life in United States after a Soviet invasion, the Soviet government saw the movie as nothing more than propaganda. A top Soviet official called the program "a disappointing event in the life of the American mass media" (Gitlin, 1987, p. 35). The condemnation was interesting because the Soviet-owned media had constantly portrayed the United States as a decadent and morally inept country.

The "Hyder Incident" also illustrates the media diplomacy struggle between the United States and the Soviet Union during the Cold War. The relative inattention Dr. Charles Hyder received from the United States media during his hunger strike in front of the White House in 1987 to protest nuclear armaments was presented by the Soviet media as an example of the United States media unwillingness to cover stories that ridicule the United States. But while Hyder's protest was constantly in the Soviet media, the story was not about his moral commitment to global nuclear disarmament. Rather, the Soviets saw in Hyder an opportunity to score a point against the United States in the I-am-holier-than-thou media diplomacy over human rights. The Kremlin even invited Hyder to visit the Soviet Union, not to dramatize his campaign, but to further embarrass the United States (CBS Evening News, March 12, 1987).

A major variable in a government's success in asserting its own version of national identity is its ability to convince both its citizens and the international community that the identity it seeks to project is legitimate. The "islamization" of the Iranian media after the collapse of the Shah's regime was an effort by the new sectarian leaders to legitimize a new islamic identity (Mowlana, 1989). Part of the goal was to use media to assure its citizens and the international community that the national identity of Iran does not violate the norms of international relationships. In Third World countries, the media, particularly television, have always played an important role in nation-building. These countries argue that the political instability and social disintegration brought about by the arbitrary demarcation of nations by colonialism makes nation-building their primary political concern (Momoh, 1987). Television and other media are important in the process because of their ability to create a sense of political and social unity when controlled by the government. For most Third World countries, freedom of the press is a luxury they cannot afford.

During the Gulf War the international media's response to Iraq's invasion of Kuwait might have been muted had Saddam Hussein been able to generate supportive coverage from the major international media for his historical claim to sovereignty over Kuwait. In fact, Hussein tried desperately to use the international media to legitimize his actions and create a positive international image for Iraq without much success. His early media diplomacy efforts were designed to engender an international image of Iraq that included the territory captured from Kuwait. Without much success, Hussein attempted to portray himself as a compassionate leader—President Bush had referred to him as another Hitler—by appearing on television with Western hostages and their children. He was shown patting the heads of some of the children in a move calculated to create a positive international image. This backfired because the television appearance portrayed him as devious man willing to use children as a pawn. He then attempted to influence American public opinion against the use of military force by recalling the Vietnam analogy, and emphasizing Iraq's greater willingness to sustain troop losses. Hussein also directed a media campaign towards the Arab world, framing the Gulf conflict as a jihad—holy war—against the West (Ebo, 1995).

Hussein's major problem was that he failed to derive support from the major international media due to their almost universal condemnation of the Iraqi invasion. Only three major daily European newspapers out of 50 sampled in one study categorically opposed the use of force to remove Iraq from Kuwait (USIA, 1990, pp. 6–10). Hussein's attempt to push for a new identity and international image for Iraq which encompassed the captured territory failed to influence the international media, and so they did not give legitimacy to the Iraqi cause. Iraq's media diplomacy, consequently foreign policy, was unable to convince the international community that it was in their interest to accept Iraq's definition of the conflict. Iraq was put at a disadvantage because of its lack of influence over the international media and lack of credible media outlets outside Iraq. Even within its own borders, Iraq was bombarded with pro-Kuwaiti information from external sources, and Hussein had to struggle to control the information that came into Iraq (Rusciano, 1993).

MEDIA DIPLOMACY AND GLOBAL POLITICAL HIERARCHY

Media diplomacy is an integral component of the global power structure in contemporary foreign policy because the hierarchical structure of international relationships reflects media dominance to a significant degree (Galtung, 1992). While military advantage still plays an important role in global power structure, superiority in communications technology equally gives a nation an advantage in exerting some influence over its national identity and international image (Albritton, Manheim and Jones, 1983). The ability of a nation to use the international media to construct an international image that complements its preferred national identity is important to the "power" status of the nation and placement on the global political hierarchy (George, 1991).

Global political agenda, hence global political power, is more than ever influenced by the structure of the global information order (Bonkovsky, 1980; Lee, 1980). Media diplomacy, foreign policy and transnational corporate culture exhibit a mutuality of purpose that shapes the global flow of information in line with national interests (Golding, 1979, Schiller, 1976). The global allocation of resources and investments by transnational companies, including media organizations, involve the transfer of technology and business etiquette that encase political philosophies (Lee 1980). Thus, the global flow of news embodies an inherent transfer of media artifacts that prescribe a certain ideological leaning that favor certain global power alignments (Peterson, 1979; Ostgaard, 1965).

The political significance of a country or a geographical region raises the newsworthiness of that country or region and provides political incentives for international media to allocate media resources and attention to that country or region (Galtung, 1971; Tatarian, 1978, p. 3). Also, choices of countries and geographical regions to cover are influenced by political affinity and socio-cultural mutuality (Peterson, 1979; Ostgaard, 1965). Western media coverage of Chad, Angola, Grenada, Philippines and Panama during political strife in those nations reflected political alignments. These obscure and ordinarily politically insignificant countries gained lavish attention from Western governments and media because they become crisis centers that threatened Western political interests (Ebo, 1992). Chad received a lot of Western media coverage because of Libyan involvement in the crisis and Libya's strong anti-Western sentiments (Breslau, 1987; Nelson, 1981). Grenada received lavish coverage from Western news media because of Cuban involvement in the civil war and the long-standing animosity between United States and Cuba (Cuthbert, 1985). As soon as the temporary political significance of these countries died down, they lost their generous limelight in the news.

Even though Third World countries have developed a reputation for openly treating media as an official arm of the government, historically Western governments have actively used broadcast services for diplomatic functions. Indeed, media diplomacy was a big part of the intense ideological struggle between the Western Alliance and the Soviet-led Warsaw Pact during the Cold War for control of global political agenda. Radio Free Europe and Radio Liberty, sponsored by the United States and Western alliance, broadcast promotional democratic messages into former Warsaw Pact countries for four decades to discredit communism (Merrill, 1995, pp. 159–160). Understandably, the fund for Radio Free Europe and Radio Liberty was slashed by the United States congress after the collapse of communism in Eastern Europe. Both operations have moved to Prague from Munich, with reduced diplomatic function. Philosophically, the United States still sees such ventures as a significant part of media diplomacy. The senate approved Radio Free Asia in January 1994 to broadcast into China (Merrill, 1995, p. 301).

The British Broadcasting Corporation international radio network has served as an official arm of British foreign service since the British colonial ventures. The Voice of America and Radio Moscow play the same role for the United States of America and Russia respectively. Because of the sour relationship between Fidel Castro and the United States, Cuba has been a particular target of United States broadcast service (Frances, 1967). Since 1984 Radio Marti, located in South Florida and named after Jose Marti, the revered organizer of Cuba's war of liberation from Spain, has broadcast anti-Castro information into Cuba (Head, 1985, p. 139). The official United States television service, WORLDNET, disseminates foreign policy information in multiple languages all over the world. The president occasionally uses the network to discuss foreign affairs. The United States Armed Forces Network also disseminates foreign policy information to locals and military personnel stationed overseas.

National governments and multi-national corporations achieve and maintain ideological hegemony using media diplomacy apparatuses such as advertising agencies, market surveys, opinion polls, public relations and technological transfer (Lee 1980, p. 619). Western international news agencies, as part of multi-national corporate system, are inseparable elements in the worldwide capitalist system of resource allocations, and invariably provide imagery and messages that create and reinforce their audiences attachment to the media's country of origin. This explains why many Third World governments are reluctant to import media technology and artifacts from the West. In fact, some sectarian governments in the Middle East such as Saudi Arabia and Iran have national decrees that prohibit importation of media artifacts such as television programs and movies from the West. These governments subscribe to the inherent link between ideology, media artifacts and foreign policy.

The intense debate in the United Nations in the 1970s for a New World Information Order (NWIO) was really a fight for redistribution of advantages of media diplomacy between the West and the Third World (MacBride, 1980). Third World countries argued that the four major Western international news agencies—Associated Press, United Press International, Reuters and Agence France Press—controlled eighty percent of global news flow, and that the West was using this advantage to maintain a tight grip over global political agenda (Fenby, 1986; Boyd-Barrett, 1980). For Third World countries, this global information structure is only another form of political, economic and cultural colonization (Masmoudi, 1979).

Except during periods of crisis that threaten Western interests, Africa ordinarily does not command significant Western media attention. Western media diplomacy tends to play down or ignore African concerns and the role of Africa in the world community. Smiley (1982, p.70) observed that, "Africa, vast as it is, no longer seems of great importance to the rest of the world. Journalists know that the great power game will not be played out there." Fitzgerald (1987, p. 24) similarly observed that "For the most part, Africa... is not a player in the great global power game, and... is not deemed to be newsworthy because it is not high on the foreign policy agenda of the West."

The proliferation of national and regional news agencies in the Third World in the late 1970s and 1980s was an attempt to address this media diplomacy disadvantage after the collapse of the movement for a New World Information Order (NWIO). Third World countries felt that these news agencies would reduce or eliminate their dependence on Western international news agencies, an important step towards improving their media diplomacy capability. The Non-Aligned Nations Agencies Pool (NANAP) was a news clearinghouse set up by a conglomeration of Third World countries to collect and circulate news stories primarily among member nations (Pinch, 1978; Ivacic, 1978).

More regionally oriented news agencies sprang up in different parts of the Third World to cater to the specific concerns of those regions. The PanAfrican News Agency

(PANA), set up in 1979 by the Organization of African Unity, was envisioned as a continental media diplomacy vehicle for African nations to counteract negative images in the West (Africa Communications, 1993; Wauthier, 1987). Other Third World regional news agencies include the Caribbean News Agency; the Latin American news agency, Accion de Sistemas Informativos Nacionales; Federation of Arabic News Agency; Middle Eastern news agency, OPEP and Islamic International News Agency (Cuthbert, 1985; Cholomondeley, 1977). While the effectiveness of these Third World news agencies is still open to debate, their formation at least indicates the importance of media diplomacy for contemporary international relations.

Media diplomacy has become an important part of national movements and guerrilla warfare because of the power of the international media to legitimize political platforms. The label the major international media ascribe to a national or guerrilla movement influences the global recognition and legitimacy of that movement. Whether guerrilla fighters are called "terrorists" or "freedom fighters" influences its placement in global political agenda. The Western international news agencies legitimized the Contras when they were fighting to overthrow the Sandanista government of Nicaragua by calling them "freedom fighters," while delegitimizing the Sandanista government by labeling it "communist." The media treatment of the Contras and Sandanista paralleled the foreign policy of the United States. The Reagan administration had argued that the Contras were the moral equivalent of the founding fathers because of ideological compatibility with the United States. Unita's Jonas Savimbi received global legitimacy during the Angolan civil war because Western governments effectively used the media to present him as a "freedom fighter" and an anti-Communist crusader (Jennings, 1992; Windrich, 1992).

Western media coverage of South Africa during apartheid was couched in ways that did not compromise Western economic benefits from South Africa. Apartheid was portrayed as a system of racial discrimination rather than economic domination (Schechter, 1987, p. 6). Such emphasis ignored how the West was benefiting from the economic exploitation of blacks under apartheid. The coverage reflected the position of the South African government and the Reagan administration that the African National Congress' inclination towards communism constituted a major threat (Windrich, 1989). Schechter (1987, p. 6) observed that, "...just as the Reagan administration bought the South African line that the African National Congress was a communist front, so much of the media uncritically parroted the same view." As a result, "The ANC was invariably described as 'pro-Soviet' or Marxist. Yet, other groups were rarely called 'capitalist,' 'racist' or 'pro-American'" (Schechter, 1987, p. 6). The consequence was that for a long time following the lead of the U.S. Government, the Western news media did not legitimize the ANC's efforts to dismantle apartheid despite its condemnation of racial practices in South Africa.

International Western media coverage of the Iranian revolution in 1979 also illustrates the relationship between media diplomacy, foreign policy and global political power. Iran was a valuable clandestine post for the United States because of its proximity to the Soviet Union and the Shah was a strong ally, so the United States government was determined to keep him in power. The United States government used the international Western media to orchestrate an effective media diplomacy that played down the domestic protest against the Shah (Smith, 1980, p. 102). Instead, he was portrayed as firmly in charge even though there were indications that the supporters of Ayatollah Khomeni were mounting an effective underground media diplomacy by smuggling audio tapes of his speeches into Iran. Until the Shah was finally dethroned, the Western media had portrayed the protesters as a handful of disgruntled religious zealots without wide support from the Iranian people (Smith, 1980, p. 102). During the Iranian hostage crisis, both U.S. and Iran also tried to use the international media to campaign for the appropriate label for the hostages. The United States government officially classified them as "hostages" while the Iran government called them "spies." Much of the international media, particularly the powerful international Western media, went along with the United States classification.

During the Gulf War the Western alliance used the international media to promote a notion of international consensus for military campaign against Iraq (Hinckley, 1991). The West presented the war as a conflict between Saddam Hussein and the international community, thus invalidating Iraqi claim to the captured Kuwaiti territory (Ebo, 1995). The major international media barely examined the nature of the international consensus. The fact that the United States government acquired Egyptian support for the War by forgiving $8 billion in debts or that the United States government was willing to ignore the well-documented Syrian reputation for sponsoring international terrorism to gain Syrian support were not important. Similarly, the fact that the United States government gained Russian support for the war by ignoring the Soviet crackdown in the Baltic regions, and granted China a high-level diplomatic contact to gain its support, reversing the post-Tiananmen Square policy, did not receive any significant international media coverage (Ebo, 1995). The U.S. and Western governments effectively used the international media to promote the notion of complete Arab support for military action against Iraq, although Yemen, Morocco and Tunisia opted for economic sanctions (Ebo, 1995).

Western media diplomacy successfully portrayed Iraq as a reckless military power because the media virtually ignored the role the United States government played in facilitating Iraqi arms build-up in the first place. Efforts by the Iraqi government to focus some attention on the historical context for the Iraqi-Kuwaiti conflict in terms of the perennial territorial dispute between the two nations were over-shadowed by intense Western media diplomacy. Western media diplomacy masterfully constructed an image of Saddam Hussein that fit into pre-existing stereotypes of Arabs as terrorist (Ebo, 1995; Said, 1981). One source noted that "media coverage of the war, by and large, was led by the U.S. media, and to a lesser degree, by the British and French. The rest of the world literally relied on a few powerful news organizations, primarily from the U.S., which had the technology and were favored by the military" (Media Development, October 1991, p. 1). In essence, "The military superpower made sure that all the world's media became American" (Media Development, October 1991, p. 1).

DISCUSSION AND CONCLUSION

Media diplomacy has become an important component of contemporary foreign policy because of the information revolution. Media have become a dominant source of information for people and a powerful player in international relationships. The traditional idea of global power, determined primarily by military advantage, no longer sufficiently explains the nature of contemporary international relations and foreign policy. The ability of a nation to use the media to construct an international image that complements its preferred national identity is now an important function of foreign policy. Thus, media diplomacy constitutes a predominant factor that moderates the sense a nation has of itself and the image the rest of the world has of it.

If a nation is to create and maintain a favorable international image in the world community, it must have the ability to project its preferred national identity onto the global arena. The implication, of course, is that superiority in communications technology may allow a nation to exert some control over the flow of global information and its international image. Thus, while every nation will have some power to construct its national identity internally by exerting control over domestic forces, including national media, nations with dominant global media advantage will have a better chance of shaping their international image and placement in the global political hierarchy.

The dynamics between media diplomacy and foreign policy must be a significant part of any analysis of contemporary international relations. National dignity and the placement of a nation in the global political hierarchy are influenced as much by the international image of the nation. Indeed, a nation's global political "power" in the information age emerges, in part, from the interaction between national identity and international image, to the extent that the nation could use the media to align them. The dynamics between media diplomacy and foreign policy must be examined in the context of national identity, international image and global political power. In this sense, media diplomacy is indispensable to foreign policy because of the power of the media to shape the international image of a nation.

REFERENCES

Adams, W. C. (1982). *Television coverage of international affairs*. Norwood, NJ: Ablex Publishing Corporation.

Africa Communications (1993, May-June 8). PANA agency on the road to revival.

Albritton, R., Manheim, J. & Jones, R. (1983, October 21). *Public relations and the control of external national images: an added dimension in international communication*. Paper presented at the Conference on Communications, Mass Media and Development, Northwestern University, Evanston, Illinois.

Altschull, J. H. (1995). *Agents of power: The media and public policy*. New York: Longman.

Apple, R. W. (1991, December 2). Correspondents protest pool system. *New York Times*.

Bloom, W. (1990). *Personal identity, national identity and international relations*. Cambridge: Cambridge University Press.

Bonkovsky, F. (1980). *International norms and national policy*. Grand Rapids, MI: Eerdmans

Boyd-Barrett, O. (1980). *The international news agencies*. Beverly Hills, CA: Sage.

Breslau, A. (1987, March–April). Demonizing Qaddafy. *Africa Report,* 32, 46–47.

Brice, K. (1992, July–August). Muzzling the media. *Africa Report* 37, 49–51.

Cholomondeley, H. N. J. (1977, April). CANA: An independent news agency launched by the English-speaking Caribbean countries. *Unesco Courier*, 10–11.

Chomsky, N. (1990). The invasion of Panama. *Lies of Our Times*, (2).

Cohen, B. C. (1963). *The press and foreign policy*. Princeton, NJ: Princeton University Press.

Cuthbert, M. (1981). The Caribbean news agency: Third world model. *Journalism Monographs*, (71). Columbia, SC: Association for Education in Journalism and Mass Communication.

Cuthbert, M. (1985). Journalistic perspectives on the Grenada crisis: Media coverage in the Caribbean, Canada, the United States and Europe. *Press Association of Jamaica.*

Davison, P. (1975). Diplomatic reporting: Rules of the game. *Journal of Communication, 25*(4), 138–146.

Delaney, R. F. (1968). Introduction. In Arthur Hoffman (Ed.), *International communication and the new diplomacy*. Bloomington, IN: Indiana University Press.

Domatob, J. K. (1987). Propaganda techniques in black Africa. *Gazette, 36*(3), 193–212.

Ebo, B. (1983). *Africa and the West in the new world information order.* Paper presented at the Northwestern University Conference on Communication and Development. Chicago, Illinois.

Ebo, B. (1992). American media and African culture. In Beverly Hawk, (Ed.), *Africa's media image*. New York: Praeger.

Ebo, B. (1995). War as popular culture: the gulf conflict and the technology of illusionary entertainment. *Journal of American Culture. 18*(3).

Fenby, J. (1986). *The international news services*. New York: Schocken Books.

Fisher, G. (1972). *Public diplomacy and the behavioral sciences*. Bloomington, IN: Indiana University Press.

Fitzgerald, M. A. (1987, March–April). In defense of the fourth estate. (reporter's notebook). *Africa Report,* 32, 24–26.

Fletcher, R. (1981, December 18). How the Secret Service shaped the news. *The Guardian* (London).

Frances, M. J. (1967). The U.S. press and Castro: A study in declining relations. *Journalism Quarterly, 44*, 257–266.

Galtung, J. (1971). A structural theory of imperialism. *Journal of Peace Research, 82*(2), 81–117.

Galtung, J. (1992). *Global glasnost: Toward a new world information and communication order?* Cresskill, NJ: Hampton.

Galtung, J. & Ruge, M. H. (1965). The structure of foreign news. *Journal of International Peace Research, 1*, 64–90.

George, A. (1991). *Forceful persuasion: Coercive diplomacy as an alternative to war*. Washington, D.C.: United States Institute of Peace Press.

Gitlin, T. (1987, January). Invaders from ABC: A study in the pathology of network television. *Mother Jones.*

Golding, P. (1979). Media professionalism in the third world: Transfer of an ideology. In J. Curran, M. Gurevitch, & J. Woolacot, (Eds.), *Mass communication and society.* Beverly Hills, CA: Sage.

Hachten, W. (1971). *Muffled drums: The news media in Africa.* Ames, IA: Iowa State University Press.

Hansen, R. D., Fishlow, A., Pearlberg, R., Lewis, J. P. (1982). *U.S. foreign policy and the third world.* New York: Praeger.

Harris, P. (1974). Hierarchy and concentration in international news flow. *Politics, 9,* 159.

Head, S. (1985). *World broadcasting systems.* Belmont, CA: Wadsworth.

Hinckley, R. (1991, May). World public opinion and the Persian Gulf crisis. *Proceedings of the American Association for Public Opinion Research.* Phoenix, AZ.

Huntington, S. (1993, Summer). The clash of civilizations? *Foreign Affairs, 72* (3) 22–49.

Ivacic, P. (1978). The flow of news: Tanjug, the pool and the national agencies. *Journal of Communication, 28*(4), 157–162.

Jennings, K. (1992). Jonas Savimbi's media image analyzed. *Africa Today, 39*(1–2), Second Quarter, 145–146.

Kellner, D. (1992). *The Persian Gulf TV war.* Boulder, CO: Westview Press.

Kern, M., Levering, P. W., & Levering, R. B. (1983). *The Kennedy crises: The press, the presidency, and foreign policy* University of North Carolina Press.

Lee, A., & Astrow, A. (1987, March–April). Togo: In search of friends. *Africa Report, 32,* 51–53.

Lee, C. (1980). *Media imperialism reconsidered.* Beverly Hills, CA: Sage.

Loory, S. (1974). The CIA's use of the press: A 'mighty wurlitzer'. *Columbia Journalism Review, 13.*

MacArthur, J. (1992). *Second front: Censorship and propaganda in the Gulf War.* New York: Hill & Wang.

MacBride, S. (1980). *Many voices, one world: Communication and society, today and tomorrow.* Paris: UNESCO.

Manheim, J. & Albritton, R. (1983, September). *Changing national images: Public relations campaigns and the foreign policy agenda.* Paper presented at the annual Meeting of the American Political Science Association, Chicago.

Masmoudi, M. (1979). The new world information order. *Journal of Communication, 29*(2), 172–185.

McPhail, T. (1987). *Electronic colonialism.* Beverly Hills, CA: Sage Publications.

Merrill, J. C. (1995) *Global journalism: A survey of international communication* (3rd ed.). New York: Longman.

Mickiewicz, E. (1988). *Split signals: Television and political life in the Soviet Union.* New York: Oxford University Press.

Momoh, P. T. (1987, March–April). Nigeria: the press and nation-building. *Africa Report, 32,* 54–57.

Mowlana, H. (1989, October–November). The Islamization of Iranian television. *InterMedia, 17*(5), pp. 38.

Mowlana, H., Gerbner, G. & Schiller, H. (1992). *Triumph of the image: The media's war in the Persian Gulf—a global perspective.* Boulder, CO: Westview.

Nelson, L. (1981, December 9). The Khadafy plot: fact, fiction and fear, *New York Daily News.*

O'Heffernan, P. (1991). *Mass media and American foreign policy: Insider perspectives on global journalism and the foreign policy process.* Norwood, NJ: Ablex.

Ostgaard, E. (1965). Factors influencing the flow of news. *Journal of Peace Research, 1,* 47.

Peterson, S. (1979). Foreign gatekeepers and criteria of newsworthiness. *Journalism Quarterly, 56.*

Peterson, T., Schramm, W., & Siebert, F. (1956). *Four theories of the press*. Urbana, IL: University of Chicago Press.

Pinch, E. (1978). The flow of news: an assessment of the non-aligned news agencies pool. *Journal of Communication, 28*(4), 163.

Preston, W., Herman, E., & Schiller, H. (1989). *Hope and folly: The United States and UNESCO, 1945–1985*. Minneapolis, MN: University of Minnesota Press.

Ramaprasad, J. (1983). Media diplomacy: in search of a definition. *Gazette, 31,* 69–75.

Rosenblum, M. (1979). *Coups and earthquakes*. New York: Harper and Row.

Rosenthal, H. F. (1983, May 30). U.S. devotes millions to PR, experts, *Washington Post*.

Rusciano, F. (1992, November). *World opinion on the Kuwaiti-Iraqi question: Does the third world have a voice*. Paper presented at the Annual Meeting of the Association for the Advancement of Policy, Research and Development in the Third World. Radisson Hotel, Orlando, Florida.

Rusciano, F. (1993). Media perspectives on world opinion during the Kuwaiti crisis. In R. E. Denton (Ed.). *Media and the Persian Gulf War*. New York: Praeger.

Rusciano, F., & Ebo, B. (1993, Summer). *National consciousness, international image, and the construction of identity*. Paper presented at the American Political Science Association Convention in Washington, D.C.

Said, E. (1981). *Covering Islam: How the media and the experts determine how we see the rest of the world*. New York: Pantheon.

Schechter, D. (1987, March–April). How we cover southern Africa. *Africa Report, 32,* 4–8.

Schiller, H. (1976). *Communication and cultural domination*. White Plains, NY: International Arts and Sciences Press.

Schiller, H. (1992). *Mass communications and American empire* (2nd ed.). Boulder, CO: Westview.

Serfaty, S. (Ed.) (1990) *The media and foreign policy*. New York: St. Martin's Press.

Servaes, J. (1991, October). Was Grenada a testcase for the 'disinformation war'? *Media Development*, Special Issue.

Skurnik, W. A. E. (1981). Foreign news coverage in six African newspapers: The potency of national interests. *Gazette 28,* 117–130.

Smiley, X. (1982, September). Misunderstanding Africa. *The Atlantic Monthly*, 70.

Smith, A. (1980). *The geopolitics of information*. New York: Oxford University Press.

Stein, R. (1970). *Media power: Who is shaping the picture of the world?* Englewood Cliffs, NJ: Prentice-Hall.

Tatarian, R. (1978). *The multinational news pool*. Medford, MA: Tufts University.

Tehranian, M. (1990). *Technologies of power: Information technologies and democratic prospects*. Norwood, NJ: Ablex.

Tunstall, J. (1977). *The media are American*. New York: Columbia University Press.

Wauthier, C. (1987, March–April). PANA: The voice of Africa, *Africa Report, 32,* 65–67.

Wilcox, D. (1975). *Mass media in Black Africa: Philosophy and control*. New York: Praeger.

Windrich, E. (1989). South Africa's propaganda war. *Africa Today, 36*(1), First Quarter, 51–60.

Windrich, E. (1992). Media coverage of the Angolan war. *Africa Today, 39*(1–2), 2nd Quarter, 89–99.

chapter 4

information liberalization and the restructuring of international relations

Shalini Venturelli
The American University

INTRODUCTION

In a recent essay on the spread of liberal internationalism, Stanley Hoffman observes that the conscious neglect of self-determination and human rights in the foreign policy agenda of advanced, industrialized liberal states since the post-Cold War, is being "rationalized with the argument that the propagation of political liberalism will ultimately result from the spread of global economic liberalism" (Hoffman, 1995, p. 169). Recognizing the deficit of this assumption, he nevertheless sees no alternative to liberalism, calling it "the only comprehensive and hopeful vision of world affairs" (p. 177) which has "succeeded in removing a vast number of barriers to trade and communications" (p. 174). Even while admitting that "the global economy is literally out of control, not subject to the rules of accountability and principles of legitimacy" (p. 175), Hoffman maintains that the transnational economic order "constitutes a triumph of the liberal vision that first appeared in the eighteenth century" (p. 174). Ultimately, Hoffman has no answer to the problem of regulation or governance over the forces of international liberalization since he reverts to the example of liberal realism as the only model for world development.

While the theory and practice of international realism has been around for some time, contemporary liberalization has transformed the realist basis of interstate relations into a set of powerful forces for compelling nations worldwide into a single design of the social order. It is the argument of this paper that information liberalization applied through the emerging framework of the "global information highway" is one of the most important forces for advancing the political aims of liberal internationalism which predominantly favor the reconstitution of the world system on the basis of large-scale proprietary interests. The argument will be demonstrated by analysis of the basis of contemporary liberal internationalism and its manifestation in the restructuring tendencies of global communication policy within areas involving the problem of democracy, the politics of competition policy, telecommunication liberalization, the minimization of universal service, and institutionalization of information liberalization by means of the world multilateral system on most nations and regions of the world. The chapter concludes by suggesting a few central issues that are being effaced in the global information liberalization debate because they lie outside the logic of the liberal internationalist agenda for reconstituting interstate relations.

THE BASIS OF LIBERAL INTERNATIONALISM

Hoffman's account overlooks the central question of the relation between liberal internationalism and modern communications: namely, the extent to which information liberalization enhances or even further alienates citizens' rights to participate in the decisions of political association. As seen in this inquiry, current "information revolution" or technological innovation arguments justifying a radical restructuring of the relation between the state and society, are generally employed to emphasize how liberalism would be strengthened by the universal propagation of communication technologies which, by virtue of their technological components, transfer power of decision making and oversight to individuals worldwide. The argument that participatory democracy is no longer an issue because it will be implemented by technological means is put forward by liberalization policies (see Commission of the European Communities, 1995a, 1995b, 1994a, 1994b; U.S. Congress, 1995a, 1993a; U.S. Government, 1995, 1995a, 1993) and their conceptual justifications (see, for instance, Noam, 1995, 1989; Pool, 1990) though unproved by the social order of liberal internationalism.

As demonstrated in the analysis here, these proposals fail to address the profound contradiction between liberal internationalism and the democratization of nation states. The seemingly straightforward technological solution of the spread of computing and interactive devices that possess the inherent capacity to democratize public space, public policy, and even the practice of voting, disallows some essential questions to be raised. These include, for instance: (a) Why do extensions of information technology mostly give rise to the servicing of large-scale proprietary preferences as opposed to broad societal development through access to information and the advancement of democratic participation; or why does the process of innovation seem to favor the growth of commercial penetration as against non-commercial, associational organization? (b) Will information liberalization allow societies to transform, in any way at all, the existing conditions by whom and how issues of common concern in the public arena are to be formulated? and (c) For all societies affected by the forces of information liberalization—viz., by consenting to global communication policy regimes—will there be actual enlargement and advancement in how individuals learn of the arguments for and against the various proposals for the development of their societies? An engagement with these questions in international relations is more likely to establish whether liberal internationalism and its mechanism of information liberalization point to a substantive improvement in the prospects for democracy and global development than do policies which merely reference dramatic advancements in technological innovation. This section takes up some of these questions by examining the basis of liberal internationalism and its realist thesis.

The realist approach to foreign policy is the notion that among societies and states power is the predominant currency and self-interest the predominant motivation (Walker, 1993). While this is also an ancient, neo-classical idea of world affairs (see Machiavelli, 1985/1513; and discussion of Thucydides in Bruell, 1974), in the late twentieth century it has fully merged with liberal internationalism (Forde, 1995) because of the essential consistency with liberalism's postulates of competitive private self-interest and the preservation of existing conditions of social power as the basis for the organization of society. This view presupposes the negation of any competing moral outlook regarding the nature of international relations. For instance, contemporary international realism treats liberalization as justified in shedding normative concerns regarding the ethical basis of interstate relations because of liberalization's increasing reliance on the scientific grounds of technological innovation and market economics. A cornerstone of contemporary liberal internationalist theory and practice is the principle that truly scientific processes at work in the logic of economic competition and technological innovation is inherently value free with respect to political constitutions and power, proprietary conditions, culture, religion, or social development, and hence applicable to all human societies as a scientific, and value-neutral path to a global model of interstate relations. An important defense of this view argues that the only alternative to liberal internationalism in the post Cold War is the existence and persistence of anarchy (Grieco, 1988). Only if states respond to the (inevitable) conditions of international anarchy by the terms of this late modern form of international realism—which emphasizes private proprietary relations on a world scale as the basis of interstate relations—can nations hope to establish behavioral regularities that are rational, thereby peaceful, scientific, and mutually beneficial to all societies.

Thus universal imperialism via liberal internationalism is justified on the rational grounds of proprietary self-interest held to be a progressive force which deserves liberation on its own account through a foreign policy constituted in realist bilateralism and multilateralism in trade and economic arrangements. What gives modern liberal internationalism its scientific character is its grounding in necessity—the fundamental liberal defense of a theory of nature organized around the processes of competitive self-interest. Natural compulsions for private self-interests mainly with respect to issues of property and accumulation arising from the state of nature induce both individuals and states to act in the ways described by realist liberalism. Information liberalization grants profound legitimacy to the arguments and reality of liberal internationalism because it is a verification of this natural necessity of market economics and of its consequences. If the liberalization of trade and information services, or more generally, the exercise of power based only on private interest, constitutes a genuine law of international behavior in the sense argued by liberal realists (Donnelly, J. 1992), no state can be blamed for acting in accordance with liberalization. To the extent that the imperialist behavior of expanding, large-scale proprietary interests under contemporary information liberalization is referred to nature, hence scientific necessity, it is removed from the realm of ethical discourse, for it is its own exoneration.

The goal of the science of liberal internationalism is to guarantee the survival of existing proprietary structures and the liberal state laboring on its behalf, which can be accomplished only by the pursuit of economic power and the practice of universal preemptive imperialism in global communications markets. This realist environment continually threatens the genuine moral achievement represented by democratic community, and the two irreconcilable poles of morality and necessity suggest an almost tragic perspective for the "global information highway" and the information age. This issue of the global human achievement of democracy and its irreconcilable conflict with the realist basis of information liberalization oriented to a set of private proprietary ends that are not necessarily democratic, should be explored in the discussion of liberalism's model of democracy constituted in global communication policy and arrangements.

LIBERAL INTERNATIONALISM VS. DEMOCRACY

Schumpeter (1947) defends the core of liberalism's model of democracy which he describes as "the democratic method of institutional arrangements for arriving at political decisions in which individuals acquire the power to decide via a competitive struggle for the people's vote" (pp. 232–302). Democracy is defined by Schumpeter not as a kind of society or a set of moral ends or even as a principle of legitimacy but rather as a method of competitive struggle. The liberal model, therefore, claims the advantages of realism in its emphasis on the descriptive, pragmatic, and as the sole model appropriate to modern international relations. Thus the realist model of democracy prides itself on providing an operationalizable and empirically descriptive account of the needs and behaviors of nations considered to be democratic. In short, the realist theory of liberal democracy tends quite openly to reduce the normative meaning of the term to a set of minimum procedures for bargaining and competition derived from the preeminent realism of the market than from any model of citizenship or participation.

Competitiveness in acquiring power is, of course, the core of this model of democracy. The competitive element is deemed to be the source of creativity, productivity, responsibility, and responsiveness but is first and foremost the only legitimate behavior in international relations. Indeed, participation theorists argue that the realist model has denuded the concept of democracy of so many of its elements that it has lost any connection with its original meaning (Cohen & Arato, 1992). In short, the price of the realist model of democracy and international relations is the loss of what has always been taken to be the core of the concept of democracy, namely, the citizenship principle (Arendt, 1958; Habermas, 1989) that carries definite normative assumptions of justice, participation, access, and common interest. For these reasons, among others, liberal internationalism along with the forces of information liberalization to which it gives rise lose all criteria for distinguishing between public communications systems comprised of formalistic ritual, systematic distortion, choreographed consent, manipulated public opinion, on the one hand, and systems of participatory communication structures, on the other.

The practice of international realism today by liberal states—principally in the form of information liberalization—involves either some rather undemocratic adjustments to the exigencies of advanced industrial societies coupled with an abandonment of the normative core of democracy—which does not necessarily imply liberalism,—or it proffers somewhat hollow normative visions, such as the realist recourse to free trade, that cannot be reconciled with the institutional requirements of modern nation states (Habermas, 1973) confronting the challenges and realities of the information age. Liberal internationalism's supply-side economics seeks to dismantle the welfare state in order to eliminate the "disincentive" for capital investment, but to do so would be to abolish precisely those structures which stabilize the social order (Offe, 1985). If the role of the state in regulating the worst irrationalities of the market and defending the public interest in modern societies are terminated by the globally accelerating forces of liberalization in the name of the preconditions and demands of international capital, the compulsion of the market will certainly return, but so will the gross injustices, dissatisfaction, social instability, and class confrontations derived from widening inequalities that characterized the liberal economies prior to welfare-state policies and public-interest regulation.

Liberal internationalism's realist attack on the fundamental responsibility of the state is predicated on the idea that there is an unlimited growth potential for commercial goods and services that would be unleashed, but only on the condition the state is pushed back to its proper minimal terrain of guaranteeing property rights and law and order (for a justification of this view, see Locke, 1960/1690; Hobbes, 1991/1651; Gray, 1989). Privatization and deregulation, the principal strategies of liberalization, would allegedly restore competition to its natural state and end the inflation of political demands. However, the political presuppositions of this global policy conflict with the goals of democracy. Necessarily repressive policies on the right to participate in the public sphere, for the non-commercial sector, and efforts to abolish social rights ranging from social security to unemployment compensation to universal service, are scarcely conducive to citizenship and the creation of consensus.

The export worldwide of the liberal realist model of democracy and civil society through trade and communication policy—information liberalization,—a model essentially of "society against the state," is often based on a model in which civil society is either equivalent to market or proprietary interests or to some notion of an essential inherited, natural non-political culture. Thus policies of deregulation and privatization enforced by contemporary liberal internationalism on many societies are based on the defense of re-creation of a traditionalist and authoritarian social order.

Social integration is undermined by the expansion of an increasingly illiberal corporate economy, fostering new forms of dependency and unaccountable structures of governance on existing or emerging civil societies in the post Cold War.

The way in which liberal realism mobilizes the forces of information liberalization as a new form of international relations is better understood by examining the political uses of competition policy in the communications sector, particularly as the latter is employed to force fundamental social transformation on nation states and regions. Yet other mechanisms of contemporary communication policy for the "global information highway" are also significant to this transformation, including telecommunications liberalization, universal access, and multilateral information liberalization arrangements. Each of these aspects of global communication policy in international relations is taken up in the following sections.

COMPETITION POLICY IN INTERNATIONAL COMMUNICATION

To illustrate the ascendancy of communication policy in the political aims of liberal internationalism, this section will examine the application of notions of competition to information liberalization policies in the United States and the European Union. The parameters of the regulatory debate have been broadly sketched by the European Commission's White Paper on the information society (Commission of the European Communities, 1993a) and its related initiatives, by the U.S. National Information Infrastructure agenda (U.S. Government, 1993), and by the U.S. Congress information superhighway legislation proposed in 1995 (U.S. Congress, 1995a). These policy directions now serve as the basis for assessing a few of the central issues at stake both for regulatory design of the intelligent network and for the organization of interstate relations in the information age.

The 1984 breakup of AT&T monopoly into regional telephone companies (see U.S. Government, 1982) and the Commission's 1987 Green Paper on telecommunication services liberalization (Commission of the European Communities, 1987) are commonly thought to forecast the worldwide competitive environment of the "information superhighway." Yet in light of recent communication policy developments, these initiatives must instead be reassessed as representing the last historical achievements of competition or anti-trust law and the transition to an entirely different approach to the spread of market forces under international liberalism in the information age. Competition law through most of this century has imposed a responsibility on liberal states to intervene in civil society for creating democratic conditions in economic participation and for ensuring that markets work in practice as they should in theory. Yet new digital highway liberalization proposals in the international arena—originating from advanced industrialized states—seem to indicate that principles of competition and competitive conditions mandated by policy may, in fact, constitute an obstacle in the development of a global broadband network acceptable on the terms of liberal internationalism which is now thought to be better served by a so-called "tear up the rule books" argument (Noam, 1995, 1989) for sweeping withdrawal of national and international regulatory restrictions.

Thus the first political dilemma of liberal international regulation for the digital revolution is, what I call, the "paradox of competition law" whose dimensions are as follows:

1. Even as the significance of competition law applied to a number of communications industries ranging from broadcast to telecommunications is widely debated, it is becoming irrelevant to market players. Actions of the U.S. Federal Communications Commission in auctioning spectrum for the cellular market (*Congressional Quarterly*, 1994), various US House and Senate communications bills (U.S. Congress, 1995a, 1994a) rolling back monopoly restrictions, and the Commission's orientation (Commission of the European Communities, 1995a, 1994b, 1994d, 1990) in assimilating the US communication policy paradigm to mobile, telecommunication, and broadband infrastructure development in Europe, indicate competition legislation is being overtaken by policies favoring capital consolidation upheld by liberal internationalism.

2. Whereas industry and governments in advanced industrialized states at one time pressed for the extension of competition law in interstate relations to cover growing areas of communication infrastructure and services, the utility of such laws in prying open markets for global players is now over. Once the concept of dismantling public sector monopolies has gained international validity in communication policymaking and trade negotiations, the political aim of competition law to advance liberal internationalism has been achieved. As new information liberalization initiatives in the US and EU show, hereafter strict principles of competition superimposed to correct the invisible hand of the market will be regarded as counter productive to global infrastructure development and economic growth.

3. Competition law is being displaced by information liberalization and the two do not necessarily reinforce each other nor do they constitute related processes; they may even be logically opposed. Competition rules emphasize the public interest in discouraging unfair distortions, uneven development, and unacceptable domination by a few market entities, thus attempting to force the market to behave as its ideal says it should. Information liberalization, however, favors the aims of global strategy in breaking up worldwide public monopolies while simultaneously taking their place with private monopolies. Evident in the Commission's infrastructure green paper (Commission of the European Communities, 1995a, 1994b) and in proposed U.S. legislation (U.S. Congress, 1995a, 1994a) communications industries are being released both from non-commercial public interest obligations as well as sector ownership barriers into a state of new oligopolistic freedoms for positioning themselves in the battle over global market share.

4. The other major rationale of competition law, which is to benefit consumers by provoking downward pressure on tariffs, is also being effaced in the arguments suc-

cessfully advanced by liberal internationalist policies and major information industries (Commission of the European Communities, 1994e; U.S. Chamber of
Commerce, 1995; International Chamber of Commerce, 1992). The greater the
diversity of players competing over provision of services, liberal internationalism
holds, the fewer the chances of high profitability incentives to finance technological
innovation and development. Thus competition rules must be suspended in order to
guarantee compensation for industry above the market level in the global arena, on
the assumption that liberalization policies nurturing the global strategy of larger
economies of scale will result in the necessary technological investment to stimu-
late economic—i.e., proprietary—growth.

These are reasons that both the US and EU may invoke competition as a public
interest anchor to rationalize information society policies—starting with Vice President
Al Gore's vision of the rewiring of the information society by a diversity of competitors rather than by previous "natural monopoly" providers (Congressional Quarterly,
1994), and rearticulated as well in the mobile and infrastructure green papers of the
Commission (Commission of the European Communities, 1995a, 1994b, 1994d). But
the actual provisions of emerging legislation is to sanction a new age of monopoly by
flexible modes which will permit vertical and horizontal integration of communication
sectors within single proprietary structures and a restructuring of economic relationships toward concentration in a range of industries.

Among the conclusions one may draw from the digital revolution regulation trend
on both sides of the Atlantic is that states are being forced to recognize the anti-monop-
oly political movement of the last decade led by the forces of liberal internationalism
was only able to address through competition policy the problem of *public* communications monopoly but not the condition of monopoly as such. This is because foreign
relations in the post Cold War conducted by the terms of liberal realism centered on the
global communications market for particular international ends, make it virtually
impossible for network development and advanced information services delivery structures to emerge on a national or transnational scale except in the context of immense
economies of scale, capital concentration, and the intertwining of industry sectors; in
other words, by substituting public with private monopoly, which must then be provided a new framework of regulatory legitimacy. The role of the liberal state, therefore,
is rapidly being redefined as a shift from guaranteeing the conditions of democratic
participation in economy and society to guaranteeing freedom from regulation for
global oligopolies.

The pressure to maintain Europe's place in the liberal international market will de-
emphasize competition rules in public policy and oppose industrial policy to competition policy. This mirrors US communications policy history which has been largely
unsuccessful in distinguishing between supporting industry economic growth and the
requirements of social and economic democratization of information space for citizens,
users, and providers.

The "limited government" claims of liberal internationalism suggests that information liberalization brings about the generalization of competition in interstate relations. Yet the basis of information liberalization policies point to its realist defense of the conditions of proprietary consolidation, that is to say, of monopoly. The direction of global communication policy under liberal internationalism is developing toward the absolute freedom of proprietary accumulation and concentration, a global oligarchic logic for which the dissolution of all alternative models of social development—including democracy—in the modern world would now seem inevitable. Concrete areas in the communications sector where it is evident that information liberalization is moving in such a direction, are taken up below.

TELECOMMUNICATIONS LIBERALIZATION

Realist liberal internationalism seems to have won the battle on the question of ownership of public communications. Because the global advance of this form of realism has made it illegitimate for governments to own non-commercial communications networks and services, the battle to protect public ownership of information industries has been lost in international relations. Hence, nations are now being asked to negotiate beyond the mere question of ownership and agree to a single framework for regulating communications evolving in the multilateral arrangements of the World Trade Organization (Beardsley & Patsalos-Fox, 1995). Yet, the needs of many countries in communications development may be quite diverse, with objectives ranging from local telephony development to cultural, legal, and political development under different conditions. Some nations have a need for extending their basic telecommunications services and raise quality standards to minimally acceptable levels, while others already possess a solid infrastructure and need to modernize their networks and develop advanced services. The vast majority of countries fall into the first category, according to the International Telecommunications Union (International Telecommunications Union, 1993) which has tracked the telecommunication needs of 132 countries. Evidence indicates more than half the world's population live in countries with not even one telephone to a hundred citizens (International Telecommunications Union, 1993), pointing to a division of the world into information-rich and information-poor communities.

It is in this broad context that telecommunications liberalization in advanced industrialized regions must be considered. In the European Union, for instance, four fundamental strategies to advance information liberalization are identifiable:

1. The twin mechanisms of competition and harmonization policies: The European Commission has targeted the use of competition clause in Article 90 of the Treaty of Rome (Commission of the European Communities, 1993b) to force the dissolution of the public service monopolies (Commission of the European Communities, 1995a, 1994b), despite the reality that it is becoming increasingly difficult to specify anti-competitive practices by private monopolies. Simultaneously, however, the Commission has defined Article 100A of the Treaty (Commission of the European

Communities, 1993b) on its responsibility to establish the internal market, as the mechanism for achieving the second and larger goal of liberal internationalism, viz., to create a policy and legal architecture for liberating the forces of proprietary consolidation. Labeled "harmonization" in EU liberalization policies, this process requires a broadening and equalizing of European communications law that favors the interests of large-scale private proprietors of the communications industry (see discussion in Venturelli, 1996a, 1996b).

2. The separation of operation and regulation of telecommunication industries: This policy (Commission of the European Communities, 1990a, 1987) has been implemented only in the UK, and is intended to lead eventually to the establishment of regulatory authorities in all member states. But the history of independent regulation of communications, drawn primarily from the example of the U.S. FCC (see Horwitz, 1989, 1986; Middleton & Chamberlin, 1994), indicates that regulatory agencies can work entirely on behalf of private communications entities without ever having to take into account the public interest and/or non-commercial needs of citizens and users. Liberalization policies for telecommunications in the EU are forcing states to harmonize regulation without legally clarifying the central mission of regulatory authorities. It is just such ambiguity in the 1934 U.S. communications statute (U.S. Congress, 1934) that has contributed to the inability of the FCC to interpret its central mission of the protection of public interest (see Horwitz, 1989).

3. Application of the subsidiarity principle: This principle requires decision-making in the EU to be undertaken at the most appropriate level, whether transnational, national, regional, or local. The Commission has employed the subsidiarity principle to determine which institutional level has the authority for regulation of frequency allocation, numbering, rights of way, licensing, and so on, with frequency allocation reserved to the EU level and the others to the national level. While the subsidiarity principle in information liberalization can be very functional to stabilizing regulatory mechanisms across national boundaries—it even emerges under various forms in the GATT multilateral agreement—it can also be employed by the very same policies to weaken national law protecting the rights of citizens for access, reasonable rates, and service, while simultaneously strengthening the interests of transnational capital for minimum standards of regulation and maximum conditions of remuneration.

4. Coordination with global communication policy initiatives: The calibration of information liberalization across the European continent with the political and economic objectives of liberal internationalism (see speech by Jacques Santer, and by Michel Carpentier, Commission of the European Communities, 1995b, 1995c) renders the global dimension of information liberalization preeminent and unavoidable for all regions of the world. The export of the western information liberalization model originating in the EU and the U.S. to the rest of the world via the WTO practically assures the victory of the liberal internationalist project of interstate relations based solely on the grounds of proprietary interests and the removal of all barriers to commercial consolidation.

The adoption of these strategies has been of crucial importance to modern international relations constituted under liberal internationalism in the post cold war. This is evident in the multinational communications industry demands for a certain form of trans-European and global regulatory framework. For instance, the International Communications Round Table, an organization of thirty multinational communications entities from European, Japan, and North America, has demanded that the EU and its member states harmonize interstate and intrastate rules to guarantee conditions favoring high rates of return on capital investment in the communications sector (see *European Report*, 1995a), ranging from telecommunication services and audiovisual production to intellectual property, internet, and on-line services. These demands represent a massive redistribution of social power from the public to the private sector but even further, they represent the systematic closing down of non-commercial sectors in international communications. Recognizing the implication, the European Telecommunications Network Operators Association recently warned (*European Report,* 1995b) that in a private competitive environment, capital investment will respond only to the market demand of high-end users. Faced with this inevitability, nation states are being left with fewer and fewer options under the policies of liberal internationalism, to avoid a split society of information haves and have-nots, at the same time as they are being asked to ensure transborder interoperability of networks conducive to economies of scale. In order to ensure the survival of a minimal non-commercial sector in the information age, the association has asked (*European Report,* 1995a) the European Parliament to pass at the very least, minimal communications conditions such as the maintenance of universal service.

MINIMIZATION OF UNIVERSAL SERVICE

The question of universal service is central to understanding the social model exported worldwide by the information liberalization movement under the realist structures of liberal internationalism. The European Commission has left "universal" telecommunication financing to the states in its application of the subsidiarity principle to this political and social concern (see Commission of the European Communities, 1995a, 1994b). While the EU has decided to guarantee industry interests through harmonization of legal conditions conducive to capital investment, it has bounced the problem of regulation in the interests of citizens—the public interest—back to individual states themselves. The EU has even further delimited citizens' freedoms in the information age by constraining the scope of state regulation to protect universal service if it infringes in any way on commercial freedom.

The coalition of U.S. industries has warned the EU it must roll back all non-commercial burdens of universal service and retrench to an even more minimal standard. The American Chamber of Commerce in Brussels expressed its concern for allowing the issue to devolve to the states lest universal service tilt in favor of citizens' rights (*Europe*, 1995a). These rights are now termed "pretexts" or "obstruction to competition" that the multinational communications industry has threatened to fight in multi-lateral and bilateral fora of international relations. U.S. communications entities with European branches have supported the Commission's idea of moving away from across-the-board subsidies, to a system of targeted subsidies through a universal service fund (see proposal in Commission of the European Communities, 1995a, 1994b). However, these entities insist the EU needs to preempt nation states from taking a stronger approach to universal service beyond the minimal service of voice telephony (see *Europe*, 1995a).

The Commission has already secured these limits on the meaning of universal service by prohibiting member states from placing any non-commercial, public interest obligations on communication industries, public or private, if such obligations lead to the creation of barriers to market entry (Commission of the European Communities, 1993c:6). Since the Commission and the European Court of Justice reserve the right to define, by the terms of the Treaty (Commission of the European Communities, 1993b), what constitutes at any given time a "barrier to market entry," EU policy upholding universal service "making available a defined minimum service of specified quality to all users at an affordable price" (Commission of the European Communities, 1993c:4), is assuming more the form of a political declaration rather than policy fulfillment of the claim of an information democracy (see assurance, for instance, in the "Bangemann Report," Commission of the European Communities, 1994a). Moreover, the untenability of conceptualizing universal service that is *also* not a non-commercial burden—now implanted in policy, statute, and case law—will make it exceedingly difficult later to accommodate, even in moderate terms, the demands of governments, citizens and social groups, i.e., of civil society, for enhanced democratic benefit from the information age.

The approach to public policy in the information age revealed in telecommunications deregulation in the EU, provide a further boundary to the problem, insofar as statutory documents of information liberalization already appear to define the scope of permissible arguments on minimum information rights. These limits arise from Article 1 of the "services directive" (Commission of the European Communities, 1990a) which reserves the temporary—up to 1998—statutory monopoly for voice telephony on highly narrow and specific terms. In fact, voice telephony services may not be subjected to the universal service requirement except where

> The commercial provision for the public of the direct transport and switching of speech [is] in real-time between public switched network termination points, enabling any user to use equipment connected to such a network termination point in order to communicate with another termination point. (article 1)

Thus the question of identifying which voice services carry public service obligations, is not broad but prescribed with exactitude. No doubt, the scope of reserved services, i.e., information categories assigned to non-market imperatives for the benefit of civil society without distinction, must be narrowly defined given that they are an exception to the general objective of information liberalization. Nevertheless, the specific form in which services are defined as reserved for the interim until full-scale liberalization in 1998, has also established the meaning and potential of universal service for the "information superhighway" as evident in the Commission's proposed legal framework on communication infrastructure for the next century.

The green paper on liberalization of telecommunications infrastructure and cable television networks in two parts (Commission of the European Communities, 1994b, part 1, and 1995a, part 2) had as its goal the task of balancing, on the one hand, residual public service needs remaining from the PTO mandate which market competition cannot address, such as the non-commercial needs of civil society, including education and information exchange, information rights of citizens, and democratic requirements of access to the public realm; and on the other, the overriding objective of placing development of the information age wholly within competitive market processes. The infrastructure green paper stresses its responsibility to this end in the recognition "that full scale network liberalization can only proceed after a satisfactory solution to this problem" (Commission of the European Communities, 1994b, p. 29), and that "maintenance of universal service is an essential part of the infrastructure liberalization" (p. 30). Despite this seeming effort to explore a basic definition of approach toward minimum conditions of information without distinction to all in the EU, the formulation of the universal service problem in relevant statutes already both delimits as well as resolves the issue, with little for the infrastructure green paper to do but to make the policy explicit.

This policy on universal service, after several years of debate, seems to mean, therefore, voice telephony in real time only. The EU has experienced a rich debate in recent years over a more enlightened social approach to the information age than may be emerging in the U.S. and Japan, evidenced in the assurances of governments, the urgency of technological convergence and digitization articulated by communications industries, and in the Commission's profession of an information revolution to socially, culturally, and economically benefit and uplift all EU citizens (see "Bangemann Report," Commission of the European Communities, 1994a; the "White Paper," Commission of the European Communities, 1993a; and council resolution on universal service, Commission of the European Communities, 1993c). Despite the democratic and social consciousness scattered through these arguments, the infrastructure green paper guarantees no more for the democratization of information—which intelligent networks and multimedia, interactive contexts supposedly could potentially provide in an unlimited sense—than the same service mandated for universal provision a century ago as well as reserved by EU statute from commercial forces until 1998 (Commission of the European Communities, 1995a: section 5, pp. 41–47). Thus, while "The Commission reaffirms the fundamental importance of maintaining and developing universal service in the European union, on the basis of a common minimum set of services and infrastructure," the elements of "minimum service" in the information age advance no further in a century than the "obligation to provide a basic voice telephony service at an affordable price to all customers, which is but a 19th-Century promise (section 5, p. 41).

However, even the concept of obligation is reduced to conform with assurances made to private operators and providers for a fully market-driven sector and thus to the true spirit of the temporary exemption to voice services granted under the "services directive" (Commission of the European Communities, 1990a). Communication competitors, both public and private, will not be "obliged to provide service to customers whom they would otherwise have insufficient economic incentive to serve" (Commission of the European Communities, 1995a, section 5, p. 41); that is, they are not asked to bear the burden of providing information service to social sectors and regions with a rate of return less than more profitable market sectors could provide. Rather, market competitors are free to operate by profitability determinants and commercial rivalry, and thus the guarantee of basic voice telephony to all will be financed through "other mechanisms... while ensuring compliance with competition rules" (p. 41).

Mechanisms for fulfilling democracy's constitutive commitment to citizens, is defined in the infrastructure green paper as "targeted schemes for needy citizens and uneconomic customers instead of favoring general subsidies for [universal] access" (Commission of the European Communities, 1995a, section 5, p. 82). While the precise form of mechanism is still to be proposed, once more the scope of options have already been decided in existing statutes and related policies including the infrastructure green paper. The general aim, it seems, is to establish a fund for universal service to which operators who originate or terminate calls on the public switched network would contribute (p. 84). The "common fund" approach to universal service under liberal internationalist proposals, frees communications industries from all non-commercial obligations—such as equality and adequacy of minimum service, and affordable tariffs—in order that large-scale proprietors be governed solely by rivalry over the market share of high-end, more profitable users and thus gain greater incentives for technological innovation. A similar solution to the universal service dilemma of liberal democratic states is proposed in the U.S. Congress (1995a).

INFORMATION LIBERALIZATION AND THE
MULTILATERAL SYSTEM

The preceding directions in telecommunications liberalization have been reassembled at the global level for export worldwide. This section will assess the expansion of liberal internationalism through the framework of the WTO multilateral system, particularly as it involves the regulation of communication according to some of the central concerns of information liberalization, such as, for instance, existing foreign ownership restrictions in national laws. Restrictions against foreign ownership of licensed broadcast and common carrier facilities dates to the early days of broadcasting, as with statutory restrictions specified in the U.S. 1934 Communications Act (U.S. Congress, 1934) for reasons that the radio spectrum implicated questions of national security and national public resources. However, new U.S. initiatives (see U.S. Government, 1995a; U.S. Congress, 1995a) constituted on modern realist grounds, have recast these restrictions into eminently functional tools for furthering liberal internationalism in the multilateral and interstate arena.

These initiatives (see U.S. Government, 1995a; U.S. Congress, 1995a) would repeal the foreign ownership restriction and apply them only to owners from countries which resist the new realism. To force social and political change upon nation states dependent on access to new communications technology and services, the U.S. proposals insist on "reciprocal market access" for U.S. communications industries. Thus the ownership restriction on communications industries now functions as a powerful bilateral foreign policy mechanism (Lopatkiewicz, 1995), in effect, allowing the new rules to upgrade communications policy into international U.S. foreign policy. These rules allow the FCC to amend its entry standards for authorization of foreign carriers in the U.S. market to include determining whether "reciprocal market access" exists for U.S. carriers in the foreign applicant's "primary market" (U.S. Government, 1995a). "Effective market access" would include such factors as whether U.S. carriers can offer, in the foreign country, international facilities based services similar to those the foreign carrier seeks to offer in the U.S.; whether safeguards exist in the foreign market against "anti-competitive" or discriminatory practices, such as cross-subsidization; whether protection is afforded in the foreign market for the carriers' and customers' proprietary information; and whether an independent regulatory body with "fair and transparent" procedures exists to enforce competitive safeguards.

The initiative manifests a virtual blueprint for the liberal internationalist agenda, for it is evident from this developing U.S. policy that the thrust of administrative rulemaking and legislative action is an attempt to impose the U.S. regulatory paradigm on foreign communications systems; to the point of suggesting that the U.S. model of regulation, with its orientation towards furthering the political interests of large-scale private proprietors as the general interests of civil society, is also the most effective social-political model for mankind. The campaign to export the liberal internationalist agenda through the U.S. model for telecommunications regulation, represents through the G-7 group of industrialized nations, a major influence on a multilateral design of a "global information infrastructure" or GII (see U.S. Government, 1995).

The U.S. approach to realist international relations via information liberalization, demonstrates the emergence of the GII as a vehicle by which to achieve the aims of liberal internationalism, primarily by leveraging the proprietary power of the U.S. telecommunications marketplace in order to secure fundamental social restructuring in most regions of the world and to compel transformations in the role of the state and the political arrangements of civil society.

This basis of international relations has not gone unchallenged, though any resistance can only be mounted from within the wealthy industrialized states. The European Commission, for example, has insisted (*European Union News*, 1995) bilateralism should be abandoned as a mechanism to achieve information liberalization, arguing instead for a EU model rooted in the principle of uniform transnational harmonization as a concept better suited to the multilateral system. Rather than pursue realist bilateralism, the EU has proposed the strategy of developing an international legally enforceable form of information liberalization (*European Union News*, 1995). This global policy strategy includes pressing for: (a) making illegal any restrictions on foreign ownership of communications industries in all nations; and (b) eliminating licensing regulations worldwide (*Europe,* 1995b).

The EU thus regards itself as the true leader of a multilateral project for institutionalizing the legal basis of liberal internationalism within all participating nations. The EU's initial offer on telecommunications liberalization in the WTO gives rise to a category of questions concerning the implications of this approach for the fundamental constitution of the nation-state. Base on a resolution by the European Council of Ministers in June, 1995 (reported in *Europe,* 1995c) for the creation of an international regulatory framework for telecommunications liberalization, the EU's offer proposes the linkage of global liberalization in the WTO with dates for liberalization in the EU itself. Since public service entities will be dissolved by 1998 in all EU countries—with a few exceptions—the EU favors liberalization based on total deregulation corresponding to the 1998 date to be adopted worldwide through the multilateral accord. Fixing the concept of total deregulation into international law as the standard for the world does more to advance the historical and social interests of modern liberal internationalism than even the most calculated strategic use of bilateral reciprocity wielded by the U.S.

Thus the ostensible disagreement between the U.S. and the EU in WTO negotiations over the telecommunications sector, is not a disagreement at all, in the sense of competing visions. It is merely an exploration of the most effective mechanisms for the achieving the political aims of liberal internationalism. The Telecommunications Negotiating Groups within the WTO have, in fact, admitted that developing countries are silent as viable participants in the evolving arrangements (*Europe,* 1995d), and that no alternative proposals to the development of the global information highway have emerged from their number—thus suggesting the liberalization debate is closed and almost entirely appropriated by the U.S. and the EU.

CONCLUSION

The chapter concludes with a brief discussion of the central questions which affect all global communication policy issues invoked in the liberal internationalist vision of a worldwide multimedia network, questions which may be distilled to a debate between commercial vs. non-commercial development of the digital bandwidth.

In the information infrastructure policy framework still emerging in international relations, communications industries have successfully convinced nation states that universal service and public interest criteria are, in general, becoming less relevant as a policy concern since technological innovations allow the market to address these aims without the necessity of non-commercial, public interest obligations. If fixed into the information superhighway regulatory design, this dramatic proprietary tilt could mean the end of a public interest rationale in public policy, resulting in significant reconstruction of the role and responsibility of the democratic state through the next century and a reassessment of the place and value of the individual in free societies.

Developing nations have an opportunity to take note of U.S.–EU historical and contemporary experience and forge a regulatory framework for the information society that can set a global standard and serve as a model for regions of the world where such a debate will soon be inevitable. Diverse public interest traditions for communications policy in different democratic states can become the basis on which to develop a set of shared, common principles for the information age. A few key public interest issues— which the logic of liberal internationalism will eventually efface if left unchallenged—that ought to be accounted for in such a framework, include, for example:

1. Promoting non-discriminatory access. Barriers to access by societies and social groups can result from limited spectrum access which has been a major obstruction to non-commercial speech in the US since the advent of broadcasting. Since digital services delivery will basically evolve into point-to-point rather than broadcast modes, public policy should seek to ensure complete and broad common carriage to both commercial and non-commercial speakers, rather than permit private industries a reclassification according to the model of the print press which is what they very much seek in order to be released from public obligation.
2. Preventing redlining. Since the broadband network is currently being designed according to the needs of high-end and corporate users, public policy must fairly quickly, before structures become irreversible in the growing liberal internationalist environment, establish regulation to prevent discrimination based on residence, income, and other socio-economic demographics. Engineers, economists, and the industry have argued that unlimited capacity of the digital bandwidth will automatically solve problems of access in the future. Technological assurances aside, public policy must establish the rules by which the non-profit sector can access the spectrum for enabling participation by non-commercial voices, as well as clarify the grounds of the public's right to receive information.
3. Creating parameters for oligopolistic practices. Structural regulation for defining the boundaries of vertical and horizontal integration of communications sectors must be formulated. If governments lift all structural regulations on the communications industries, compelled through the emerging multilateral liberalization framework for regulating ownership, concentration and content, the notion of competition will be effaced both in fact and in principle with serious regression to market conditions which prevailed in the West towards the end of the 19th Century. For instance, regardless of the forms of technology, the number of networks, services, and programs a corporate conglomerate can own and offer in any market should remain at one. Otherwise, significant political and social consequences are bound to arise from distortions and domination of societies and economies nurtured along through the restructured form of contemporary international.

There is urgent need for assessing the regulatory framework of the information age, which will fix the structures of public communications for the next century, in terms of its potential for addressing the technological promise of enhanced participation and the policy claim that the digital revolution can make possible a new age of public freedom in a plurality of decentralized, interactive contexts. This chapter has attempted to suggest that the reconstruction of contemporary interstate relations has cast information liberalization as a mechanism central to the global political aims of liberal internationalism. The analysis of the realist forms of information liberalization also suggests a basis for asking in what form a coherent conception of enlarged participation is accounted for in the liberal internationalist design of a global communication system in the digital age.

REFERENCES

Arendt, H. (1958). *The human condition*. Chicago: University of Chicago Press.

Beardsley, S. & Patsalos-Fox, M. (1995). Getting telecoms privatization right. *The McKinsey Quarterly, 1*(1), 3–26.

Bruell, C. (1974). Thucydides' view of Athenian imperialism. *American Political Science Review, 68*, 11–17.

Cohen, J. & Arato, A. (1992). *Civil society and political theory*. Cambridge, MA: MIT Press.

Commission of the European Communities (1987). Green Paper on the development of the common market for telecommunications services and equipment (COM(87) 290).

Commission of the European Communities (1990). Commission Directive on competition in the markets for telecommunications services (90/338/EEC).

Commission of the European Communities (1993a). White Paper on growth competitiveness, and employment: The challenges and ways forward into the 21st century (the "Delors White Paper"), (COM(93) 700 final).

Commission of the European Communities (1993b). "Treaty establishing the European Community (signed in Rome on March 25, 1957)," in *European Union: Selected Instruments taken from the treaties, book I, vol. I*, pp. 91–669. Luxembourg: Office for Official Publications of the European Communities.

Commission of the European Communities (1993c). Communication from the Commission to the Council, the European Parliament and the Economic and Social Committee on developing universal service for telecommunications in a competitive environment (COM(93) 543 final, 15 November, 1993).

Commission of the European Communities (1994a). Status report on European Community telecommunications policy (DGXIII/A/1, January). Brussels: Commission of the European Communities.

Commission of the European Communities (1994b). Europe and the global information society, Bangemann Task Force Report to the European Council. *Cordis*, Supplement 2, July 15: 4–31. Brussels: European Commission, DG XIII/D-2.

Commission of the European Communities (1994c). Green Paper on the liberalization of telecommunications infrastructure and cable television networks, part 1. October 25. Brussels: European Commission, DG XIII.

Commission of the European Communities (1994d). Green Paper on a common approach in the field of mobile and personal communications in the European Union, (COM (94) 145).

Commission of the European Communities (1994e). Information and communication highways: Background documents of the Davignon working party. Brussels meeting, March 23.

Brussels: European Commission, DG XIII.

Commission of the European Communities (1994f). Green paper on strategy options to strengthen the European programme industry in the context of the audiovisual policy of the European Union, 7 April, 1994. Luxembourg: Office for Official Publications of the European Communities.

Commission of the European Communities (1995a). Green Paper on the liberalization of telecommunications infrastructure and cable television networks, part 2: A common approach to the provision of infrastructure for telecommunications in the European Union, (COM(94) 682 final, January 25.

Commission of the European Communities (1995b). Chair, Mr. Jacques Santer's conclusions, G-7 Ministerial Conference on the Information Society, Brussels, February 25–26. Office of the President of the European Commission, Brussels.

Commission of the European Communities (1995c). Speech by Michel Carpentier, Director General DG XIII of the European Commission, Brussels, June 22. Brussels: DGXIII.

New telecommunications age hits a snag in the Senate, 2 July. (1994). *Congressional Quarterly*, *52*(26), 1776–1780.

Donnelly, J. (1992). Twentieth-century realism. In T. Nardin and D. R. Mapel (eds.), *Traditions of international ethics*, (85–111). Cambridge: Cambridge University Press.

EU telecoms offer in the WTO. (1995c). *Europe* (6576), October 4, (p. 9).

Sir Leon Brittan leads WTO negotiations. (1995b). *Europe* (6525), July 19, (p. 9).

Telecommunications negotiating groups. (1995d). *Europe* (6580), October 9/10, (p. 12).

US industry response to universal service. (1995a). *Europe* (6554), September 2, (p. 10).

Industry demands for a European regulatory framework. (1995a). *European Report* (2076), October 18, (p. 2).

Public telecommunications operators have their say. (1995b). *European Report* (2073), October 7, (pp. 7–8).

World deal on telecommunications. (1995, July 17). *European Union News* (49/95), p. 1.

Forde, S. (1995). International realism and the science of politics: Thucydides, Machiavelli, and neorealism. *International Studies Quarterly*, *39*(2), 141–160.

Gray, J. (1989). *Limited government: A positive agenda.* London: Institute for Economic Affairs.

Grieco, J. M. (1988). Anarchy and the limits of cooperation: a realist critique of the newest liberal institutionalism. *International Organization*, *42*, 485–507.

Habermas, J. (1973). *Legitimation crisis*, T. McCarthy (trans.). Boston: Beacon Press.

Habermas, J. (1989). *The structural transformation of the public sphere*, T. Burger (trans.). Cambridge, MA: MIT Press.

Hobbes, T. (1991/1651) *Leviathan*, R. Tuck (Ed.). Cambridge: Cambridge University Press.

Hoffman, S. (1995). The crisis of liberal internationalism. *Foreign Policy, 98,* 159–177.

Horwitz, R. B. (1986). Understanding deregulation, *Theory and Society*, *15*(1–2), 139–174.

Horwitz, R. B. (1989). *The irony of regulatory reform*. New York: Oxford University Press.

International Chamber of Commerce (1992). Toward greater competition in telecommunications, position paper no. 17, Brussels: International Chamber of Commerce.

International Telecommunications Union (1993). *Yearbook*, 14–15. Geneva: ITU.

Kaplan, L. (1994). The European community's 'television without frontiers'directive: stimulating Europe to regulate culture. *Emory International Law Review*, *8*(1), 255–346.

Locke, J. (1960/1690). *Two treatises of government.* New York: Cambridge University Press.

Lopatkiewicz, S. M. (1995, March). *The U.S.: A laboratory for change?* Paper presented at the International Institute for Communications' Digital Media Forum, Washington, DC.

Middleton, K. R. & Chamberlin, B. F. (1994). *The law of public communication.* New York: Longman.

Noam, E. (1989). Network pluralism and regulatory pluralism. In P. R. Newberg (Ed.), *New directions in telecommunications policy, 1,* 66–91. Durham, NC: Duke University Press.

Noam, E. (1995). The stages of television: from multi-channel to the me-channel. In C. Contamine & M. van Dusseldorp (Eds.), *Towards the digital revolution,* (49–54). Published proceedings of the 6th European Television and Film Forum, Liège, Belgium, November 10–12, 1994. Düsseldorf, Germany: European Institute for the Media.

Offe, C. (1985). *Disorganized capitalism.* Cambridge: MIT Press.

Pool, I. (1990). *Technologies without boundaries.* Cambridge, MA: Harvard University Press.

Schumpeter, J. (1947). *Capitalism, socialism, and democracy.* New York: Harper & Row.

U.S. Chamber of Commerce (1995). Report of findings of the national information infrastructure survey, U.S. Chamber of Commerce Telecommunications Infrastructure Task Force. Washington, D.C.: U.S. Chamber of Commerce.

U.S. Congress (1934). Communications Act of 1934, Public Law No. 416,73rd Coress, June 19, 1934. Washington, DC: U.S. Government Printing Office.

U.S. Congress (1993). U.S. telecommunications services in European markets. A report of the Office of Technology Assessment, TCT-548, August. Washington,DC: U.S. Government Printing Office.

U.S. Congress (1994). "The information superhighway and the national information infrastructure (NII)," *CRS Report for Congress,* March 22. Washington, DC: Congressional Research Service, Library of Congress.

U.S. Congress (1995). Proposed telecommunications deregulation bill, S. 652. Washington, D.C.: U.S. Government Printing Office.

U.S. Government (1982). *United States v. AT&T,* CA No. 82–0192 (DDC) Modification of Final Judgment. United States District Court of the District of Columbia, 24 August.

U.S. Government (1993). The national information infrastructure: agenda for action. Information Infrastructure Task Force, September. Washington, D.C: U.S. Government Printing Office.

U.S. Government (1995a). Global information infrastructure: Agendafor cooperation. Information Infrastructure Task Force, February. Washington,D.C.:U.S. Government Printing Office.

U.S. Government (1995b). Notice of proposed rulemaking in the matter of market entry and regulation of foreign-affiliated entities. Federal Communications Commission, IB Docket No. 95-22, FCC 95-53, February 17, 1995. Washington, D.C.: U.S. Government Printing Office.

Venturelli, S. (1996). The information society in Europe: conflict of regulatory paradigms. In G. G. Kopper (Ed.) *European media and journalism yearbook,* Vol. 1. Berlin: Vistas.

Venturelli, S. (In press). The information society in Europe: Passing of the public service paradigm of European democracy. In A. Cafruni & C. Lankowski (Eds.). *Europe's ambiguous unity: Conflict and consensus in the Post-Maastricht Era,* Boulder, CO: Lynne Rienner Publishers.

Walker, R. B. J. (1993). *Inside/outside: International relations as political theory.* Cambridge: Cambridge University Press.

chapter 5

social identification and media coverage of foreign relations

Nancy Rivenburgh
University of Washington

U
nited States media play a variety of roles—observer, interpreter, actor, and at times, catalyst—in regards to foreign policy. Because these roles have been linked to both public opinion and policy making in the international sphere, it is imperative that communication researchers continue to refine their understanding of media presentations of foreign affairs.

The purpose of this chapter is to argue that the study of social identification offers a largely unexplored framework for analyzing media within the foreign policy process. The general logic to this recommendation comes from the view that the analysis of foreign policy is essentially the study of social or intergroup behavior—in this case, the relations among nation-states. Further, the existence of patterns of representation in international news suggests that the producers of media (i.e., journalists, editors, etc.) engage in identifiable cognitive processes related to foreign affairs. Analysis of the link between intergroup behavior and cognitive processes finds its most active home in social psychology—and more specifically in theories related to social or collective identity.

Much social psychological study related to international relations is based on the idea that the "perceptions, cognitions, attitudes, and values held by individual actors" link to conflict or cooperation at a national level (Fisher, 1990, p. 6; also Jervis, 1976). In fact, political scientists have long looked to social psychology in an effort to better understand how, for example, nationalist ideology can mobilize citizens to war or how leaders behave in their capacities as representatives of national collectives (e.g., Kelman, 1964). Yet communication researchers have largely missed the potential relevance of collective identity as a cognitive process that may be an important influence on the construction of the external world through media content. Assuming that media presentations are influential in the formation or maintenance of perceptions of other nations, this literature is potentially very useful to communication researchers interested in the media and foreign relations. Schlesinger (1991, p. 150) summarized the need for such an approach when he said that communication research has tended to focus on communication and its supposed effects on collective identity instead of first investigating how collective identity might influence communicative practices.

The type of collective identity considered here is that of national identity, as it is central to any inquiry regarding media and foreign relations. National identity is a fundamental type of collective identity (Schlesinger, 1991). It will be argued that, according to principles of social identification, producers of media are influenced by this aspect of identity in consistent, observable, and even predictable ways. And, as will be discussed, existing research on media presentation of foreign relations seems compatible with the hypotheses this approach would generate concerning media content. This is not to usurp other approaches to explaining the complexity of media coverage of foreign relations, but rather to add a needed, and it is believed, conceptually useful dimension to our understanding of media and foreign affairs.

MEDIA PRESENTATIONS OF U.S. FOREIGN POLICY

Contrary to the complaints of politicians about media undermining foreign policy efforts through their criticisms of U.S. government actions abroad, research demonstrates that mainstream media are largely supportive of U.S. foreign policy goals and initiatives and display a distinct deference to official views in terms of both attention and credibility relative to alternative voices. Despite media attention to tactical miscalculations, international news and editorial content remains steadfast in its portrayal of the United States as a well-meaning and benign actor in the international sphere.

The shape of these general findings crystallize significantly during times of military action when media willingness to support the government line—or, conversely, when government ability to manage the media—tends to become even more pronounced. Analyses of the coverage of the Cuban missile crisis, invasions of Panama and Grenada, the Gulf War, and even the first stages of the Vietnam war show a national mainstream media system choosing the role of U.S. government supporter over watchdog in times of real or government-defined threat to national interests. As stated by Iyengar and Simon (1993) at the conclusion to their study of media and the Gulf War:

> As the recent examples of Grenada, the Gulf crisis, and Somalia make clear, print and broadcast news coverage of world events involving the use of U.S. military force have propagated the worldview and policy preferences of the incumbent administration. The media portrayed Grenada as a hotbed of communist insurgents hatching terrorist plots and jeopardizing American lives. Saddam Hussein was portrayed as a modern Hitler, bent on annexing Kuwait and controlling the world's supply of petroleum. In Somalia, the deployment of U.S. troops was seen in exclusively humanitarian terms. (Iyengar and Simon, 1993, pp. 381–382)

It is important to note that such findings do not characterize media coverage of domestic policy issues where critical perspectives may be expressed in media content from the initial stages of policy articulation. This is encouraged by, among other reasons, easy access to domestic interest groups and more internal political debate from the outset. As is implied in the forthcoming discussion, this would also occur because media personnel unconsciously draw on different, more salient social identities than national identity to influence their interpretation of domestic policy issues. In fact, domestic politics represent, to a large extent, the internal squabbling between various groups trying to garner support for their preferred versions of national identity (Neumann, 1992, p. 222). One role of media as a domestic actor in a democracy is to keep citizens abreast of this struggle.

MEDIA PRESENTATION OF NATIONAL OTHERS

A fundamental aspect of media coverage of U.S. foreign policy is media representations of others in the international sphere. Research into the presentation of other nations in news content shows that media not only select, but position and evaluate others relative to the perspective of the home nation. For example, U.S. news attention tends to be skewed toward elite nations or those which hold some particular economic, political, or geographic salience in terms of U.S. interests or security. Once selected for coverage, nations are not simply described, but often positioned *vis-à-vis* the home nation in cooperative (friend, ally) oppositional (enemy, threat) or stratified (developing, admired) postures (Rivenburgh, 1995). Further, nations considered "more like us" in terms of economic philosophy, political system, values, language, and so forth tend to be evaluated more favorably relative to those "least like us," for example developing nations, in international news content (e.g., Stevenson and Gaddy, 1994; Larson, 1982; Dahlgren with Chakrapani, 1982).

Also relevant to this discussion is the observation that group membership and unity are overemphasized in coverage of foreign affairs even to the point of, inaccurately, portraying the nation as psychological unit—"Today France denied U.S. allegations that..." or "Japan asked for a continuation of trade talks on..." or "Zambia's attitude toward South Africa recently took a turn for the worse...". This is consistent with Goffman's (1959) observation that group membership tends to be over communicated in public rituals—in this case, in media discourse of international relations.

APPROACHES TO UNDERSTANDING MEDIA COVERAGE OF FOREIGN AFFAIRS

To help explain the above findings related to media coverage of foreign relations much research has pointed to the social organization of news work: the professional norms, organizational routines and operations which guide news production. These include issues related to accessibility, timing, relations with sources, budgetary constraints, and so forth (e.g., reviewed in Schudson, 1989). Some of these organizational conditions—such as reliance on government sources or use of stereotypes in situations of time or space pressures—become particularly influential in the coverage of international events.

A more critical, and no less apt, approach links the institutions of media and government more broadly to their governing political and economic ideologies—and thus to each other—to explain media coverage of government foreign policy activities (e.g., Hallin, 1987). This approach, for example, interprets presentations of instability, conflict, or corruption in other nations as not only justifying U.S. intervention in the affairs of others, but socializing citizens to believe that a capitalist, representative democracy—where the representatives are members of or beholden to the existing power elite—is prerequisite to a stable, rational, and peaceful society. This approach is often supported by research which shows that truly alternative views or systems find no place in mainstream media content. Bennett (1990, 1994) suggests that the boundaries of acceptable discourse found in media coverage of foreign policy tend to be "indexed" to internal Congressional debate. Further, these debates rarely question basic assumptions concerning U.S. policy, but come from disagreements as to resource allocation, tactics, or domestic political squabbles.

A third approach, broadly stated, is that which considers media content and its makers as inextricably linked to dominant cultural discourses, symbols, myths, and values. Schudson (1989) labels this a "culturological" understanding of the production of news. Researchers have long identified that national media express "qualities of their nations" through news values based on national political philosophy, common social heritage, and values of its constituent audience (e.g., Schramm, 1956; Head, 1985; Gans, 1979). Similarly, news selection processes have been shown to be based on local salience and cultural orientation (Peterson, 1979). For example, U.S. media pay attention to elections in other nations—whether they are meaningful or not in that context—because they hold high symbolic value here. Further, with the exception of a handful of elite media stars, journalists are "disproportionately white, male, middle-class, and middle-aged" and, as such, subscribe to traditional national myths and values with elements of both liberal and conservative ideology (Paletz & Entman 1981, p. 4; Weaver & Wilhoit, 1993; Gans, 1979).

This is to suggest that the producers of media, at an individual level and reflected in the unwritten expectations that media organizations have for news presentation, view international affairs through a culturally biased lens. Berry (1990), in his analysis of *New York Times* coverage of five foreign policy "failures," named cultural bias as a key variable in media support *and criticism of* foreign policy. He characterizes the media as largely a "home team" supporter—particularly in the initial stages of foreign policy articulation. Berry found that it is when U.S. foreign policies begin to fail that coverage becomes more critical. At that time, he says, criticism occurs not just because of the presence of internal debate as suggested by Bennett, but because American journalists, by and large, do not want to see the United States fail.

A journalist's cultural bias is not "my country right or wrong." It is, instead, a natural bias to have the United States succeed, so that it is secure, prosperous, prestigious, and contributing to world progress. Reporters, like everyone else, rally around the president... when confronting hostile forces.... However, at the outcome stage, when policy appears to be failing, reporters' cultural bias drive them to critical analyses. They do not want their country to continue down a dead end path. Flagging ineffective or costly foreign policy is patriotic. (Berry, 1990, pp. 141–142).

This view has been echoed by others—both reporters and researchers alike. According to Robert Manning, former editor of the *Atlantic Monthly*, there is a fundamental tension that journalists feel between not wanting to do something that will harm Americans or American policy and the obligation to disclose information (Manning, 1968). McCartney's (1994) analysis of the Cuban missile crisis, among others, provides an example of this tension at work where the press chose to "rally around the flag" and never questioned President Kennedy's account of that crisis. This does not suggest that harmful disclosures never occur, but rather that American media personnel possess some level of emotional connection to the United States that biases media content.

What the above, more cultural approach to understanding media content lacks is a theoretical base from which to generate specific hypotheses for predicting and explaining more discrete patterns and dimensions of international news coverage bias. The literature in social identification offers that potential.

SOCIAL IDENTIFICATION: THE GROUP IN THE INDIVIDUAL

People actively seek identity for a variety of reasons most often related to the desire for security and a stable sense of self. Self identity comprises both personal (one's sense of uniqueness from other ingroup members) and collective identity (also variously referred to as social identity, group identity, or self-categorization) or that part of identity derived from one's knowledge of their membership in a social group or groups (e.g., Turner, Oakes, Haslam, & McGarty, 1994). Each person has the capacity to self identify with numerous groups as part of their social self although the balance, value, and character of one's collective identity as part of self vary significantly by person and situation. Even so, collective identity, as it is used here, requires the sharing of some emotional involvement in each ingroup, as well as some degree of social consensus about the evaluation of that group (Tajfel and Turner, 1986, p. 116).

Miller and Prentice (1994) state that the above conceptualization represents a shift in regard to research on self identity. Researchers in this area have become more interested in group identity as part of self. Rather than asking, "How do individuals behave within groups?" social psychologists now ask, "How do groups behave within individuals?" Or, as stated by Turner et al. (1994) collective self is every bit as "real" as personal self. As an example they point to the effects of collective identity on individual behavior during Operation Desert Storm when people tied yellow ribbons on mailboxes and trees in a patriotic gesture of support of U.S. troops in the Middle East. Such displays of "collective emotion," they claim, show that the attachment to the collective has its own psychological and imagined reality distinct from one's attachment to individual group members.

Collective identities are also relational in that they require the recognition of collective "others" who are different. A primary function of this process of social identification is to allow people to organize their world and, in doing so, define both the boundaries and nature—e.g., the goodness—of one's own group. But researchers in this area insist that social identification is not merely the calling forth of stored "attributes" of self or other, but rather a dynamic process in which collective identities are continually being reconsidered, renegotiated, and recomposed relative to other groups. This idea seems critical to better understanding of the nature of media presentations of international affairs by suggesting more complex cognitive processes than simply stereotyping are at play.

Dahlgren (1982) attempts to elucidate this complexity in his analysis of U.S. television news coverage of the Third World. He argues that the portrayal patterns of the Third World as inherently troubled by social disorder, flawed development, and primitivism serve a social psychological function. Such news portrayal patterns self-define the U.S. as superior through the implied bipolar opposites of such characterizations—in this case, the U.S. is implied to be stable, rationally developed, and modern relative to the Third World. Although not explicit about the underlying principles at work, Dahlgren connects the concept of collective identity to the cognitive processes of journalists by suggesting that the representation patterns found across media are an unconscious aspect of media production with a function related to self identity.

> It must be underscored here that this way of seeing the Third World and the West does not function on an analytical level, but rather a mythic one. The perspective is more unconscious than conscious... (Dahlgren with Chakrapani, 1982, p. 53)

A SOCIAL IDENTIFICATION APPROACH TO MEDIA COVERAGE OF FOREIGN RELATIONS

National identity is a fundamental aspect of journalists' identity. Katz (1965) describes two particular situations when national identity becomes highly relevant as part of one's self identity. The first is the case of personal and direct contact with people of another nationality. The second situation is the "world created by the mass media and communications from leaders [where] the sense of national identity is aroused by perceived matters of national interest and national security in relation to other nations" (p. 366). For correspondents abroad, as well as domestically stationed journalists and editors producing international news, both or either of these situations are a daily occurrence. Nationality is clearly a relevant identity ingroup for these media personnel and one that Katz suggests will be highly influential whenever it is salient. He says, "One is either a loyal citizen or not.... The realistic alternatives to rejecting the system are forbidding…" (Katz, 1965, p. 368). Or, as Bloom (1990, p. 74) puts it, "To avoid citizenship and national identity is extremely difficult—so difficult, in fact, that in the contemporary world, to be without nationality is to be perceived as almost without identity."

Not only is national identity an unavoidable aspect of identity, but Bloom (1990) suggests that because people are motivated to maintain positive social identities, they will potentially act to preserve, defend, or enhance national identity. He has named this potential for action the "national identity dynamic" (Bloom, 1990, p. 53). He says that explicit conflict or external threats are not necessary for this to occur because the modern international system provides ever-present images of national competition and threat in politics, sports, and economics.

When related to media coverage of foreign relations, Bloom's idea of a "national identity dynamic" predicts that journalists confronted with opportunities to preserve, defend, or enhance identity—whether they realize it or not—will tend to "act" through the construction of media presentations biased toward those ends. Further, this will result in overall patterns of such presentations across U.S. media outlets because of the shared nature of national identity.

This general proposition, however, just opens the door. Of more specific interest is that research into social identification has generated a list of properties of collective identity that have implications for new types of useful analyses of media presentations of foreign relations. Social psychologists are careful to note that variability in social identification and characterization is not arbitrary and chaotic, but is systematic and related to variation in context (Turner et al, 1994). This means that principles of social identification may be empirically explored in the form of patterns of presentation in media content. Some of the most relevant principles related to national identity and their possible links to communication research are reviewed below.

National identity is evaluative and competitive

Ingroup bias is an omnipresent feature of intergroup relations. The research of Tajfel and Turner (1986) and others demonstrate that direct conflict or incompatibility are not even necessary to generate intergroup discrimination. Simply an awareness of an "other" is sufficient to trigger discriminatory responses. In this sense, national identity is not only evaluative, but essentially competitive. An important corollary here is that our representations of others are naturally biased to achieve, maintain and, when possible, enhance a positive social self-identity through techniques of differentiation.

To demonstrate this in terms of national identity, Forgas and O'Driscoll (1984) found that people not only tend to magnify distinctions between their nation and others, but choose to emphasize those areas in which their country does better than the other. In other words, if the intergroup comparison isn't favorable for the ingroup, people will seek other criteria for comparison *or* even focus on other outgroups.

Kitabayashi's (1995) findings from a study of news coverage of Japan demonstrates that the above principle might be presented as hypotheses regarding media content. She found that articles involving the presentation of Japanese economic success in both *Newsweek* and *New York Times* (1989–1991) were consistently tempered by attention to related, but negative dimensions of such success, such as increased pollution, the personal price of workaholic lifestyles, or housing problems now present in Japan. That is, journalists' sought to diminish the impact of Japanese economic success in ways that served to protect U.S. identity.

The above ideas are also compatible with existing research, summarized above, concerning the presentation of other nations in news content whereby others are "positioned" relative to a home nation in ways that tend to confirm and favor its own value perspective.

National identity is context dependent

Social identity is not only relational, but situational and as noted previously, dynamic. For example, Haslam, Turner, Oakes, McGarty, and Hayes (1992) found that people's perceptions of self and other nations varied significantly from the beginning to the end of the Gulf War. National identity attributes, such as aggressive or ambitious, when associated with the U.S., Iraq, Russia, and Great Britain relative to each other, changed significantly throughout the course of the war.

Here there is much that could be investigated concerning both the nature of change in media presentations of national others relative to specific times and events and in terms of the sphere of international interaction. For example, one might ask, "How does coverage of foreign relations change (or how is national self and other redefined) when the sphere of interaction moves from economic to military, political or social?"

Or even more basic to this, when is national identity activated in media content? While government officials routinely are portrayed as national representatives in international coverage, the media can appropriate any international issue or event or actor and use it to defend or enhance national identity. Depending the circumstance, sports teams, celebrities, or even tourists might suddenly become a symbol of nation in news coverage. When does this happen? The U.S. servicemen convicted of raping a girl in Japan in 1995 were decidedly not presented as national representatives in U.S. media coverage. However, when an American couple touring in Italy saw their 7-year old child killed in a robbery attempt, then donated his organs to an Italian hospital, the media coverage elevated that gesture to a representative symbol of a humanitarian and selfless United States (Cowell, 1994).

Context also affects what is considered the "typical" of a outgroup. According to principles of social identification, if more extreme members of a group are repeatedly seen in the intergroup context then those extreme members will gain in relative "prototypicality" over more moderate members of that group. As more extreme members become more representative, the judgment of the category as a whole will change (Turner et al., 1994). This has obvious implications for the effects of repeated media attention to the activities of terrorists or other types of extremist groups on the perception—and subsequent media presentations—of their nation of origin on the part of media producers.

National identity is linked to emotion and self esteem

While varying significantly across individual members, some level of emotional significance is attached to national membership. As such, the fortunes or misfortunes of one's ingroup affect feelings of pride and self esteem. For example, research consistently reveals that people take more personal responsibility for group successes than failures (Kowalski & Wolfe, 1994). Related to this is the finding that ingroup successes tend to be attributed more to ingroup character and ingroup failures to external circumstance. The opposite, of course, holds for outgroups; successes tend to be characterized as situational, failures as dispositional. Entman's (1991) comparison of U.S. media framing of the 1983 Soviet shootdown of 269 crew and passengers on KAL flight 007 as an act of aggression and "wanton killing" versus the framing of a near identical event involving the 1988 U.S. Vincennes shootdown of 290 passengers and crew on Iran Air flight 655 as an "understandable accident" could be easily re-conceptualized in terms of this social identification principle. Throughout the media coverage of the KAL shootdown, the Soviets were presented as knowing actors, internally disposed to aggression, secrecy and criminal acts. The media presentation of the U.S. Vincennes incident by contrast focused on external circumstances—technological complexity, Iran Air flight path, etc.—and the "collision of random events" that led to the shootdown of that civilian plane. Other comparisons of international events might also be approached using this basic hypothesis.

Tajfel and Turner (1986) distinguish between "social" competition motivated by a desire for positive self-evaluation through intergroup comparison and "instrumental" competition based on realistic self interest (e.g., material gains). Their research shows that the desire for positive self esteem holds even when it conflicts with personal self-interest (i.e., citizens will sacrifice personally for group identity enhancement). Stagner (1967, p. 51) cites the case where citizens will follow a belligerent leader into battle because he promises the aggrandizement of the nation, over a more pacifist leader who is perceived as weak. Relative to this idea one might revisit the conclusions of Berry (1990) and others who suggest that journalists will criticize policy once it begins to flounder because they do not want to see their country fail or look weak in the international sphere. Here a variety of hypotheses might be formulated concerning media attention and support of "high profile" policy activities that make the U.S. look prominent or strong in the international sphere versus "low profile" policy activities which are more mundane in terms of international impact.

These properties of social identification related to social self esteem also suggest possible comparative analyses of media coverage of international problems worked out through cooperation and compromise compared to problems confronted with economic might or military intervention. For example, does successful U.S. leadership in battle attract more media plaudits than U.S. involvement in negotiation that avoids conflict?

NATIONAL IDENTITY, NEWS MANAGEMENT, AND
PUBLIC EXPECTATIONS

These propositions related to social identification may also help to explain the ability of the government to manage news by framing a policy issue in a way that activates a national identity dynamic. In order to attract media and public support, an international problem may be presented by government sources in such a way that creates a sense of threat to national identity—e.g., the spread of communism—or offers an opportunity to enhance national prestige—e.g., sending troops to Somalia as a humanitarian effort. According to Bloom (1990), as long as such presentations remain within the parameters set by shared ideas of national identity, they will tend to be effective. Of course, this strategy of news management is hardly a new observation. Manheim (1994, p. 152) refers to this idea in when he discusses making "psychological contact" through media content by associating emotionally potent national symbols ("democracy," "freedom," etc.) with foreign policy initiatives. However, principles of social identification may help to explain the repeated success of this strategy in the face of media professionals arguably in a position to recognize and criticize such manipulations.

In domestic reporting, media personnel are seen as a distinct outgroup from the public and, at times, criticized by various domestic groups as taking too liberal or conservative, too critical or non-critical stances. However, when national attention turns to U.S. actions and interests abroad, then journalists share membership in a national group with the public. Thus, international events which emotionally involve the public would, according to dynamics of social identification, also alter public expectations of media behavior to support that common national group. Some evidence of this ingroup "pressure" occurred during the Gulf War when public opinion generally supported the need for government control of the news as part of the war effort and even criticized media for not "supporting our troops" once they were deployed. Soderlund and Briggs (1995) are quite direct in their assessment of this shift in public expectation of media where policy is concerned:

> On domestic ground, politicians are fair, and often eagerly sought, game. It is not only perfectly fair to denounce the administration's bungling of health care or agricultural policy, it is expected.... All of that is within the family and therefore both legitimate and necessary if integrity (democratic principle) is to be maintained.
>
> When an external enemy is sighted, however, the family naturally closes ranks. Against this outsider—essentially all other states in the international system—a united front must be presented. To fail to report, and at least tacitly support, the undoubtedly righteous national position, is tantamount to treason. (p. 19)

A RESEARCH AGENDA FOR A CHANGING
INTERNATIONAL SPHERE

Ideas related to social and collective identity also link to another arena of exploration: that of role theory in international relations (e.g., Walker, 1987). While it is not possible to examine the potential of this here, it is a view that sees the international system as a social structure whereby nations occupy "positions" and "role relationships" to other nations, as well as to other ingroup members. It makes sense that these roles are articulated, debated, and mediated through media content.

Further, with the real strength of U.S. hegemony coming increasingly under challenge, questions concerning U.S. national identity and roles *vis-à-vis* foreign policy should only become more pronounced in the international sphere and offer exciting research possibilities. Using social identification as a framework for analysis communication researchers might, in addition to the hypotheses generated above, have the possibility of tracking patterns of renegotiation and recomposition of U.S. national identity as expressed through media content. In other words, with the post-Cold War world order experiencing change and conflict concerning global power distribution and balance, a research agenda that considers the representation of relationships in media content as the focus of analysis seems to make sense.

The next step, of course, is to embark on some of the research paths suggested here using empirical means. While a first look at existing research of international news shows promise for the applicability of a social identification framework, there are clear limitations to trying to re-conceptualize studies designed for other purposes. New research designs need be developed which more directly address the concepts and propositions related to social identification in such a way that can better characterize the dynamic, relational, and situational nature of national identity as expressed in media coverage of foreign relations.

REFERENCES

Bennett, W. L. (1990). Toward a theory of press-state relations in the United States. *Journal of Communication, 40*(2), 103–125.

Bennett, W. L. (1994). The media and the foreign policy process. In D. Deese (Ed.), *The new politics of American foreign policy.* (pp. 168–188). NY: St. Martin's Press.

Berry, N. O. (1990). *Foreign policy and the press: An analysis of the New York Times' coverage of U.S. foreign policy.* New York: Greenwood Press.

Bloom, W. (1990). *Personal identity, national identity and international relations.* Cambridge: Cambridge University Press.

Cowell, A. (1994, October 4). Italy moved by boy's killing and the grace of his parents. *New York Times*, p. A1.

Dahlgren, P. with Chakrapani, S. (1982). The third world on TV news: Western ways of seeing the 'other.' In W. Adams (Ed.), *Television coverage of international affairs* (pp. 45–63). Norwood, NJ: Ablex.

Entman, R. M. (1991). Framing U.S. coverage of international news: Contrasts in narratives of the KAL and Iran Air incidents. *Journal of Communication, 41*(4), 6–27.

Entman, R. M. (1993). Framing: Toward clarification of a fractured paradigm. *Journal of Communication, 43*(3), 51–58.

Fisher, G. (1990). *Mindsets: the role of culture and perception in international relations.* Yarmouth, ME: Intercultural Press.

Forgas, J. P. & O'Driscoll, M. (1984). Cross-cultural and demographic differences in the perception of nations. *Journal of Cross-Cultural Psychology, 15*(2), 199–222.

Gans, H. (1979, January–February). The messages behind the news. *Columbia Journalism Review,* 40–45.

Goffman, E. (1959). *the presentation of self in everyday life.* Garden City: Anchor Books.

Hallin, D. C. (1987). Hegemony: The American news media from Vietnam to El Salvador, A study of ideological change and its limits. In D. Paletz (Ed.), *Political communication research* (pp. 3–25). Norwood, NJ: Ablex.

Haslam, S. A., Turner, J. C., Oakes, P. J., McGarty, C. & Hayes, B. K. (1992). Context-dependent variation in social stereotyping. *European Journal of Social Psychology, 22,* 3–20.

Head, S. (1985). *World Broadcasting Systems: A Comparative Analysis.* Belmont, CA: Wadsworth Publishing Co.

Iyengar, S. & Simon, A. (1993). News coverage of the Gulf crisis and public opinion. *Communication Research, 20*(3), 365–383.

Jervis, R. (1976). *Perception and misperception in international politics.* Princeton, NJ: Princeton University Press.

Katz, D. (1965). Nationalism and strategies of international conflict resolution. In H.C. Kelman (Ed.), *International behavior: A social-psychological analysis* (pp. 354–390). New York: Holt, Rinehart, and Winston.

Kelman, H. C. (Ed.). (1965). *International behavior: A social-psychological analysis.* New York: Holt, Rinehart, and Winston.

Kitabayashi, W. (1995). *An analysis of the richness of Japanese national images as portrayed in the U.S. print media from 1989 to 1991.* Unpublished master's thesis, University of Washington, Seattle, Washington.

Kowalski, R. M. & Wolfe, R. (1994). Collective identity orientation, patriotism, and reactions to national outcomes. *Personality and Social Psychology Bulletin, 20*(5), 533–540.

Larson, J. F. (1982). International affairs coverage on U.S. evening network news, 1972–1979. In W. Adams (Ed.), *Television coverage of international affairs* (pp. 15–41) Norwood, NJ: Ablex.

Manheim, J. B. (1994). *Strategic public diplomacy and American foreign policy.* New York: Oxford University Press.

Manning, R. (1968). International news media. In A. S. Hoffman (Ed.), *International communication and the new diplomacy* (pp. 147–167). Bloomington: Indiana University Press.

McCartney, J. (1994). Rallying around the flag. *American Journalism Review,* 40–46.

Miller, D. T. & Prentice, D. A. (1994). The self and the collective. *Personality and Social Psychology Bulletin, 20*(5), 451–453.

Neumann, I. B. (1992) Identity and security. *Journal of Peace Research, 29*(2), 221–226.

Paletz, D. & Entman, R. (1981). *Media power politics.* New York: The Free Press.

Peterson, S. (1979, Spring). Foreign news gatekeepers and criteria of newsworthiness. *Journalism Quarterly,* 116.

Rivenburgh, N. K. (1995). Images of others: The presentation of nations in the 1992 Barcelona Olympics. *Journal of International Communication, 2*(1), 6–25.

Schlesinger, P. (1991). *Media, state, and nation.* Newbury Park: Sage.

Schramm, W. (1959). *A day in the world's press.* Stanford: Stanford University Press.

Schudson, M. (1989). The sociology of news production. *Media, Culture, and Society, 11,* 263–282.

Soderlund, W. C. & Briggs, E. D. (1995, Spring). Left, right and center: Cold War press portrayals of Caribbean and Central American leaders. *International Communication Bulletin, 30*(1–2), 18–22.

Stagner, R. (1967). *Psychological aspects of international conflict.* Belmont, CA: Brooks/Cole Publishing Co.

Stevenson, R. L. & Gaddy, G. D. (1984). "Bad news" and the third world. In R. L. Stevenson and D. L. Shaw (Eds.), *Foreign news and the new world information order* (pp. 88–97). Ames: Iowa State University Press.

Tajfel, H. & Turner, J. C. (1986). The social identity theory of intergroup behavior. In S. Worchel and W. G. Austin (Eds.), *Psychology of intergroup relations* (pp. 7–24). Chicago: Nelson-Hall.

Turner, J. C., Oakes, P. J., Haslam, S. A., & McGarty, C. (1994). Self and collective: Cognition and social context. *Personality and Social Psychology Bulletin, 20*(5), 454–463.

Walker, S. G. (Ed.). (1987). *Role theory and foreign policy analysis.* Durham, NC: Duke University Press.

Weaver, D. & Wilhoit, G. C. (1993, January–February). Who are we? *Quill,* 45–47

part II

empirical studies

chapter 6

the president, congress, and the media in global affairs

Dom Bonafede
The American University

> —(Edmund) Burke said there were Three Estates in Parliament; but in the
> Reporters' Gallery yonder, there sat a Fourth Estate
> important far than they all.
> —Thomas Carlyle

The emergence of advanced mass communications technology following World War II, with its emphasis on imagery and symbolism, and the new awareness regarding the value of public opinion, compelled foreign policy decision-makers to be skilled communicators and to establish a symbiotic relationship with an increasingly pervasive news media.

Throughout the Cold War and its aftermath, it became evident that the media, long perceived simply as observers and instant chroniclers of events, had become an integral player in foreign affairs. It was widely recognized that the media were part of the process, for impressions and perceptions conveyed by the media directly affect public opinion, and without public endorsement there can be no foreign policy consensus. As President Truman acknowledged, "The major decisions in our foreign policy since (World War II) have been made on, the basis of an informed public opinion and overwhelming public support." (Bonafede, 1990, p. 10)

Previously, as implausible as it may seem, the prevailing attitude of U.S. government officials was that public opinion was irrelevant in foreign policy decision making; their principal concern was public acquiescence.

Now, ever conscious of the news media's influence, world leaders communicate with each other, as well as with their own people and their rivals, foreign and domestic, through the media and engage in what has been commonly called "media diplomacy." For centuries, diplomacy was traditionally dependent on quiet consultation, private negotiations and secret intelligence. But increasingly it has entered the frenzied age of mass communications as a blend of statecraft and media relations and, in effect, become one of the performing arts. Television particularly has had a profound effect on international affairs—for good and ill. As a visual medium, television is subject to the tyranny of the camera. Unless a story can be accompanied by pictures, it is not a story. Hence, TV news attracts the viewer with dramatic and oversimplified presentations of pictorial events, normally without adequate explanation, or underscoring their significance, or providing a full range of potential repercussions. Also, TV has difficulty unraveling complicated, intellectual issues. Frequently, it fails to distinguish between the trivial and the significant; each is given the same amount of time.

Because of the constraint of time, TV news is unable to project the full litany of facts, or portray them in an organized context. The viewer, thus, receives the scene but not the sense of an event.

This contraction serves to distort the news, if only by what is omitted or left unexplained.

By its very nature, the progression in television is from images, sound and color, to impressions and emotional response. Fleeting images require less concentration, reflection, and reasoning than the passive printed word.

Not unnaturally, this creates anxieties and urgencies. Accordingly, world leaders, pressured by swift public reaction when a crisis erupts, no longer enjoy what author Theodore White called "the consoling filter of time." Hence, caught in a time bind, sometimes because of political exigencies, they are often provoked into making quick, unwise decisions based on insufficient information and unconfirmed intelligence, without adequate mediation and consultation.

Yet, we now know that, as in the physical sciences, observing an event changes it. Moreover, we are aware that much of what the mass of society knows or believes of people, places, and events is filtered through the news media. Unquestionably, this popular consciousness impacts on public attitudes and eventually contributes to the molding of government policy.

In essence, public opinion, shaped to a large extent by the media, has become the common arbiter among competing policies, politicians, and statesmen.

Consequently, it is universally acknowledged in the current information era that there exists a mutually dependent relationship between the news media and the government, although the ambitions of each are institutionally different and, as a result, adversarial tension is endemic. Namely, the government wants to get its message out to the public and solicit support; the news media want access, information, and a full accounting.

These objectives inevitably conflict, yet the practitioners are perforced to coexist in a sort of loveless marriage since they need each other and feed off of one another to ensure a democracy in which the citizenry can make informed choices.

This tense but vital relationship is the moving force in the renovated art of diplomacy—from the days when formally attired envoys followed rigid protocol to today's political public affairs officers and economic specialists who perceive the national interest in global terms and are sensitive to the value of public opinion abroad and at home through the interaction of statecraft and media relations.

SHARED—OR SEPARATE POWERS?

Among the fateful decisions reached by the delegates to the Constitutional Convention in 1789, none was more critical than the debate over the form and authority of the Chief Executive. With the abuses of King George III and the royal governors fresh in mind, most of the colonists feared and despised any concept of government which conferred absolute power in a supreme executive. As presidential scholar Edward S. Corwin pointed out, "The colonial period ended with the belief prevalent that 'the executive magistery' was the natural enemy, the legislative assembly the natural friend of liberty, a sentiment strengthened by the contemporary spectacle of George III's domination in Parliament." (Corwin, 1957, pp. 5–6) However, the experiment under the Articles of Confederation disillusioned many concerning the viability of a governmental structure dominated by the states.

Several authors of the *Federalist* papers, among them James Madison, Alexander Hamilton and John Jay, maintained that a strong executive chosen independently of the legislature was necessary to forge a union and impart a sense of cohesion, with common goals and an ability to insure a national defense. Madison warned against the "danger from legislative usurpation." Gouverneur Morris, of New York, wrote that the "Executive Magistrate should be the guardian of the people, even of the lower classes, agst. Legislative tyranny, against the great & the wealthy who in the course of things will necessarily compose—the Legislative body." Hamilton suggested that a President be chosen for life, but was firmly rebuffed.

Advocates of a strong central government found inspirational support in British philosopher John Locke's argument, as enunciated in his *Two Treatises of Government*:

> The good of society requires that several things should be left to the discretion of him that has the executive power. For the legislators not being able to foresee and provide by laws for all that may be useful to the community, the executor of laws, having the power in his hands, has by the common law of Nature a right to make use of it for the good of society. (Corwin, 1957, p.7)

Taking an opposing view, Roger Morris, of Connecticut, proposed that the presidency should be "nothing more than an institution for carrying the will of the Legislature into effect."

The result was a compromise, with the adoption of the doctrine of separated institutions sharing power. In practice, however, the two branches are natural antagonists which jealously protect their prerogatives and compete for power. This "invitation to struggle" is enhanced by the language of the Constitution, which is vague and overlapping in places, and unclear in others. As governmental scholar James L. Sundquist observed, "On essential matters that would define the boundaries between the branches, and the relations between them, the Constitution was silent, or ambiguous. The opponents would have to settle those through combat." (Sundquist, 1981, p.16)

Clearly, the founding fathers did not intend to be wholly definitive; they did not claim omniscience nor provide provisions for every possible governing or political problem. In such an eventuality, they left it up to the two branches to strive for supremacy.

A reading of the Constitution, however, suggests that it does not grant the president extraordinary powers over foreign policy; rather they are mainly subjected to checks and balances under the shared powers doctrine.

Modern American presidents nonetheless, have gained primacy in foreign policy via numerous sources: judicial interpretation, historical custom, established precedence, the superpower status of the United States, control over nuclear arms, the symbolic nature of the White House office as a unifying force and the reverence in which it is held, the constant and saturated coverage of the nation's highest elected official, and significantly, the vast communications resources at his command. Additionally, the president presides over a massive federal bureaucracy of an estimated 2 million civilian employees designated to provide him with intelligence, information and advice, and support and promote his policies and programs.

It should further be emphasized that the presidency is an amalgamation of the man and the office. He alone can speak as the national leader of the country. As the British scholar and activist Harold J. Laski noted, "Whatever voice is drowned amid the babel of tongues, his (the president's)... can always be heard." (Laski, 1940, p.275)

Congress, on the other hand, is an amorphous institution of 535 individuals, divided by ideological and regional concerns, without a recognized leader who can speak for the whole legislative branch, without strict party loyalty, without a large, supportive bureaucracy, and minus the aura of the presidency.

Therefore, perhaps it is not surprising that Congress is inclined to forfeit or surrender its prerogatives to the President during perilous crises, such as those involving the Great Depression, World War II, the containment policy *vis-à-vis* the communist threat, the Vietnam War, control of nuclear proliferation and military action to halt terrorism and hostile acts by countries like Iran, Libya, and Iraq. Powers once loaned are difficult to reclaim.

Moreover, the President has at his disposal an inordinately large press public-affairs staff whose paramount function is to sell and promote the chief executive, his decisions and policies. At least, two-thirds of the White House Office (whose numbers range from 350 to 600 or so members) are engaged in such tasks, prompting one prominent writer, educator and former assistant to President Johnson to assert, "We have today what might be called government by publicity." (Cater, 1965, p. 10)

Another respected scholar maintained, "The whole of the White House is an institution for communicating on behalf of the President." (Rose, 1988, p. 128)

While the President cannot control the news media, he can to a large extent influence it by: setting the news agenda by centering on a particular issue; holding press conferences, greeting popular celebrities, delivering speeches in world-recognized arenas such as the United Nations, traveling to international summit conferences, meeting with national leaders in global capitals, speaking on weekly radio programs, and holding interviews with selective members of the media.

Each of these appearances are precisely planned and orchestrated to derive the greatest amount of public visibility and media attention under controlled scenarios.

A memory bank recreates scenes of recent Presidents starring in what political scientists call "going public."

1. Nixon at the Great Wall during his celebrated trip to China.
2. Reagan, "the Great Communicator," televised posing on the Normandy cliffs on the anniversary of D-Day, appearing as the very essence of the commander-in-chief.
3. Reagan, standing tall and formidable at the DMZ line peering across towards North Korea.
4. Ford, shortly after assuming the presidency, allowing cameras into his home to film him cooking his own breakfast—invoking the impression of a man of the people.
5. Bush, accompanied by his wife, Barbara, visiting American troops over Thanksgiving against a backdrop of tanks and other combat material during the Persian Gulf War— an ideal tableau reminiscent of a Norman Rockwell scene reflecting American family values and the bond between the soldiers and their commander-in-chief.
6. Clinton, prominently positioned in the East Wing of the White House during the signing of the peace accord between Israeli Prime Minister Yitzhak Rabin and PLO Chairman Yasser Arafat—a perfectly conceived photo opportunity suggesting the President's renewed interest in international affairs, fortuitously just as his 1996 reelection campaign was getting underway.

To the White House's undoubted pleasure, the Clinton photo on the first page of the *Washington Post* carried the headline: "Clinton Continues Building Case For His Foreign Policy Successes." (*Washington Post*, Sept. 27, 1995)

If not in reality but in perception, Clinton was clearly intent on buttressing his image in the foreign policy area—the transparent weak spot in his presidency.

Perhaps, he, as all of his predecessors learned—many too late—or intuitively understood, the president's power is less on paper and than in the perceptual, and more in the abstract than the absolute. His success is less in legislation won or lost than in his ability to make his presence felt in setting the national tone, instilling trust and confidence, mobilizing public opinion, offering a vision of the future, and affecting a national coalition. And this he must do through the strength, charisma and credibility of his persona, his prowess as a political leader and his skill as a communicator.

Consequently, there is an ambivalence about the office, which forceful Presidents understand and use to their advantage, dating back to Andrew Jackson, Lincoln, Theodore Roosevelt, and in more recent times, Wilson and FDR.

At one extreme, Teddy Roosevelt insisted the President could do anything that the needs of the country demanded, unless specifically forbidden by law or the Constitution. John F. Kennedy similarly stated he was prepared to exercise the fullest powers of his office—"all that are specified and some that are not."

At the other extreme, William Howard Taft claimed that the President did not have the right "to play the part of a Universal Providence." He altered his view after becoming Chief Justice.

"Strong" presidents inevitably concur with Woodrow Wilson: "The President is at liberty, both in law and conscience, to be as big a man as he can be."

THE CYCLICAL PATH IN FOREIGN POLICY

Scholars and statesmen generally agree that the controlling branch in foreign policy is not constant, but rather is cyclical—depending in part on events and political developments abroad, and the popularity and quality of leadership demonstrated by the incumbent President. Congress is constantly alert to filling a political vacuum should the President fail to achieve an overarching national objective or loses the trust and esteem of the American people because of a personal or political flaw. A classic example was the undercutting of Lyndon Johnson's presidency and the alacrity with which Congress sought to assert control in foreign affairs as a result of the Vietnam debacle.

The running battle between Congress and the President has been going on since 1789 when George Washington entered the Senate chamber to propose a treaty. To his chagrin, he was compelled to stand helplessly by as the Senate debated and revised the provisions of the treaty without conferring with him and he vowed never again to return to the Capitol on similar business.

That set a precedent which stands today. More importantly, it established a custom whereby Presidents, notwithstanding the Constitutional "advise and consent" mandate, have virtually ignored provisions requiring Senatorial advice in regard to appointments and treaties. Hence, only the consent portion is faithfully complied with.

Even Thomas Jefferson, an heir of the Enlightenment, acknowledged that while serving as President he had gone "beyond the Constitution" in negotiating the Louisiana Purchase with France and had not sought the advice of the Senate beforehand.

While Congress was acknowledged as a co-equal with the Executive Branch in foreign affairs policy throughout most of the 19th century, the presidency gained supremacy during the Cold War era when the United States represented the free world's best, if not only, hope against communist incursions around the globe. To counterbalance the threat posed by the Soviet Union, the United States established massive foreign aid and economic development programs, created an elaborate network of overseas military bases, and assumed leadership in a series of international commitments and collective security pacts.

A top priority consideration throughout this period of international ferment was the danger of nuclear war, for geopolitics was irrevocably changed by the development, or feared development of the atomic bomb by peripheral foreign nations. Domestically, congressional authority was offset a marked degree by the sole prerogative of the President to use nuclear weapons, to commit U.S. military forces to meet unexpected crises and to fight "limited wars." Foreign and military affairs, thus, became a larger part of the totality of U.S. public policy, further expanding the President's sphere of authority as commander-in-chief.

At the same time, foreign policy turned more on enlightened public opinion and international relations became more reliant upon information and interpretations as reported by the news media.

This was apparent as early as 1945 following World War II. A large majority of Americans was wholeheartedly in favor of U.S. participation in the United Nations. Subsequently, they endorsed the European Recovery Program, U.S. membership in the North Atlantic Treaty organization, the Truman Doctrine to rehabilitate Greece and Turkey, and the economic rebuilding of Japan.

For four decades, from the rise of FDR to the fall of Richard Nixon, the powers of the executive branch were steadily extended beyond recognized legal and traditional boundaries. The doctrine of separate branches sharing powers fell into virtual disuse as the executive arm assumed authority, or was bequeathed it by a directionless and quiescent Congress.

Then, in reaction to the flawed presidencies of Johnson and Nixon, Congress, shaking off years of compliance and acquiescence, set out to retrieve its constitutional powers. In 1970, it repealed the Tonkin Gulf Resolution, passed in 1964 in support of Johnson's Vietnam War policies; and in 1973, over President Nixon's veto, it adopted the War Powers Resolution, designed as a check on the President's ability to involve the country in armed combat without consultation with Congress.

Next, amid the mass media clamor, Congress moved into the political void created by President Nixon's resignation on August 9, 1974. Its role in the special Watergate inquiry and impeachment proceedings seemed to give the legislative body new life and it became intent on redressing the imbalance of power.

"We do not have an imperial presidency; we have an imperiled presidency," cried President Ford.

Later, Ronald Reagan, whose anti-big government campaign carried him into the White House, tipped the scales of foreign policy decision-making back in favor of the presidency. Arraigned against the mystique of a President who was part pragmatist, part visionary, and part showman, Congress retreated into its reactive mode.

But the cycle took still another turn during the Clinton presidency, when the Republicans achieved majority control in both the House and Senate in the 1994 midterm elections, elevating Senator Jesse Helms, R-N.C., a quintessential neo-isolationist, as chairman of the Senate Foreign Relations Committee.

Above all, the principal lesson of cyclical leadership is that shared powers does not ensure shared decision making.

THE MEDIA, IMAGERY & PERSUASION

Constantly reminded of their power and prestigious rank, Presidents become exasperated because, while they can, to a large degree, set the nation's news agenda, they cannot control the press. This inability exposes their vulnerability and tends to mock the grandeur of their office.

All Presidents, at some time or another, become frustrated at what they perceive as unfair treatment by the press, even while acknowledging its vital function in a free society. They are also aware of what it can do for them—and to them.

The relationship, strained, ritualistic and alternately bitter and cordial, has changed little since the birth of the Republic.

George Washington, irritated by the lies, unfounded rumors and vitriol of the early journals, described attacks by the press as "outrages on common decency." He further criticized the press in the draft of his Farewell Address, but deleted the section at the urging of Alexander Hamilton.

A strong defender of a free press, Thomas Jefferson wrote, "Were it left to me to decide whether we should have a government without newspapers, or newspapers without a government, I should not hesitate a moment to prefer the latter."

Scholars, however, note that Jefferson added, "But I should mean that every man should receive those papers, and be capable of reading them."

They further point out that Jefferson made the statement prior to becoming President and that, unlike many of his contemporaries, he had few contacts with the press and seldom wrote for it. (Pollard, 1973, pp. 53–54)

Some also contend that Jefferson was merely uttering a bon mot, for which he is justly renowned.

More than a century-and-a-half later, Harry Truman remarked he was "saving up four or five good, hard punches on the nose" for reporters who, he felt, had been unfair to him; John F. Kennedy, in a fit of pique, canceled the *New York Herald Tribune*; Richard Nixon compiled an "enemies list" liberally sprinkled with the names of reporters, a reflection of his distaste for the press which permeated his administration and nurtured a conspiratorial mind-set among his aides; Jimmy Carter maintained the news media were not interested in substantive issues; Ronald Reagan, hounded by the Iran-Contra affair, rarely held press conferences towards the end of his presidency, and once referred to reporters as "sons-of-bitches" when he thought the microphone was turned off.

The success of a modern President, in an age when perception equates with reality, and imagery with fidelity, depends in a large measure on his persuasiveness as a communicator to mobilize a national constituency—or, in the event of a foreign issue, to forge a multinational coalition. Not unexpectedly, every President wants his proposals, decisions, and actions couched in terms compatible with administration policy.

To an immeasurable degree, the business of government is public relations. Hence, the elaborately staged events and sophisticated attempts by incumbent administrations to manage the news and gloss its content.

Seeded throughout the federal landscape, from the White House to the gargantuan cabinet departments to the mini-agencies cloistered in the bureaucratic depths, is a complex network of civil servants whose chief mission is to package and dispense information about government policies, services and programs at one level, and to promote and "sell" them on another. The former is essentially an educational function; the latter is primarily political in nature. It is this dichotomy that has traditionally bred confusion and suspicion about federal public affairs operations.

Part of the problem is that the line between the need to inform as a public service, and the desire to gain popular support for political objectives has never been satisfactorily delineated.

Presidents mainly perceive communications in terms of helping or hindering them in quest of their goals. As often documented, the government may withhold information, distort it, classify it or, on occasion, lie about it. Prohibited by the First Amendment from censoring the press or invoking prior restraint, it may dress the news in favorable designs and shades.

In their zeal to protect and enhance their image, presidential administrations have resorted to untruths, half-truths, intentional obfuscation, and outright deception and distortion. At times, they have operated in secret under the cloak of national security.

Prominent examples include: Franklin D. Roosevelt's covert aid to the British, including 50 destroyers and other arms, prior to the United States entry in World War II; the Eisenhower Administration's misleading explanation of the American U-2 spy plane shot down over the Soviet Union in 1960; President Kennedy's secret approval of the Bay of Pigs invasion, following which Adlai Stevenson, U.S. envoy to the United Nations, unwittingly lied to the international body concerning America's intimate role in the unsuccessful operation; President Johnson's attempts to conceal the escalation of U.S. involvement in the Vietnam War; President Nixon's secret bombing of Cambodia, as well as his efforts to block the release of the Pentagon Papers, and his personal role in the Watergate cover-up; President Reagan's news blackout during the 1983 Grenada invasion and the participation of several of his chief advisers in the Iran–Contra arms sales conspiracy.

These undercover incidents were mainly disclosed by an intrusive, aggressive contemporary news media. Yet, U.S. Presidents have long been involved in subterfuges. President Grover Cleveland, for example, in 1893 had a cancerous growth in his mouth surgically removed while on a yacht off New York City, which was kept secret from the public and press for fear of creating domestic unrest, economic instability and foreign turmoil. The incident was not fully disclosed until more than 20 years later.

News of President Wilson's incapacitating stroke in the final year of his presidency, and FDR's crippling polio were also kept from the public, in each instance by an accommodating press which held privacy of public figures in higher regard than their successors.

Not until 1960 did most Americans learn for the first time that their government resorted to lying as a dark side of the governing process. On May 1, 1960, Francis Gary Powers, flying a CIA U-2 photographic intelligence plane high over the Soviet Union was downed by a Russian missile. Four days later, Soviet Premier Nikita Khrushchev announced that an American plane had crashed inside Soviet territory, without further elaboration. In Washington, official spokesmen reported that a NASA "weather reconnaissance plane" was missing while on a flight inside Turkey. On May 6, the State Department's chief public affairs officer told reporters,, "There was no—N-O-no deliberate attempts to violate Soviet air space. There never has been."

The next day, Khrushchev jubilantly revealed that the Russians had captured both Powers and the plane, which was virtually intact. Shortly afterwards, an embarrassed President Eisenhower admitted that the U-2 was a "spy plane" on an espionage mission. It was additionally learned that the CIA had been engaged in Soviet overflights for the previous four years, thus compounding the web of deception in view of the State Department's claim that there never had been "deliberate attempts to violate Soviet air space." (Wise, 1973, pp. 34–35)

As a result of the incident, a Paris summit meeting, at which Eisenhower and Khrushchev were scheduled to attend, collapsed. Media critic A.J. Liebling observed that the disclosure marked the "beginning of wisdom" in the media's attitude towards the government. Others saw it as the moment America lost its innocence.

In swift succession other ingenious fabrications—euphemistically called "cover stories" by the intelligence sector—occurred in the realm of foreign affairs, a policy area where the President can act with minimal restraints.

Briefly after taking office, John F. Kennedy's bright and shining moment was shattered by the bloody repulse of the 1961 Bay of Pigs invasion intended to topple Cuban leader Fidel Castro. The operation was feebly portrayed by the Kennedy White House as a unilateral expedition by Cuban exiles, despite universal knowledge that U.S. government forces had trained, financed and supported the rebel invaders.

Kennedy would redeem himself the following year when, in a test of iron wills, he stared down Premier Khrushchev during the Cuban missile crisis.

His successor, Lyndon Johnson, dispatched a contingent of U.S. Marines to the Dominican Republic in April 1965, ostensibly to save American lives, but it widely suspected that the real reason was fear of a Communist takeover.

In an apparent attempt to roil public opinion, Johnson reported that Americans in the capital city of Santo Domingo were in such grave peril that the U.S. ambassador was forced to dive under his desk when shots were fired at the American Embassy.

As one author–journalist wrote, "Within days more than 24,000 troops had invaded the small Caribbean country; the President spent hours personally attempting to convince newsmen that this was justified because 'fifteen hundred innocent people were murdered and shot, and their heads cut off,' which turned out later to be pure myth." (Hodgson, 1980, pp. 188–189)

Even more duplicitous and crucial was the Tonkin Gulf incident which Johnson used to rally public support and obtain a congressional resolution giving him carte blanche to escalate the war in Vietnam.

Essentially, the episode involved two U.S. destroyers, the Maddox and the Turner Joy, which were attacked by three North Vietnamese PT boats on August 2, 1964, in a daylight engagement. One machine gun bullet fired by a PT boat struck the Maddox, but there were no U.S. casualties. On the night of August 4, while patrolling in the gulf, a young sonarman aboard the Maddox reported they were under "continuous torpedo attack." But the ship could detect nothing on radar. And although it heard no torpedoes, the Turner Joy fired in the darkness for four hours.

In Washington, Johnson convened the National Security Council. There was no verification of enemy sightings, yet the President and Defense Secretary Robert S. McNamera made a decision to bomb North Vietnam in retaliation. Johnson had his war and persuaded Congress to back him up. In effect, he had created an event to conform to his war policy. Not until four years later would it be learned that the task force commander who was on the bridge of the Maddox had sent a cable to the Pentagon which read:

> REVIEW OF ACTION MAKES MANY RECORDED CONTACTS AND TORPE-
> DOES FIRED APPEAR DOUBTFUL. FREAK WEATHER EFFECTS AND
> OVEREAGER SONARMAN MAY HAVE ACCOUNTED FOR MANY REPORTS.
> NO ACTUAL VISUAL SIGHTINGS BY MADDOX. SUGGEST COMPLETE EVAL-
> UATION BEFORE ANY FURTHER ACTION. (Wise, 1973, p. 44)

To this day, the Tonkin Gulf incident remains as a symbol of Johnson's manipulative distortions to escalate U.S. participation in the Vietnam War, giving rise to what became known as LBJ's "credibility gap"—and more importantly, contributing to the loss of more than 55,000 Americans.

In a painful epilogue, during a trip to Hanoi thirty years later, McNamara said that after talking with North Vietnamese military commanders, "I am absolutely positive the second attack never took place... If it didn't occur, we would not have carried out the [retaliatory] military attack on their shore installations." (*Washington Post*, Nov. 11, 1995)

This leaves open the question whether the course of the Vietnam War would have gone differently without the provocation of an "incident" which may never have occurred, but was contrived as a propaganda ploy.

One of the most notable cases involving the weaving of the performance and behavior of the media and governmental accountability involved the Iran-Contra affair, which broke like a thunderstorm in November 1986. Not since Watergate in the 1970s had a story so dominated the news and monopolized the nation's consciousness. It enforced the conviction that the unfolding of events is only slightly more significant than how the events are perceived and portrayed by the media. For instance, how the media handled the 17-day ordeal of the June 1985 hijacking of TWA Flight 847 by terrorists became as much a part of the news as the event itself.

This phenomenon was raised to a new level in the Iran-Contra controversy. During the height of the inquiry, President Reagan complained to *Time* magazine's Hugh Sidey that the news media were overplaying and sensationalizing the story, comparing reporters to "sharks circling... with blood in the water." (*Los Angeles Times* syndicate, Dec. 1, 1986)

Basically, the issue revolved around secret and possibly illegal arms sales to Iran and the diversion of an undetermined part of the proceeds to the Nicaraguan contra rebels being supported by the administration.

Almost immediately, the issue took on the air of a war between the press, which zealously—over-zealously, in the opinion of its critics—pursued every thread of the story leading to the highest levels of government, and the administration, equally intent on justifying its actions as being within its constitutional mandate to promote and protect national security.

Major newspapers, such as the *New York Times*, *Washington Post* and *Los Angeles Times*, assigned from 10 to 20 reporters to the story—first disclosed by an obscure Lebanese magazine to the embarrassment of the U.S. news media—during peak news periods. A survey by the Washington-based Center for Media and Public Affairs beginning on Nov. 4 showed that the three national commercial television networks, CBS, NBC and ABC, averaged a combined 13 stories a night or 38 percent of the available news slot up until Nov. 25 when Attorney General Edwin Meese III publicly disclosed the contra connection, after which the networks collectively averaged 20 stories a night or 60 percent of the total news time.

Several observers accused the media of rushing to judgment because of the fervor with which the story was covered and the huge gaps of news space and air time devoted to it.

Widely quoted was a remark attributed to Benjamin C. Bradlee, executive editor of the *Washington Post*: "This is the most fun we've had since Watergate." Bradlee later insisted the comment was taken out of the context.

In a provocative piece by Michael Kinsley, editor of The *New Republic*, he wrote:

> The only irritating aspect of the otherwise delightful collapse of the Reagan Administration is the widespread insistence that we must all be poker-faced about it… Simple honesty requires any Washington type to admit that this is the kind of episode we all live for. The adrenaline is flowing like Perrier. Everyone—Reagan supporters no less than his opponents—is wandering around in a happy buzz induced by those oft-denounced but rarely eschewed two intoxicants, 'gossip and speculation.' C'mon, everybody, admit it. We're high. (The *New Republic*, Dec. 22, 1986)

Kinsley's comments served to confirm in the minds of media critics that the mainstream press was covertly concerned with scandal, sin and sensationalism and with slipping their ideological tilt into news articles.

In a prompt retort, Patrick Buchanan, Reagan White House director of communications, maintained in a press article, "What liberalism and the left have in mind is the second ruination of a Republican presidency within a generation."

Charles Lichenstein, former U.S. spokesman at the United Nations, claimed, "Most journalists have an ideological tendency to always exaggerate an issue to somehow prove that government is as bad as they said it was." (Bonafede, *National Journal*, Jan. 24, 1967)

While it remained debatable whether the national press sought a balance between even-handed and high-decibel coverage, there was little question about the competitiveness and race for exclusives.

The *Washington Post's* Bob Woodward was the first to report the United States was secretly providing Iraq with intelligence at the same time it was covertly selling arms to Iran, Iraq's longtime enemy; the *New York Times* disclosed that the CIA had originally proposed that U.S. arms sales to Iran be kept secret from Congress; the *Miami Herald* revealed that fired National Security Council aide Oliver North had spent three weeks in Bethesda's Naval Hospital for emotional distress six years before beginning work at the White House; the *Los Angeles Times* scored with a comprehensive report on the arms deal shortly after the story broke including information that Secretary of State George Shultz had been "completely cut out" of the negotiations.

Reflecting the highly charged tenor of the coverage, Thomas Squitieri, the sole reporter in Washington for The *Sun* of Lowell, Mass., reported on December 14 that some of the proceeds from the Iran arms sales had been diverted to right-wing groups to help U.S. electoral candidates favoring aid to the Nicaraguan rebels. The story, based on unidentified sources, was picked up by several major newspapers, including the *New York Times*, which ran a rewritten version the following day as the paper's lead story, even though it acknowledged that efforts to confirm the report were unsuccessful.

That the *New York Times*, generally considered the premier newspaper in the United States, should temporarily abandon its professional principles and standards for an unconfirmed story suggests the intense competitive climate which prevailed.
Newsweek's media analyst Jonathan Alter, meanwhile, faulted the Washington press for being late in picking up on the Iran-Contra affair. "It shouldn't have broken in a Lebanese magazine," he contended. "The fact that North was running a contra aid operation was well known: there were references to it in the press for some time. But there was never an effort by the media to follow it to its conclusion."

Throughout the controversy, Reagan persistently denied that he had been aware of the contra funding link and castigated the media for trying to undercut his credibility. Ultimately, he conceded, after a redundant series of denials, evasions and contradictions, that the arms deal was "a mistake", even as he sought to distance himself from it.

Nevertheless, the issue failed to succumb to his cinematic charm and went on to contaminate his presidency and damage his personal popularity. The Iran-Contra affair would predictably stalk him throughout history.

SHAPING THE NEWS

Shortly before the Bay of Pigs assault by the U.S.-backed Cuban exile brigade on April 17, 1961, the Kennedy White House learned that the *New York Times* was planning to publish a detailed front-page story on the operation. Concerned that the disclosure would surely result in the invasion's failure, President Kennedy personally appealed to the newspaper's publisher and top editors against running the piece, citing national security interests and the certain loss of life among the brigade members, not to mention the blow to the new administration which had taken office only a few months earlier. Furthermore, the paper would conceivably have to take a share of the blame if the assault went bad.

Kennedy prevailed and the *Times* ran a toned down story, omitting mention of the

CIA's role and the approximate date of the invasion.

But, as it so happened, Kennedy was the victim of unintended consequences. Not long after the invasion disaster, Kennedy told the *Times'* editors he regretted that they had not printed more about the operation and "saved us from a colossal mistake."

Kennedy, in effect, tried to manage the news to control events. Twenty-five years later, President Reagan tried to contrive news to create events.

In a classic case of government news management, the Reagan administration launched a concerted disinformation campaign in the mid-1980s against Libyan leader Muammar Qadhafi a "known" international terrorist and Middle East troublemaker. Yet, despite his claim of sovereignty over the Gulf of Sidra, his disruptive incursions in North Africa, and his role in driving up the price of oil, he posed no serious threat to the United States.

As noted by diplomatic writer R. Gregory Nokes, "Libya ended up paying the price for the administration's frustrations in dealing with terrorism in Lebanon, in Syria, in Iran, including the much publicized hostage takings, and the deaths of hundreds of marines. Libya's vulnerability and isolation—more than the actions of Qadhafi—made that country an inviting target for reprisals." (Nokes, 1990, pp. 36–37)

False reports were leaked to influential news publications, such as the *Wall Street Journal*, which parlayed them into headline stories that Qadhafi had sent terrorist hit squads to the United States; that he was a madman and Libya was a lawless state; and that he had trained and financed local terrorists in other countries. Tension was artificially hiked by expelling Libyan diplomats from the United States and urging Americans living in Libya to leave the country.

There was no hard evidence to support the U.S. government's planted charges, yet they tended to give credence to the administration's objective to take down Qadhafi.

Offering a rational for the disinformation campaign, Secretary of State Shultz publicly stated: "If there are ways in which we can make Qadhafi nervous, why shouldn't we? Frankly, I don't have any problems with a little psychological warfare against Qadhafi." Shultz then quoted Winston Churchill as saying in time of war "the truth is so precious it must be attended by a bodyguard of lies."

But the United States was not at war with Libya. A memo drafted by Admiral Poindexter, then Reagan's national security adviser, and obtained by the *Washington Post*, later revealed that the administration had created a phony crisis and resorted to "dirty tricks" not in the cause of the national interest but to promote its political policies.

It proposed that false information be leaked to the press with the objective of bringing down Qadhafi. The propaganda campaign was to combine "real and illusionary events— through a disinformation program—with the basic goal of making Qadhafi think there is a high degree of internal opposition to him within Libya, that his key trusted aides are disloyal, that the U.S. is about to move against him militarily." (Smith, 1988, p. 435)

The disclosure stunned many Americans since it uncovered a side of the U.S. government seldom seen and was generally identified with Soviet techniques for planting false information.

Qadhafi was the perfect scapegoat and, according to Nokes, the gullibility of the press fit in neatly with the disinformation scheme: "The press fell into the trap, as it often does, of careless reporting and careless sourcing in the heat of going after a story." (Nokes, 1990, p.45)

As commander-in-chief, a President can also use an unforeseen event to his advantage, even a minor military expedition. A boost to Gerald Ford's presidency occurred in May 1975 when he ordered U.S. Navy and Marine units to rescue the American merchant ship Mayaguez and its 39-member crew seized by Cambodian forces. The incident took place at a fortuitous moment, shortly after the U.S.'s chaotic exodus from South Vietnam when national spirits were at a low ebb. "There are limits beyond which the United States would not be pushed," announced Secretary of State Henry Kissinger with exaggerated bravado.

Although U.S. forces originally hit the wrong target and more men were killed in the operation than were rescued, it was hailed as a glorious feat and served to lift the country's sagging morale, and raise Ford's popularity rating. Realizing its political potential, White House aides painted a scenario which might have been scripted in Hollywood, with emergency National Security Council sessions at odd hours, military alerts, transcontinental communiques, congressional leaders coming and going from the White House, and a post-midnight television appearance by the President announcing the operation's success.

The episode deserves but a footnote in history, yet it had a perceptive, if only temporary, effect on Ford's presidency.

Frequently, presidential press secretaries who serve as the surrogate voice of their benefactor, are compelled to protect him by twisting the truth, and when pushed to the wall, by lying when the stakes are high.

Jody Powell, press secretary, adviser and confidant to President Carter, faced this quandary during the Iranian hostage crisis. Asked by Jack Nelson, Washington bureau chief of the *Los Angeles Times*, whether the administration was planning a military operation to free the hostages, Powell, who had been told by the President himself that a rescue attempt was imminent, denied that any such action was in the works. He camouflaged his denial by claiming that a naval blockade or the mining of Iranian harbors were being considered—options that already had been ruled out.

In a move to stifle internal speculation that something big was going down, and to head off press leaks, White House Chief of Staff Hamilton Jordan assembled a group of presidential aides and also lied there were no plans for a rescue mission.

Two days later, on April 24, 1980, a highly-trained Delta Force rescue team aboard helicopters and C-130s flew into Iran and met disaster. At the landing site, one of the copters rammed into a C-130 causing a fiery explosion and killing eight U.S. servicemen. Three helicopters were lost in the operation. The mission was aborted and the survivors returned to their bases.

Although troubled by the moral dilemma, Powell stressed in his memoirs, "It is ludicrous to argue that soldiers may be sent off to fight and die, but a spokesman may not, under any circumstances, be asked to lie to make sure that the casualties are fewer and not in vain." (Powell, 1984, p. 233)

On another occasion involving governmental deception to avoid risking disclosure of an invasion, the White House press secretary was manipulated along with the press and the public.

Larry Speakes was elevated to the position of Reagan's press secretary following the assassination attempt on the President's life in which James Brady, who held the job, was severely wounded. As a replacement through a tragic accident of history, Speakes was regularly excluded from the inner circle surrounding the President and frozen out of many policy meetings.

Consequently, it was not unusual when on October 24, 1983, CBS White House correspondent Bill Plante privately asked him about reports he had heard that U.S. forces were about to invade Grenada, and Speakes replied he didn't know anything about it but would check.

Speakes relayed the inquiry to Admiral Poindexter, newly named deputy director of the National Security Council. Poindexter replied, "Preposterous," and instructed Speakes to "knock it down hard."

As Speakes reported in a book on his White House years, "Twelve hours later, as dawn was breaking on October 25, 1,900 U.S. Marines and Army Rangers—accompanied by three hundred troops from Antigua, Barbados, Dominica, Jamaica, St. Kitts-Nevis, St. Lucia, and St. Vincents, which gave us an excuse for being involved—launched 'Operation Urgent Fury,' the invasion of Grenada."

Conceding he had been "hung out to dry" by Poindexter, Speakes declared, "I had been lied to, not the one who had been the liar." (Speakes, 1988, p. 153)

Actually, Speakes was kept in the dark about the Grenada invasion up until a scheduled 5:45 a.m. breakfast meeting with White House Chief of Staff James Baker—some two hours after U.S. troops had stormed ashore. He had been fooled not once, but twice by the top Reagan coterie. Adding to Speakes' anger over having been deceived, Baker gave him a thick file of "talking points" an hour or so before he was to brief the Washington press, whose tempers were high because of the news blackout surrounding the assault.

As battles go, Grenada ranks as a brisk skirmish, but the cloak of lies and deception woven around it made finding the truth almost impossible. Similar to Lyndon Johnson in the 1965 Dominican Republic invasion, Reagan insisted he ordered it to save American lives and prevent a Marxist takeover of the island by Cuban-trained rebels who had staged a military coup and executed the prime minister.

Reports persisted within the media, however, that it was hardly happenstance that the invasion occurred one day after shocking news reports and TV visuals of the terrorist truck bombing of the Marine barracks in Beirut killing 241 U.S. servicemen—and that Reagan hastened his decision to attack the Caribbean island to distract American outrage over the massacre.

Reagan, whose smiling countenance masked his distrust of the press, was convinced the operation could not be kept secret, backed the military, still smarting over the Vietnam coverage, in prohibiting reporters from accompanying American troops in the landing. Not until two days after the invasion was a pool of twelve reporters escorted by the military allowed to tour the island.

"I had been lied to, I had been given only an hour to brief the press, and then I had to go out and defend the administration against accusations from reporters that I had deceived them," Speakes ruefully recalled. (Speakes, 1988, p. 156).

Not only had the press been barred from covering the operation—breaking a tradition dating back to the Civil War—but several American reporters were held incommunicado after they tried to reach the island on their own. Vice Admiral Joseph Metcalf III, the commander of the U.S. task force on Grenada, further ordered his ships to fire on any boats attempting to take reporters to the island.

The acrimony between the press and the administration was inherent in a remark several weeks later by Secretary of State Shultz that reporters "are always against us and so they're always seeking to report something that's going to screw things up." (Speakes, 1988, p. 159)

Taking the high road, Defense Secretary Caspar Weinberger, who was in on the planning of the Grenada invasion, argued that the role and privileges of the press had to be weighed against other legitimate interests.

In a lawyerly fashion, Weinberger wrote:

The Founding Fathers did not proclaim freedom of the press and then resolutely stand aside. They expected government to put all constitutional rights as well as duties in a state of balance. Some (people) act as if they believe freedom of the press is the paramount freedom—so important that no other freedom can exist without it. They seem to believe that any action required to produce a story is justified by the First Amendment. Unfortunately, such an attitude promotes the trampling of other, equally legitimate public interests—the national defense, an accused's right to a fair trial free from a jury influenced by news reports, the right to privacy and others. (Weinberger, 1985, pp. 1–2)

Weinberger added that while the press is protected by the First Amendment, "such protection cannot diminish the other legitimate functions of good government—including the government's need for secrecy, especially in national defense." (Weinberger, 1985, pp. 1–2)

At first, public opinion supported the Grenada news blackout. But with disclosures of military mishaps, such as the bombing of a hospital, the difficulty U.S. forces had in defeating a small contingent of Cuban defenders, as well as a failure by the administration to offer a convincing rational for the operation, follow-up surveys showed that the public had second thoughts and was persuaded that the government was remiss in not letting reporters accompany the assault force.

Reagan administration officials, nonetheless, defended their action as a means to maintain secrecy and ensure the mission's success. They further contended they were concerned for the safety of the journalists—a notion scoffed at by members of the news media, who well know the risks they willingly accept when they venture into combat zones in pursuit of news.

As a result of the furor created by the administration's draconian press constrictions, a joint military-press commission under Winant Sidle, a retired lieutenant general, was

set up to study the problem and offer recommendations. The commission subsequently proposed that a small, rotating group of reporters be on call and alerted to imminent
hostile engagements and taken in with the first wave of troops. The primary objectives
would be access and open coverage—in exchange for which the press was to pledge
complete secrecy.

The recommendations, however, were never transformed into reality.

In the December 20, 1989, invasion of Panama ordered by President Bush, not a
single American correspondent accompanied the assault force. The Pentagon had
assembled a 14-member press pool but it arrived on the scene four hours after the
shooting began. The pool was sequestered and denied access to the combat area; the
correspondents' dispatches mainly reflected what they had been told by military
briefers. Two days later, some 200 American reporters were flown to Panama but were
prevented from leaving U.S. installations until the following day.

To their frustration, reporters were shielded by military escorts from witnessing
troops in actual combat. Nor could they see wounded U.S. servicemen or Panamanians
who had been taken prisoner. At one point, several hundred journalists quartered at the
Howard Air Force Base had access to only two telephones.

It soon became apparent that the administration, in launching the largest military
operation since Vietnam, was intent on controlling the flow of information in keeping
with its principal objective of deposing Panamanian dictator Manuel Noriega and
extraditing him to the United States on international drug dealing charges.

The reporters rarely got close to the action, or were able to cover the impact of the
fighting on Panamanian civilians.

As David R. Gergen, journalist and presidential adviser, observed:

> The Bush administration might almost be forgiven for believing that the Panama invasion
> was a textbook case of how to manage a military conflict. Keep the combat short and
> sweet; apply overwhelming force; establish goals that are clear and attainable; and keep
> the press at bay until the shooting stops and blood stops flowing. (Gergen, 1990, p. 62)

It was a lesson that Bush would later effectively apply in the Persian Gulf War.

THE "DOOMSDAY CLOCK"

Whereas TV formerly covered the news, news is now created for television.
Uppermost in the minds of the architects of foreign policy is, how will it look on TV?
And what effect will it have?

Increasingly, television has become the main conduit by which national leaders
communicate with one another and the rest of the world.

Television news has especially changed the way the U.S. government responds to
crucial events.

In a 1984 issue of *Foreign Policy*, Lloyd N. Cutler, White House counsel to
President Carter and later to President Clinton, noted that TV news directly affects

the timing and substance of policy decisions that a President must make.

Because television accelerates public awareness, he said, it creates a political need for prompt presidential reaction. This is particularly true, he suggested, of policies that place U.S. forces at risk.

Elaborating, he said:

> Sometimes TV's influence is all to the good, sometimes it is bad. But it is always present, and learning how to adjust to it is central to the art of governing today... If an ominous foreign event is featured on TV news, the President and his advisers feel bound to make a response in time for the next evening news broadcast... If he does not have a response ready by the late afternoon deadline, the evening news may report that the President's advisers are divided, that the President cannot make up his mind, or that while the President hesitates his political opponents know exactly what to do (Cutler, 1984, p. 114).

Cutler refers to this phenomenon as the "Doomsday Clock."

In a sense, policy decisions become captive to the news. Among such examples:

1. The Soviet invasion of Afghanistan on December 27, 1979, raising alarm at high U.S. government levels over a possible Soviet incursion into the Persian Gulf, the main oil resource of the free world. Shortly afterwards, President Carter announced in a TV address that he was placing an embargo of grain and other food shipments to the Soviet Union. Unknown to the White House, however, U.S. farmers and grain dealers earlier had contracted with the Soviets for billions of dollars worth of grain exports. After frantic bureaucratic juggling, the embargo was restructured.

2. The shooting down of a South Korean commercial airliner in September 1983 by Russian fighters became a TV melodrama—complete with graphic simulations of how the airliner had veered off course, recordings of the South Korean pilot's reports to Japanese air controllers, radio intercepts of the Soviet pilots and their ground command, and depictions of how the Russian fighters shot down the South Korean airliner. The world reacted with shock, anger and dismay.

   Based in part on the TV reports, U.S. intelligence agencies jumped to the conclusion that the Soviets purposely destroyed the airliner carrying innocent passengers.

   Within 48 hours, President Reagan appeared on television to charge the Soviet Union with cold-blooded murder. But, after a more deliberate analysis of evidence during the following week, it was concluded that the Russians, despite their inexcusable action, had probably mistaken the South Korean airliner for an American reconnaissance plane which had violated Soviet air space.

   As a result, the President's premature and mistaken on-camera charge unnecessarily aggravated an already tense relationship between the two superpowers.

3. Television's impact was particularly evident following the dramatic seizure of U.S. Embassy staff members in Iran in November 1979. The event dominated the news throughout the 444 days the Americans were held hostage. As time slowly passed, TV commentators subtly indicated disappointment that President Carter

failed to take forceful action. On the evening newscasts, they would ominously note, "This is the 156th day... the 221st day... the 305th day... since the hostages have been held in Iran."

Inevitably, the constant drumbeat heightened the American public's sense of anger and frustration, which in turn exerted tremendous pressure on President Carter. Many irate Americans were willing to go to war to seek the release of their fellow countrymen. Carter, hard-pressed politically since it was an election year, as well as being infused with a moral compulsion, finally abandoned any hope of release via quiet diplomacy, and agreed to a rescue attempt by a U.S. military Delta Force which ended in tragic failure, and in all probability contributed to the end of his presidency.

Later, television scenes of the June 1989 pro-democratic demonstration in Beijing's Tiananmen Square exposed to the world the repressive nature of the Chinese communist government and its disregard for universally accepted human rights.

And it was not until the TV cameras captured the horrifying scene of a slain U.S. soldier being dragged through the dusty streets of Mogadishu while being kicked and pummeled by Somalians that Americans began to question the U.S. military presence in the country, originally sent by President Clinton to provide humanitarian aid. Not long afterwards, the American forces were pulled out.

As Cutler observed, one of television's most detrimental effects on public policy, aside from its projection of skewed imagery, is its tendency to create emotions which speed up the decision making process—while correspondingly slowing down the process of dealing with other important issues that get less TV attention.

Gergen contends that foreign policy should not be dictated by what gets big play on television, but rather should be carefully thought out and crafted with an eye towards what is best in the national interest. "Officials sometimes argue that the American public demands fast answers from its government, especially in a television age," he said. "There is no evidence to support this view. On the contrary, the public seems to care more about results and consequences than about one-night headlines." (Gergen, 1990, p. 55)

During an April 26, 1994, hearing by the House Foreign Affairs Committee, its members claimed that vivid television images of war, famine and violence create a clamor for quick fixes in foreign policy.

"Pictures in Sarajevo got us more involved," declared Chairman Lee H. Hamilton.

Taking issue, ABC's Ted Koppel maintained that TV imposes its greatest impact only when Presidents fail to develop and articulate a clear and effective policy.

"When an administration fails to set forth a clear agenda of its own, it will become the prisoner of somebody else's," Koppel said. CNN executive Ed Turner noted that media coverage has always had an impact on foreign policy. "Now, it is just faster," he commented. (Kortanek, 1994, p. 1078)

MR. BUSH'S WAR

Two hours before dawn—8 p.m. Eastern Standard Time—on February 24, 1991, the biggest military attack since World War II was unleashed as thousands of U.S. and allied troops streaked into Iraq and occupied Kuwait behind a deafening crescendo of artillery and naval gunfire. It was the start of Desert Storm, the 100-hours war.

Upon arriving in Washington from Camp David, President Bush announced, "Regrettably, the noon deadline passed... I have therefore directed General Norman Schwarzkopf, in conjunction with coalition forces, to eject the Iraqi Army from Kuwait."

At the Pentagon, Defense Secretary Richard Cheney reported that to protect the safety of American troops, no details of the operation would be released for several hours and that a news blackout was being imposed, including the suspension of the daily briefings from Riyadh and Washington.

Cheney's news crackdown at a pivotal turn in the war predictably was not graciously received by the news media. However, it was not surprising, considering the Pentagon's tight lid on the press since the face-off against Iraqi President Saddam Hussein began the previous August. While Cheney, a former Wyoming Representative and Ford White House chief of staff, privately came across as a civil, open individual, he quietly harbored a lack of faith in the press on governmental matters.

In an official study of the deployment of the press in the 1989 Panama invasion, Cheney was blamed for "a secrecy-driven decision" which was responsible for the press pool being "called out too late to cover the decisive U.S. assaults in that brief war" (Hoffman, 1990, "Review of Panama Pool Deployment").

During the Gulf War reporters were subjected to extraordinary restrictive news coverage. Unprecedented tight censorship was enforced and disinformation was common fare. Journalists were barred from the battle zone, their copy and broadcasts monitored and transmission of stories and photos to their home offices often delayed or inexplicably lost. The war was billed as the first waged live on TV—but only those films approved by the military were broadcast.

To what purpose this lid was clamped on the news media was never defined and to what effect has never been ascertained. The tone and content of what Americans back home were allowed to see, hear and read about were totally dictated by the military.

At times, news became indistinguishable from propaganda and disinformation—as examples, the recurring touting of "surgical strikes" against vulnerable, high density targets, and in a deception to divert the Iraqis, the authorized leak of misleading information to the press that U.S. forces were planning a massive attack from Kuwait's east coast, when, in fact, it came from the west.

The media, in effect, became an involuntary and often unwitting collaborator in presenting sanitized tableaux of the war, in all probability to minimize its realities in order to placate potential dissidents at home. With Vietnam in mind, the Pentagon was determined not to win the desert war only to lose the battle of public opinion.

In their defense, Pentagon officials claimed that the vast desert terrain precluded traditional frontline reporting. They also stressed that surveys showed that the American people were satisfied with the war news they received. The salient point here is that the public, unfortunately, doesn't know what it wasn't told, or what disinformation was disguised as authentic news.

For example, not until after the ceasefire was it learned that: despite initial reports concerning the formidable strength of the Iraqis, there were, in the words of General Colin Powell, head of the Joint Chiefs of Staff, "a hell of a lot" fewer enemy soldiers than the 540,000 originally estimated by U.S. intelligence sources; notwithstanding Pentagon hype U.S. "smart bombs" comprised only seven percent of all the explosives dropped on Iraq and occupied Kuwait; the number of Iraqi tanks and armored vehicles that survived the allied assault was much greater than claimed by U.S. military officials, allowing Saddam Hussein to later use the weapons against insurgent Kurds and Shiites; "collateral damage"—a euphemism for civilian casualties and non-military facilities—was downplayed by military briefers, yet a post-ceasefire assessment by a United Nations inspection unit reported it was "near apocalyptic."

Several months after the war, Marlin Fitzwater, President Bush's press secretary, reported during an interview in his White House office that neither he nor Bush were involved in establishing the Gulf War press rules, and that it was his understanding they were set by Cheney, Pentagon press spokesman Pete Williams, and General Schwarzkopf's command, with the approval of General Powell (Fitzwater, Oct. 3, 1991).

THE POST-COLD WAR PRESIDENTS

President Bush's victory in the Gulf illuminated his presidency, but the luster gradually dimmed with the return to peace. It became apparent that his "personal style of diplomacy and his goal-oriented approach was ideally suited for running the war, but did not lend themselves to sudden post-war developments" (Bonafede, 1995, p. 119).

The political capital he had built up during the war was gradually eroded by a worrisome economy, a spreading savings and loan scandal, and a soaring federal budget. After a brief period of vitality, the old Bush who favored pragmatism over innovation reappeared. It was a period when the world was in an uncertain state of transformation, yet as the head of the sole remaining superpower, he failed to conceptualize a vision of a New World Order and the assuredly vital role the United States would play.

Furthermore, the joy of victory in war was tempered in peace by the constant reminder by the news media and Bush's political opponents that Saddam Hussein remained in power, diminished in global stature but still a threat in the volatile Middle East. The question persisted whether Bush should have gone all the way and toppled the Iraqi dictator.

As a candidate for reelection in 1992, the commanding figure Bush exhibited in the Gulf was replaced by the prewar fuzzy image of the man and what he stood for. Voters sought change but Bush represented four more years of the same. Moreover, he characteristically failed to stir the voters' passions by words and actions—critical ingredients in an age of communications.

Bush had his day in the sun but it did not provide sufficient sustenance to salvage his presidency and he was forced to give way to Bill Clinton, the former governor of Arkansas.

Clinton assumed the presidency at a defining moment in global affairs. The embers of the Cold War had turned to stone. The Soviet Union was fragmented into self-governing republics. Germany was reunified. The Iron Curtain was lifted and former Soviet satellites regained their independence. South Africa had broken the shackles of apartheid.

At the same time, violent strife erupted among tribal, ethnic, and religious groups. Conflicts, as often as not, were within rather than outside borders. Nationalistic fervor split Czechoslovakia, warfare between the Tutis and Hutu tribes in Rwanda led to the massacre of more than a half million people, Somalians by the thousands were dying of famine, Liberia was dissolving into anarchy, the Middle East continued to be a cauldron of turmoil and terrorism, Haiti was being driven deeper into poverty and despair, the former Yugoslavia was ravaged by war as separate ethnic and cultural factions fought over land each claimed was their's by heritage, language and religion.

Economically, Japan and Germany were beginning to overtake their benefactor, the United States. And it was becoming evident that Asia was emerging as an international trading center and China was growing exponentially as an economic and military power almost certainly to be the U.S.'s chief adversary in the 21st century.

That was part of the legacy that Bush had left his successor. At the beginning of his presidency, with its emphasis on domestic policy, Clinton appeared to be withdrawn and detached from foreign affairs. In the parlance of the day, he had put it "on the back burner." Indecisiveness and a tendency to vacillate and zig and zag on matters of grave international importance became a hallmark of his presidency.

From another perspective, it might be said that history was unfair to Clinton. After more than four decades, the U.S.'s containment policy aimed at holding back global communism was no longer a viable option. The price of success had left the United States without a doctrine by which to steer and give meaning to its foreign policy.

As the principal designer of U.S. foreign policy, the nation looked to Clinton to devise a doctrine to reflect America's values and national interests in the new era—but to no avail. He never seemed to understand the lesson defined by Clinton Rossiter: "The President is the American people's one authentic trumpet, and he has no higher duty than to give a clear and certain sound" (Rossiter, 1960, p. 31).

Not until well into his third year in office did Clinton attempt to exercise international leadership and broker a peace accord in the ethnic civil war in the former Yugoslavia, the site of brutal mass atrocities for almost four years.

Time and events would measure his success, his standing in the international community, and perhaps his own political future.

THE MEDIA FACTOR

For almost half a century, American journalism has undergone a radical transformation, conceptually, stylistically and technologically. During this relatively brief interlude, the press has become the "media," television has replaced newspapers as the most pervasive instrument in daily communications, news is relayed around the world by space satellites, and journalism has become recognized as a vital sociological, political and cultural force. Reporters, once proud, "ink-stained wretches," have been remodeled into establishment figures; many—referred to as "power journalists"—are accorded equal billing with popular rock stars and nationally known athletes. The "press lords" of newspaper lore have been succeeded by corporate giants, merger moguls, and international financiers, constituting a "media oligarchy."

With substantial justification, the United States has been called "the first media state." Traditional journalism defined as a literary genre to inform, educate and entertain is, for all intents and purposes, obsolete, a relic of the pre-television era. The sacred tenets of journalism—objectivity, impartiality, and balance—have been widely abandoned as quaint anachronisms, which cloak reality and sidestep interpretive and analytical assessments with vapid neutrality.

The dynamic changes in modern mass communications, greater in depth and breadth than the evolutionary developments of the preceding five centuries—since William Caxton constructed his printing press at Westminster, England, in 1476—have reached far beyond the media itself and perceptibly altered the system by which government decisions are made, the way electoral politics is waged, the manner foreign affairs are conducted, the perception society has of itself and the style in which people live and work.

Increasingly, there is also a conviction that the unfolding of events is only slightly more significant than how the events are perceived and presented by the media. Indeed, people today follow the news on two levels: their interest is focused on what is going on in the world, and how the media cover those events.

Thus, the media are no longer viewed merely as purveyors of news, but recognized more as a mover than a mirror of society. The contemporary media for example, are conceived in broad terms as: a platform, or forum, for public debate; an instrument to influence popular opinion; a catalyst for social, cultural and political movements; a channel for diplomatic relations; a vehicle by which government officials and agencies speak to one another; and a conduit through which many of our perspectives are filtered.

Specifically, the media perform several basic functions for government decision-makers: they keep them informed about breaking events; they keep them attuned to the major concerns of the American people; they enable them to convey their messages to the public and the political sector; and they monitor the effectiveness—and improprieties—of their official activities.

Communications and the free flow of information is essential to a free society and part of the fabric of the American character. And the media, for good or ill, have become a participant in public affairs, even if sometimes uninvited and unwanted.

REFERENCES

Bonafede, D. (1987, June 24) Scandal time. *The National Journal*, 199–207.

Bonafede, D. (1990). *Presidents and the public* (pp. 1–11). Washington, DC: Congressional Quarterly Inc.

Bonafede, D. (1995, Spring). George Bush and the Gulf War—a tainted triumph. *Miller Center Journal, 2*. Charlottesville, VA: University of Virginia.

Carlyle, T. (1955). As quoted in *Oxford dictionary of quotations,* (2nd ed.). Oxford: Oxford University Press.

Cater, D. (1965). *The fourth branch of government*. New York: Vintage Books.

Corwin, E. S. (1957). *The president: Office and powers*. (4th revised ed.). New York: New York University Press.

Cutler, L. N. (1984, Fall). Foreign policy on deadline. In *Foreign Policy*, (56).

Fitzwater, M. (1991). Interview with Dom Bonafede.

Gergen, D. R. (1990). Diplomacy in a television age: The dangers of teledemocracy. In S. Serfaty (Ed.), *The media and foreign policy*. New York: St. Martin's Press.

Hodgson, G. (1980). *All things to all men: The false promise of the modern american presidency*. New York: Simon & Schuster.

Hoffman, F. S. (1990). Review of Panama pool deployment. A Department of Defense paper.

Kinsley, M. (1986, December 22) The case for glee. *The New Republic*.

Kortanek, M. E. (1994). When pictures make policy. In *Congressional Quarterly*. Washington, DC.

Laski, H. J. (1940). *The American presidency*. New York: Harper & Brothers.

Nokes, R. G. (1990). Libya: a government story. In S. Serfaty (Ed.), *The media and foreign policy*. New York: St. Martin's Press.

Pollard, J. E. (1973). *The presidents and the press*. New York: Octagon Books.

Powell, J. (1984). *The other side of the story*. New York: William Morrow and Company, Inc.

Richburg, B. K. (1995, November 11) Mission to Hanoi: McNamera asks ex-foes to join in search for war's lessons. *Washington Post*.

Rose, R. (1988). *The postmodern president: The White House meets the world*. Chatham, NJ: Chatham House Publishers Inc.

Rossiter, C. (1960). *The American presidency* (2nd ed.). New York: Harcourt, Brace and Company.

Smith, H. (1988). *The power game: How Washington works*. New York: Random House.

Speakes, L. (1988). *Speaking out: Inside the Reagan White House*. New York: Charles Scribners Sons.

Sundquist, J. L. (1981). *The decline and resurgence of Congress*. Washington, DC: The Brookings Institution.

Washington Post (1995, September 1) Clinton building case for his foreign policy successes.

Weinberger, C. (1985). The delicate balance between a free press and national security. In *Defense/85*. Washington, DC.

Wise, D. (1973). *The politics of lying: Government deception, secrecy, and power*. New York: Random House.

chapter 7

appropriating the "public mood" of other nations in press-foreign policy management: a case study from Canadian/American relations

Richard L. Barton
Penn State University

INTRODUCTION

F oreign policymaking is a form of political communication involving strategies of persuasion among participants including policymakers, the press,
and politically interested publics. Frequently the "public mood" is not so
much served as served-up as part of a political strategist's persuasive campaign.
Public opinion is as often part of an elaborately constructed appeal in politically
motivated rhetoric to gain legitimacy for a proposed policy as it is a measurable
fact, despite the strained "objective" news ritual of dramatically displaying public
opinion polling data. Just how do policymakers use news representations of the
"public mood" of other nations in the course of their strategic communications?
How are appeals that are based on policymakers' reading of the news incorporated
into their internal and public rhetoric?

PRESS AND FOREIGN POLICY:
TENDENCIES IN THE RESEARCH

Research under the heading of press and foreign policy tends to concern itself with the likely impact of a variety of press forms in covering international relations. News and foreign policy analysis is based primarily in democratic-pluralism and bureaucratic models. There is a great deal of speculation about how the news excites public opinion and how that opinion, in turn, influences policymakers. For the most part, the research assumes a broad, pluralist perspective in which journalists are portrayed as the controlling agents of a volatile public discourse. Citizens are assumed to attend to this discourse variously, depending on a wide range of audience characteristics including their political interests and degree of political engagement. Alternately, there are studies that trace the bureaucratic steps of the policymaking process and focus on how the news media selectively cover and interpret that process, and how governments and their policy elite engage in domestic public persuasion and international public diplomacy through propagandistic uses of news media to further their political objectives (Manheim, 1994). Partridge's analysis of the orientation of past research is a particularly cogent articulation of the need to focus on the strategic, persuasive dimensions of communications and policy.

> Only the naive now entertain the model of a political system in which policy initiatives proceed from the body of the citizens and the function of government is to give the effect to the popular will. For a great number of empirical reasons we recognize that the politics of complex societies cannot work like that; that political and other organizations, leaders and elites, bureaucracies and governments necessarily assume such functions as selecting and defining issues and problems, assembling and distributing information, proposing policies and advocating them, engaging in public persuasion, demonstrating the satisfactoriness of general lines of policy by initiating practical measures that are seen to work....These are among the ways in which governments (and other influential political organizations and groups) may forge, consolidate, and expand the approval or support which enables them to continue to enjoy and deploy authority—or, as we commonly say, manufacture consent (Patridge, 1971, p. 265).

The model of democratic pluralism frequently used by analysts of the role of the press in international relations is a perspective that is likely to overstate the power of individual news reports on public opinion, to underestimate the intricacies of media form as they influence the language of politics, and to overlook the complexity with which particular audience cultures attend to and use media (Barton, 1990).

There is a trend in the research to more fully account for the consequences of the combination of strategies used by policymakers, journalists and politically active citizens by focusing on the context of the particular cultures with whom these collectives are most intimately associated. These researchers are eager to reveal the comparative levels of control and influence of participants in the policymaking process. This trend promises to lead to a more accurate assessment of the relative power of the public compared to the press; to a better understanding of the assumptions about the public made by journalists and policymakers alike. While there are few communications studies dealing directly with policymakers, studies of topics such as "interest groups and the news", "reporting and the public mind", and "policymakers and the third person effect" are adding substance to the line of inquiry raised by Partridge. Kennamer effectively reviews one branch of this research under the heading of "Policymaker's Perception of Public Opinion" (Kennamer, 1992). He points out that "some of the voices of "public opinion" they—policymakers—hear are simply their own echoes" (Kennamer, 1991). Miller and Stokes identified legislator's perceptions of opinion as being a more important policy determinant than the constituent opinion itself, and the policymaker's interpretations of opinion varied greatly from the actual opinion (Miller and Stokes, 1963). There is evidence that political leaders act according to what they think the public wants when the public has not even demonstrated any interest in that particular issue (Erikson, Luttbeg, & Tedlin, 1988). Other research has pointed to the tendency of foreign policymakers to substitute press reports of public opinion for the opinion itself (Cohen, 1973, and Cohen, 1986).

The present study connects with this research emphasis on policymaker's use of the press in strategically negotiating public opinion. However the focus of this study is not so much on the actual texts of press portrayals of public opinion as it is on how the policymaker interprets those portrayals and uses them to construct an internal rhetoric within the policymaking culture to persuade colleagues about a policy direction, and a corresponding externally directed communications strategy that serves as public relations for the policy. The intention is to reveal the patterns of strategic communications for a particular historical case of foreign policymaking in order to establish a foundation for broader, more generalizeable comparative research about this dimension of international political communications. This line of inquiry assumes that public opinion is just as much the result of strategies of rhetorical construction as it is a reflection of a quantifiable " public mood."

This historical/critical study intends to provide a detailed account of:

1. How American policymakers interpreted press representations of the Canadian public mood in preparing for a key policy development in Canadian/American relations, the Ogdensburg Agreement of 1940.
2. How those interpretations were used to construct a strategic policy rhetoric within the policymaking subculture to persuade colleagues to embrace a particular policy course.
3. How these interpretations became, eventually, part of a logic for a press management strategy to legitimate that policy in the eyes of the public.

By reviewing declassified internal documents and press releases that were essential pieces of communication during the policymaking process, and by placing these documents in a larger historical view we can gain a relatively more detailed understanding of the communication dynamics of policymaking than is the case when we are restricted to contemporary policy documents that are strategically and selectively released to the public on the basis of the political objectives of the parties involved, and whose significance has yet to be verified by the passing of time (Benson, 1967).

The method of analysis used here attempts to reveal how players in the policymaking process made judgments about the public mood as that mood was presented in news accounts, and how they selectively organized their readings of news as part of their own political communications. Edelman describes this political terrain as one in which "rationality claims" are made on public opinion and policy (Edelman, 1995). Depending on their orientation to and their objectives for a particular foreign policy, people involved in the process organize a rhetoric that they hope will persuade others to their way of thinking; in other words, they construct appeals.

Appeals are the leading edge of arguments for a policy. These appeals can be described in terms of their potential to be inviting, that is to accommodate another's political orientation, ideals and objectives. The power inherent in these "invitations" is, of course, a significant element in the overall policy process. The general audience might be invited by a newspaper editorial to observe, or be concerned, or to take political action; whereas the policy elite might be invited by a colleague to consider certain aspects of public opinion in the making of policy (Barton, 1990).

The intended audience for the appeals may be narrowly focused as in the case of one policymaker sending a personal letter or memo to another as a classified communication, or cast more broadly as a press release to the public-at-large. Both of these extremes are represented in this case study. Part of the objective of this study is to demonstrate that appeals are chosen specifically to cater to the particular audience the communicator hopes to influence. The method is decidedly comparative; it compares past with present perceptions. It compares public and private political discourse. One of the distinctive advantages of historical analysis is that we can bring into public view the private, hitherto undisclosed assumptions made about publics; whether the publics were thought to be respected, informed participants or dupes in the policy process. And, this research orientation compares actual practice with theory. Analysis of the documentary evidence allows us to see the details of the communication strategies as they unfold, to compare the internal and public communications about the proposed policy and measure the success of the entire management routine by recalling the public and press response to the policy.

THE CASE: THE OGDENSBURG AGREEMENT OF 1940

Before the Second World War, one of the key issues associated with Canada's move toward independence from Commonwealth ties was the extent to which such a posture would lead Canada further into the vortex of United States influence culminating, inevitably, in domination by the Americans. Franklin Roosevelt's meeting with Prime Minister Mackenzie King at Ogdensburg New York on August 17–18, 1940, when Canada was a belligerent already engaged in the war effort and the United States was neutral, is a key moment in the balance of political influence among the three members of the Atlantic Triangle; Canada, Britain and the United States. The entire Ogdensburg odyssey began with American diplomats crafting strategies on the basis of their reading of the Canadian public's mood at the time.

The meeting proposed by Roosevelt was part of a larger defensive military strategy by the Americans. Roosevelt was moving toward a defense agreement with Britain which involved America establishing military bases on British islands in the Caribbean and western Atlantic in exchange for fifty US destroyers that would greatly aid the British Royal Navy. Roosevelt wanted to coordinate the public announcement of this British agreement so that it would be a persuasive prelude to talks with Canada. King went to the meeting accompanied only by the American minister in Ottawa Mr. Pierrepont Moffat, Edouard Handy, secretary and J.S. Nicol, a confidential messenger (*NY Times, 8/18/40*).

One of the recurring issues associated with the Ogdensburg Agreement is the extent to which Canadian interests and particularly their relations with Britain were coopted at this point in history by an aggressive, self-serving American policymaking machine. Historians vary in their assessment as to whether the British or the Americans were most responsible for the weakening of British/Canadian ties following Ogdensburg.

Roosevelt phoned King on August 16, informing him that he was coming to Ogdensburg to inspect American troops. Roosevelt and King were described by the press as "old friends who have visited each other at least once a year for perhaps fifteen years" (*NY Times, 8/17/40*). Interestingly, while Roosevelt was on his way to Ogdensburg, Wendell Wilkie accepted the Republican nomination for the presidency, claiming that Roosevelt was "courting war". Roosevelt and his staff kept a close eye on Wilkie's speechmaking while at Ogdensburg and were elated to discover that Wilkie, in a subsequent speech, proclaimed support for the military draft and aid to the allies as proposed by Roosevelt's administration (Goodwin, 1994). The way was thereby cleared for the Ogdensburg trip to become a dramatic demonstration of Roosevelt's bold foreign policy plans. Roosevelt invited King to join him for the night in the president's private railway car. The president suggested this would be a good opportunity for them to discuss important military matters of mutual interest. King is described as responding to the invitation enthusiastically, behaving "…like a puppet which could be animated only by the President of the United States" (Creighton, 1976, p. 43). Roosevelt proposed a permanent, joint United States-Canada commission for the study of common defense issues. The body was given the name Permanent Joint Board on Defense (PJBD). As part of the deal, the Americans would have access to air and naval facilities in Nova Scotia. The nature of the commitment seemed to some to be an irrational one on King's part in light of his previous stand regarding Canadian autonomy *vis-à-vis* the Commonwealth. Canadian historian Creighton makes this assessment:

> In the past, Mackenzie King had repeatedly and solemnly assured the Canadian people that he would make no external commitments—without the concurrence of the Canadian Parliament. He had invariably rejected all proposals for a Commonwealth secretariat or

continuing committee on the ground that such a body might entangle Canada in sinister diplomatic or military engagements. (Creighton, 1976, p. 44)

Some accounts portray the Canadian prime minister as so irrationally enthralled by Roosevelt's charisma that he danced to the American tune on this occasion. He agreed to have this meeting without fully consulting with the Canadian Chiefs of Staff . Ralston, King's new Minister of Defence, is said to have learned of the meeting from the newspapers (Creighton, 1976). Others are more forgiving of King's actions at Ogdensburg. They note that he had steadfastly refused to cave-in to Roosevelt's desire to put American bases in Newfoundland, which was then a separate crown colony that Canada hoped to bring into the fold. Their conclusion is that, after all, King had secured military protection for Canada in a way that posed the least threat of American domination and allowed his country to continue to do its utmost for Britain (Granatstein & Hillmer, 1991, p. 141).

Granatstein and Hillmer, claiming that King's critics "miss the point of Ogdensburg," provide this logic in their support of King's actions:

Canada had been forced to turn to the United States because of Britain's weakness after Dunkirk. Every military action and every ounce of economic assistance to help keep Britain in the war weakened Canada further. (Granatstein and Hillmer, 1991, p. 143)

But King is remembered by many, due in part to his decisions at Ogdensburg, as " a cranky autonomist who... took a leading part in dismantling the British Empire" and one who had "...accumulated concentrated hostility to his account in the old capital of the Empire." And it is especially ironic that King, described as "one of the most unmilitary products of an unmilitary society", and "..hating war he also hated the military services", should have had his reputation so tarnished by the Ogdensburg meeting (Stacey, 1976, pp. 21–22).

THE DOCUMENTARY EVIDENCE

Documents associated with the Ogdensburg agreement reveal how the dynamic interactions of press and public opinion were strategically managed. A review of this evidence demonstrates that the American diplomats in this particular case held specific assumptions about the nature of public opinion.

MOFATT'S LETTER

The Ogdensburg meeting was encouraged by a letter from the American minister in Ottawa, Mr. Pierrepont Moffat, saying that Canadians wanted a defense agreement with the Americans (*Foreign Relations of U.S. Diplomatic Papers*, vol. 3, 1940). The letter from Moffat to Sumner Wells, the Acting American Secretary of State, uses

Canadian public opinion as the primary evidence that the time was right to go forward with the proposed Joint Board on Defense between the US and Canada. The details of his appeals and the context in which they are posed are essential to our understanding of the significance of the letter to the political communications that led to the meeting. Moffat's letter, written from his post in Ottawa, Canada on August 14, 1940 and represented here in its entirety, begins:

> Dear Sumner: Ever since I have been here, but more particularly in the last two or three weeks, there has been growing a public demand throughout Canada for the conclusion of some form of joint defence understanding with the United States. Even elements which in the past have been least well disposed toward us, such as the Toronto public and the English-speaking sections of Montreal, are now outspoken in its favor. The principal newspapers, such as the Montreal Gazette, the Winnipeg Free Press, the Vancouver Sun and such periodicals as MacLean's and Saturday night are committed to the idea. Questions have been asked in Parliament and some of the political leaders are putting pressure on the Government behind the scenes. As a matter of practical politics the Prime Minister may ultimately be forced to recognize the existence of this popular demand; if Great Britain should suffer serious reverses the demand would immediately become very acute. (*Diplomatic Papers*, p. 144)

Reviewing this first section of the document, one can immediately begin to appreciate Moffat's working theory about the connections among press form and function, public opinion and international political reality. A reading of the documentary evidence reveals how the assumptions of the diplomat's working theory are put into action in the construction of his policy rhetoric.

Public opinion by the host country's citizens was an important consideration in policy formation; it constituted a "demand" for policy action.

The press, broadly defined to include newspapers and magazines, was assumed to represent public opinion. Apparently Moffatt perceived the public mood as a patchwork construction contributed by a variety of press types, and his sense of the prevailing public mood was based on his review of all of these sources.

Public opinion was not to be read simply in terms of peak levels at a given time, but comparatively over time with attention to changes in mood on the part of particular domestic political constituencies. In this case those political subcultures were assumed to be represented by the newspapers that served them. For example, the English speaking constituency in French Canada was served by the *Montreal Gazette*, hence Moffat concluded that the paper reflected the mood of that constituency.

A pluralistic orientation was assumed by Moffat; elected politicians would be bound to represent the public will through political action. Moffat believed that the press representations of public opinion had profound domestic political power that would be recognized by Canadian members of Parliament who would manifest its importance by confronting the Prime Minister in Parliament and force him toward a military agreement with the Americans. This assumption was qualified, significantly, as dependent on the outcome of Britain's fate in the ongoing war.

Moffat's letter continued by confronting one of the most enduring and, from the Canadian perspective, most troubling issues in the history of Canadian/American relations; the threat of America's domination of Canada, in this case a domination that would weaken the cherished Commonwealth ties between Canada and Britain.

> To Canadians such a joint defense understanding, whether it took the form of a treaty or merely of publicly announced staff talks—seems a reasonable reinsurance policy. The old fear that cooperation with the United States would tend to weaken Canada's ties with Great Britain has almost entirely disappeared. Instead, Canada believes that such cooperation would tend to bring Britain and the United States closer together, rather than force Britain and Canada apart. (*Diplomatic Papers* , p. 144)

Moffat's rhetorical construction was inventive and misleading in its simplicity; he treated the issue as a past issue—an "old fear" and combined the constituent elements of public opinion into a single prevailing voice of Canada, (" Canada believes...").

Moffat only briefly acknowledged a commentary/press voice independent from the public's but he appropriated it for his own ends and eventually folded it back into his preferred reading of the press as an expression of the people's voice. Moffat recalled that the press had proposed a defense logic of its own:

> The press is increasingly pointing out that Canada has two lines of defense: the first in Great Britain, the second in a coordinated plan for the protection of North America. (*Diplomatic Papers,* p. 144)

The dominant form of appeal in Moffat's letter, constructed by his selective reading of Canadian opinion, is based on appeals to domestication as opposed to another option open to him, appeals to internationalization. Domestic appeals are relatively blind to the broader international context of policy issues, leaving out the perspectives and concerns of other nations (Barton, 1990). This tendency reflects the priorities of the Roosevelt administration which included staying out of the European conflict while presenting a strong North American defensive posture with the threat of a strong retaliation if directly attacked. European perceptions of that stance were recently illustrated in remarks by Vaclav Havel, the President of the Czech Republic who recalled:

> When Hitler was getting ready to invade Czechoslavakia, and in so doing finally expose the lack of courage on the part of the western democracies, your president wrote a letter to the Czechoslovak president imploring him to come to some agreement with Hitler. Had he... instead shown a few teeth, perhaps the Second World War need not have happened, and tens of thousands of young Americans need not have died in fighting in it. (Havel, 1995)

Fully mindful of the American determination to stay out of the war Moffat addressed the options of a hemispheric versus a continental defense plan. He dismissed the former option, privileged the other by citing the preference of the Canadian public in this way:

> A few Canadians, but still relatively few, would add a coordinated plan for the protection of the Western Hemisphere.
>
> That an understanding between Canada and the United States must necessarily be limited to the defense of North America is everywhere accepted here. Any suggestion that it would obligate the United States, even morally, to become involved overseas is recognized as outside the realm of practical possibilities. (*Diplomatic Papers,* pp. 144–145)

Moffat assumed the perspective of the "average Canadian" by concluding that: "Conversely, the average Canadian fails to see why the United States, which unanimously supported the President's Kingston pledge, should hesitate to work out ways and means of implementing the pledge" (*Diplomatic Papers,* p. 145).

The "Kingston Pledge" was an address given by President Roosevelt at Queens University, Kingston, Ontario, August 18, 1938, in which he pledged that US defenses would come to the aid of Canada in the event of an external threat against that country. Moffat puts his case in the context of that pledge by noting that

> The argument that this would be difficult while Canada is a belligerent and the United States a neutral is generally brushed aside as a technical one, which ignores the basic fact that an understanding would only become operative in the event of a physical attack on Canada or the United States. (*Diplomatic Papers,* p. 144*)*

Together these examples reveal another dimension of Moffat's rhetoric; the selective appropriation and definition of press forms to support his policy argument. He accomplished this in several ways. First by demoting the opposition to a comparative "few". Second by speaking for the "average Canadian", and most aggressively and subjectively, characterizing the argument against his preferred plan as having been "brushed aside" with little or no evidence of either the press or the public having done so.

Moffat's reading reveals a peripheral dependency perspective, one that assumes Canadians' willing domination by and orientation to the American version of political reality even as it is represented in the American press.

> The recent advocacy by the *Chicago Tribune* and the *New York Herald Tribune* (which in political philosophies are as the poles apart) of a defensive alliance between Canada and the United States has made a deep impression on the average Canadian, and that it is the Canadian Government that is holding back. (*Diplomatic Papers*, p. 145)

Moffat assumed that Canadians were avid readers of the American press, and he portrays that press as having been a primary force in shaping Canadian public opinion in favor of the American plan. Moffat's claim is an exaggeration of the power of the press in shaping Canadians attitudes, and a misrepresentation of the comparative contribution of the American press to Canadians' world view. While the Canadian press of the period used American press services, Canadian impressions about international affairs were also fully informed by a number of British and European views as represented by their major wire services which were routinely incorporated in their newspapers.

In the next section of the letter Moffat assumed several functions for the press. The press could bring pressure to bear on political leaders, and threaten to reveal behind-the-scenes diplomacy at some cost to the participants. The force of this press power in rallying public reaction Moffat argued, could be politically costly for the Canadian prime minister in one of two ways:

> Mr. Mackenzie King may well be subjected to very heavy political pressure to make some approach to us either (a) to formalize the Kingston pledge or (b) to make a public admission that "staff talks" have in fact taken place. In a war situation where the picture changes overnight, I could not hope to prophesy when the pressure on Mr. Mackenzie King might be expected to reach its maximum intensity. (*Diplomatic Papers*, p. 145)

The letter closed with a clear demonstration of Moffat's belief in the importance of public opinion to the policy being proposed in both countries. Strategies of balancing, comparing domestic and international opinion are revealed. And it is clear that Moffat believed that a key function of his diplomatic post was to interpret and report Canadian opinion to his colleagues.

> The purpose of this letter, Sumner, is merely to give you a feeling of the way Canadian opinion is growing, so that you in turn may be able to consider it in relation to the development of political opinion (pro or con) at home. (*Diplomatic Papers*, p. 145)

Moffat's letter is, of course, a highly selective reading of the Canadian press for the period. His rhetoric involves the exclusion of certain details and the reshaping of contexts. Although a detailed review of the press reports used by Moffat is not the focus of this analysis, it is interesting to note several patterns and themes in that reporting that strain against the general thrust of his reading. For example, despite Moffat's claim that "an understanding between Canada and the United States must necessarily be limited to the defense of North America is everywhere accepted here," the Canadian press during this period carried, in some detail, an ongoing debate about the implications for Canada of America's western hemispheric economic strategies for dealing with the Nazi threat and America's growing preoccupation with German fifth column activities in Latin America (*Vancouver Sun*, 6/11/40 and *Vancouver Sun*, 6/17/40. And, in contrast to Moffat's assumptions about Canada's eagerness to have America's military power available for its defense, the Canadian press portrayed the United States as woefully unprepared for war. One reporter cited the U.S. for "a lack of preparedness beyond belief," and in no position to offer any assistance to Canada, even if she asked (*Vancouver Sun*, 6/11/40). Another commentator concluded that, "There is no trace of the traditional view that the United States is our shield against aggression. The United States is unable to defend itself" (*Vancouver Sun*, 6/19/40). Moffat ignores the keen spirit of Canadian independence that was celebrated in the press as the war effort continued. Canada's confidence in its role as a key player in the war effort without the United States was served up almost daily as a reporting ritual. One particular recurring theme was Canada's full commitment to the war effort and the determination to aggressively engage the German enemy independent of the United States if need be (See for example *Vancouver Sun*, 6/22/40). Moffat's claim that American newspaper editorials advocating an alliance were changing Canadian public opinion loses force in light of the fact that Canadian editors saw those same American editorials as "striking evidence of the recent change of public opinion in the United States in regard to the war" (*Montreal Gazette*, 6/20/40).

THE STRATEGY OF THE PRESS RELEASE:
"GOING TO THE PUBLIC"

The press release is acknowledged by practitioners and media analysts alike to be an effective form of information management. Policymakers can use the press release to take advantage of their power as sources of tightly controlled information. This news management routine usually does not include the opportunity for on-the-spot questioning of government officials (Graber, 1993). Furthermore, the press release allows government officials the opportunity to take full advantage of the dimensions of source power, including having the exclusive opportunity to define the political situation to the public and thereby set the parameters of the public debate (Lemert, 1981).

The Ogdensburg Declaration which announced the results of the meeting was actually a short press release which is represented here in its entirety:

White House Statement on Establishment of Joint Board on Defense of Canada and the United States. August 18, 1940.

The Prime Minister of Canada and the President have discussed the mutual problems of defense in relation to the safety of Canada and the United States.

It has been agreed that a permanent Joint Board on Defense shall be set up at once by the two countries.

This Permanent Joint Board on Defense shall commence immediate studies relating to sea, land and air problems including personnel and materiel.

It will consider in the broad sense the defense of the north half of the Western Hemisphere.

The Permanent Joint Board on Defense will consist of four or five members from each country, most of them from the services. It will meet shortly. (*The Public Papers and Addresses of Franklin D. Roosevelt*, 1940, p. 331)

The announcement of the agreement came at a time of increasing international tension and diplomatic strategizing as the war intensified. For example, the announcement came shortly after Germany declared a total blockade of the British Isles (*NY Times*,

8/20/40). But the broader foreign policy implications of the pact were barely apparent in this brief document. This was not a treaty but an executive agreement; there was no time limitation and the agreement cleared the way for an enduring American military presence in Canada. One commentator implies that the form used to bind the agreement was not coincidental; that this was an instance of diplomacy by press release.

> The Ogdensburg Declaration was not a treaty; it was an executive agreement disguised in the disarming form of a press release. Yet it effectively bound Canada to a continual system dominated by the United States and largely determined Canadian foreign and defence policy for the next thirty years. (Creighton, 1976, p. 44)

Equally significant are Roosevelt's personal notations about this document, written in late 1940. He is careful to maintain the preferred slant on the policy. His gloss of the document suggests that the agreement was the result of an opportunity that presented itself in the midst of general discussions. In fact, the agreement and the meeting at which it became reality were both the result of a series of carefully developed strategies engineered by him and his associates (*NY Times*, 8/20/40).

> The foregoing statement was issued after a conference between the Canadian Prime Minister, the Right Honorable W. L. Mackenzie King, and myself in August 1940. I had invited him, while I was on an inspection tour of some defense establishments near the Canadian border, to meet with me and discuss problems of defense common to Canada and the United States. (*Public Papers and Addresses, 1941*, p. 331)

Roosevelt explains the agreement as a natural and logical outgrowth of the close working relationship between the two countries:

> The adoption of these joint defense efforts is another proof of the solidarity existing among the American Republics, which has been even more closely cemented by the danger and threat which loom up from the swift movement of events in Europe and in the Far East. (*Public Papers and Addresses, 1941*, p. 331)

The consistency of the public appeals made by the policymaking constituency, including the President, works to lend credence to their claim that their interpretation of public opinion and international relations policy was rationale and in the country's best interests.

CLOSING THE STRATEGIC LOOP: THE PRESS RESPONSE TO THE POLICY STATEMENT AS A TEST OF POLICY MANAGEMENT SUCCESS

To what extent had the strategy of the press release, and the meeting itself, been a power play directed by Roosevelt that involved a self-serving rush to an agreement that precluded the full public discourse and congressional review that one would expect in typical U.S. treaty-making? This point was not overlooked by the domestic and international press. The New York Times reported that:

> The London press hailed the joint defense plan as of "far-reaching import" and said that the suggestion to give the United States air and naval bases in the West Indies has "been received sympathetically." (*New York* Times, 8/20/40)

But, for the most part, the international press began to suspect that there was another motive behind the policy that led to the agreement, namely the American desire to establish a closer relationship with Canada for purposes of long-term economic development. Again, the earlier concern about the impact of this agreement on the long history of Canadian/British relations as a special case under the British Commonwealth began to emerge. After the fact of the agreement, just how credible was Moffat's assertion that it would serve to bring Britain and the United States closer together? Winston Churchill's initial reaction was obviously sensitive to just this issue, and reveals his contempt for America's self-serving behavior in this case. He was not pleased by the agreement or the conditions under which it was negotiated, and understood full-well its implications for the future of Canadian/British relations. It marked the end of an era.

> He (Churchill) observed grumpily that there might be "two opinions" about some aspects of the Ogdensburg arrangement. No doubt he perceived that from that moment it was likely that American influence would increase faster in Canada, and British influence would decline. He was displeased at not having been consulted. (*Stacey, 1976, p. 52*)

As the British forces were engaging in night raids on Germany, and British citizens were recovering from German bombs dropped during the night in South London, the British newspapers were reporting the agreement in considerable detail. The press was keen to note that British interests were not the top priority for the Americans. "Whatever the United States might do to strengthen Great Britain would at the same time strengthen Canada, in whose protection the United States is primarily interested" (*The Times, 8/19/40*).

Moffat's assessment of the Canadian concern for the potential threat of the agreement to British/Canadian relations as expressed in his letter to Sumner is at odds with the early reactions to the announcement of the policy. In fact, other documents from the period reveal America's intention to exclude Britain's involvement in the PJBD and raise questions about Moffat's insight if not his sincerity about the threat posed to British/Canadian relations. Just how opportunistic was the rhetoric of his letter? Later that year, in October of 1940, the Secretary of the American Section of the PJBD, John D. Hickerson disclosed in a memo that the Chief of Staff of the Canadian Army, General Cerar, had remarked to the Ambassador to Argentina that he favored including the British in the PJBD. Hickerson's advice leaves little doubt about his feeling regarding British involvement.

This is the first suggestion of this sort which I have heard, and I earnestly hope that the Canadian Government will not raise such a question; I do not believe there is much chance of their doing so. May I point out, against the possibility of someone raising this question with you, that such an addition would virtually destroy the premise on which we have thus far worked in the Joint Board. We have stated quite frankly to the Canadian Section that the job of the Joint Board is to consider the *defense* of Canada and the United States from attack, and no other question. We have added that it is of course the policy of the American Government to give every possible assistance short of actual participation in the war to the British Government and to the Canadian Government in its overseas effort, but that such assistance will be given by agencies other than the Permanent Joint Board on Defense. (Diplomatic Papers, 1940, pp. 147–148)

If the British were looking for American encouragement to use the PJBD to strengthen British ties with either the United States or Canada, they would find none here.

Once the agreement was signed, the Canadian press response to it was generally positive. A week after the agreement, *Saturday Night* , a leading Canadian magazine concluded that the informal manner in which the two leaders had achieved the agreement worked to Canada's favor:

The difference between a treaty and the present friendly collaborations is that the latter can be carried on by the American Executive, in whom Canada has entire confidence, whereas treaties have to be made by a two-thirds majority of the American Senate, a majority which can hardly ever be secured except for a treaty in which the United States gains everything and the other party little or nothing. (*Saturday Night,* 8/24/1940)

Here the Canadian press portrays a public that prefers efficiency to a policy process, that carefully weighs public concerns as they might be represented through congressional and parliamentary deliberations. The irony of this portrayal in the context of Moffat's concern for public opinion reveals the realpolitick of a rhetoric of opinion management.

As a further demonstration of political agility in fashioning rhetoric that appears to accommodate the public good, it is informative to note that by August 20th, Churchill's bleak mood at the time of the Ogdensburg announcement had changed dramatically when it was disclosed that Britain would lease to the Americans island territory from Newfoundland to the Caribbean for military bases. The British too, he seemed to proclaim, could play a pivotal role in the defensive planning of the Atlantic triangle.

Utterly confident, Prime Minister Churchill used his disclosure of the plan for air-naval base leases to declare that the British Empire and the United States 'will have to be mixed up together for some of their affairs for mutual advantage. No one can stop it!" he cried, "Like the Mississippi, it just keeps rolling along! Let it roll! Let it roll on, full flood, irresistible, to broader lands and better days!" (*Washington Post,* 8/21/40)

But, in reality, the tightening Canadian-American embrace was not to be loosened. The Ogdensburg agreement would draw Canada closer to the United States in ways that went beyond mere defense arrangements. The implications for a greater American influence over Canada are apparent in this report some 10 days after the formal announcement. "While the Joint Defense Board is theoretically limited to military and naval considerations, it is believed certain that the President will be informed on economic and industrial aspects" (NY Times, 8/28/40).

And the Americans industrial development with Canada served to establish patterns that would persist long after the war. "There are plans to gear Canadian and American industry more closely to eliminate unnecessary duplications in defense plants" (The Washington Post, 8/21/40).

In early September, as Canadian squadrons were successfully engaging Dormier bombers over the Thames in the heart of London, the work of the Joint Defense Board was well underway. Its chairman was Mayor La Guardia who issued the following statement on the occasion of the second official meeting of the group:

Our task is to utilize the gifts of nature for the defense of our two countries, Canada and the United States. When we are through, the dictators will think twice, or half a dozen times, before they attack the Western hemisphere. (NY Times, 9/10/40)

During the early period of the Second World War, after the Ogdensburg Agreement, Canada was beginning to feel its muscle as an international force of some consequence.

Canadians realize that the temporary eclipse of so many of the smaller Powers, and the circumstances created by her individual contribution to the war, have made Canada the greatest of the small powers and closer to the great Powers than any of the smaller Powers are to her. In the second place, Canada has special relations with each of the three great Powers. She is the Commonwealth partner of Great Britain; she is geographically in intimate relations with, and has a permanent defence agreement with, the United States; she is Russia's northern neighbour, a fact which will become increasingly significant in the years ahead. (Macadam, 1941, p. 520)

And her determination to be seen as an independent participant in the war is evident in this commentator's remarks.

The present outlook of Canadians, or of a great many of them, can best be exemplified by the way some of them feel about Canada's entry into the war. Nothing is more infuriating to many Canadians than to be thanked by Englishmen for coming to the help of England by entering this war. Canadians believe that they are fighting in this war, not because they want to be good to England, or because of any debt they owe to England, but because this war is Canada's own war, just as it is a British war, a Russian war, and American war. Canada entered the war because she felt that her vital interests were endangered. (Macadam, 1941, p. 520)

Canada was fully engaged in the process of striking a posture of independence from Britain and the Ogdensburg agreement marks the turning point in their long relationship. That agreement was the result of a combination of American strategies that carefully orchestrated policy and public opinion. Further proof that a new Canadian/American train was on the rails and gathering steam was to come less than a year after the Ogdensburg Agreement when Mackenzie King again met with Roosevelt in the United States. This time they collaborated at Roosevelt's Hyde Park, New York home to seal the Hyde Park Declaration which promised even closer coordination between the countries in the production of defense articles.

CONCLUSIONS

This particular case suggests that the Roosevelt administration's management of public opinion during the period of the Ogdensburg agreement rested on a number of assumptions. Taken together, these assumptions reveal two main dimensions, a comprehensive theory of political communications that was the basis for the construction and coordination of internal and public policy rhetoric and, secondly, a set of political communication strategies based on that theory. The theory had several aspects:

1. Public opinion constituted a central consideration in the making of policy, and American diplomats posted in Canada were expected to monitor and interpret public opinion of the citizens in the host country and report their interpretations to their colleagues.
2. Canadian public opinion was assumed to represent viable citizen power in the formation of Canadian policy.
3. American policymakers assumed that the press was the representative of the public mood; that there was in fact no distinction between press and public attitude toward a policy, and that a selective use of these press representations of the public's mood could be effectively incorporated into arguments for a particular course of action.

The political language constructed to appeal to particular constituencies was built upon these assumptions and employed a number of rhetorical strategies for purposes of constructing a version of what would appear to be "objective reality." The strategies that underlay the language intended for the subculture of policymaking colleagues included the following:

1. Selectively Defining the "Public Mood."
2. Devaluating Contentious Public Opinion. For example, Moffat relegated to the past Canadian concerns that might challenge the proposed policy when he described Canadian public fears of weakening ties to Britain as "an old fear."
3. Selectively Priviliging and/or Constructing Public Opinion Constituencies. For example, those who opposed the proposed policy were relegated to the category of "the bare minority," and their arguments were described as having been dismissed by the majority. The process of constituency construction is represented by this pol-

icymaker having conveniently lumped all of the various constituencies that contribute to Canadian opinion to a single Canadian opinion and constructing arguments that include the image of a unified Canadian voice as in "Canada believes…"

4. Playing the Advocacy Role. In this case the policymaker demonstrated intercultural empathy and credibility by assuming the "public advocacy" role and arguing on behalf of the "average Canadian."

5. Assuming a Peripheral Dependency Perspective. Moffatt presumed that Canadians were willing to be oriented to and dominated by America.

The public relations strategies used to announce the policy after-the-fact included:

1. Going Public. This strategy avoided the complications associated with following traditional policymaking channels and procedures.

2. Choosing a Defining Moment. This strategy involves announcing the policy at a time when the dynamics of international relations lend credence to both the policy and the expeditious manner in which it was approved.

3. Providing an International Relations Political Logic. The policy is described as a logical step in the pattern of relations between the countries involved.

Finally, as a response to both the theoretical assumptions and the practiced strategies of the policymakers, press coverage of the announced policy demonstrated several patterns of interpretation:

1. The American press was supportive and celebratory in its coverage while fully reporting Britain's negative response to the policy.

2. The British press response cycled through a period of resentment, resignation, and finally, guarded acceptance. The agreement was seen as primarily serving American interests; it threatened the future of British/Canadian relations. But, the British press in general seemed to conclude that accepting the agreement with a minimum of rancor on the part of the British government was but another of the many compromises required in the current struggle for survival.

3. The Canadian press was generally supportive, lending credence to American diplomatic management of that country's opinion about this policy issue.

The communications strategies that culminated in the creation of the Permanent Joint Board on Defense at Ogdensburg were successful for the Roosevelt administration. While the process of American diplomats constructing a policy rhetoric based on Canadian public opinion was certainly politically opportunistic and self-serving for American interests, it was treated by these same politicians as sufficiently important to demand great care in its execution. The documentary evidence reveals a public opinion management routine that is convincingly circumspect and sophisticated in its approach. Public opinion was interpreted carefully over time with a particular attention to the contributions of specific presses and the ethnic and regional constituencies they represented, all in the context of changes in mood that were occasioned by political developments nationally and internationally. However, the evidence also reveals the political objectives of the players in this historical drama and the reality of political communications becomes apparent when we realize that the care in monitoring public opinion was undertaken more for purposes of constructing a politically expedient image of Canadian public opinion than accurately reporting it.

The dynamics of the Ogdensburg case are peculiar to the management of that policy for that time period. We must, of course, be careful in generalizing beyond this case. The objective of this study was to isolate rhetorical patterns in a particular case to establish a baseline for further comparative study. Additional research along the lines proposed here might usefully reveal how typical, how idiosyncratic, how historically bound were the routines of political communications that interpreted and appealed to public opinion to formulate the Joint Defense Board policy of 1940.

While irony and skepticism are possible responses to this kind of historical analysis as it reveals an American-centered appropriation of Canadian public opinion, this kind of study also has the positive potential to lead us toward a reflexive consciousness, one which encourages international policy analysis and press coverage that is informed by the knowledge of historical precedent. The dismal and divisive alternative is to assume that we are passive victims of the acts of others.

REFERENCES

Barton, R. L. (1990). *Ties that blind in Canadian/American relations: Politics of news discourse.* Hillsdale, NJ: Erlbaum.

Benson, L. (1967–68) An approach to the scientific study of past public opinion. *Public Opinion Quarterly, 31,* 522–567.

Board to stress Canandian coast. (1940, August 28). *New York Times,* p. 7.

Canada must go all out, editorial. (1940, May 22). *Vancouver Sun,* p. 1.

Canada to get U.S. assistance. (1940, August 21). *Washington Post,* p. 1.

Cohen, B.C. (1973). *The public's impact on foreign policy.* Boston: Little Brown.

Cohen, Y. (1986). *Media diplomacy.* London: Frank Cass.

Creighton, D. (1976). *The forked road: Canada 1939–1957.* Toronto: McClelland and Stewart.

Edelman, M. (1995). The influence of rationality claims on public opinion and policy. In T. Glasser, & C. Salmon (Eds.), *Public opinion and the communication of content.* New York: Guilford, 1995.

Erikson, R.S., Luttbeg, N.R., & Tedin, K.L. (1988). *American public opinion: Its origins, content, and impact* (3rd ed.). New York: Macmillan.

Foreign Relations of the United States: Diplomatic papers (volume 3). (1940). pp. 144–148.

The front page, editorial (1940, August 24). *Saturday Night,* p. 3.

Goodwin, D. K. (1994). *No ordinary time. Franklin and Eleanor Roosevelt: The home front in World War II.* New york: Simon & Schuster.

Graber, D. (1993). *Mass media and American politics.* (4th Ed.). Washington: Congressional Quarterly Press.

Granatstein, J. L. & Hillmer, N. (1991). *For better of for worse: Canada and the United States to the 1990's.* Toronto: Copp Clark Pitman.

Havel, V. (1995July–August) Civilizations thin veneer, *Harvard Magazine.*

Hurd, C. (1940, August 18). U.S.–Canada ties welded by president and premier. *New York Times,* p. 1.

Hurd, C. (1940, August 20). President hurries U.S.–Canada plan. *New York Times.*

Hutchison, B. (1940, June 1). U.S.–Canada defense pact. *Vancouver Sun,* p. 1.

Hutchison, B. (1940, June 17). U.S. proposes all Americans join in big economic pool. *Vancouver Sun,* p. 1.

Hutchison, B. (1940, June 11). Call to America. *Vancouver Sun,* p. 8.

Kennamer, J. D. (Ed.). (1992). *Public opinion, the press and public policy.* Westport, CT: Praeger.

Kennamer, J. D. (1990). Self-serving bias in perceiving the opinion of others. *Communication Research, 17,* 393–404.

La Guardia warns invaders to pause. (1940, September 10). *New York Times,* p. 7a.

Lemert, J. B. (1981). *Does mass communication change public opinion after all? A new approach to effects analysis.* Chicago: Nelson-Hall.

Macadam, I. S. (1941). Canada and the Commonwealth *International Affairs,* VI.

Manheim, J. (1994). *Strategic public diplomacy and American foreign policy.* New York: Oxford.

Miller, W. E., & Stokes, D. (1963). Constituency influence in Congress. *American Political Science Review, 57,* 45–56.

Partridge, P. (1971). *Consent and consensus.* London: Macmillan.

Plan to lease lands proves no one can stop the fusion of interests he (Churchill) holds. (1940, August 21). *Washington Post,* p. 1d.

The Public Papers and Addresses of Franklin D. Roosevelt, 1940 (1941). volume 'War and Aid to Democracy' Macmillan, NY. p. 331.

Roosevelt to see Mackenzie King. (1940, August 17). *New York Times,* p. 1.

Stacey, C.P. (1976). *Mackenzie King and the Atlantic triangle.* Toronto: Macmillan/Maclean-Hunter.

U.S. aid to Canada by naval patrol studies in capital. (1940, August 20). *New York Times,* p. 1.

U.S.–Canada defense alliance, editorial. (1940, June 20). *Montreal Gazette,* p. 8.

chapter 8

the press and foreign policy dissent: the case of the gulf war*

Robert A. Hackett
Simon Fraser University

One intriguing—if backhand—way of assessing the press/foreign policy relationship is to examine how the press treats opposition to the state's foreign
policy. For both the state and for journalism as an institutionalized way of
making sense of the world, no foreign policy decision is more fundamental than a commitment to wage war. Such a crisis may reveal characteristics which are latent during
more "normal" times. The 1991 Gulf War, when Iraqi forces were driven from Kuwait
by a U.S.-led multinational coalition under the rubric of the United Nations, was just
such a moment of truth.

This chapter, which summarizes case studies of American and Canadian press
framing of domestic opposition to the Gulf War, is intended to shed light on three conventional perspectives on the relationship between the press and foreign policy. What
are those perspectives?

First, the dominant position, often labelled *liberal-pluralism*, sees the media as an

* This chapter is based largely on three previous publications listed in the references: Hackett 1993a,
Hackett 1993b, and Hackett and Zhao, 1994. The author is grateful to the Center for War, Peace, and the
News Media at New York University, Robert Elias of Peace Review, and Sage Publications, publisher of
Discourse and Society, for copyright approval. Hackett gratefully acknowledges financial support for this
study from the abovementioned Center, as well as the Fund for Investigative Journalism, the C.S. Fund, the
Canadian Institute for International Peace and Security, and the Social Sciences and Humanities Research
Council of Canada. Thanks are also due to Alan Etkin, Debra Pentecost, David Robinson, Myles Ruggles,
Jim Sands and Yuezhi Zhao for research assistance and/or comments, and to the dozens of government and
military officials, peace activists and journalists he interviewed in both Canada and the U.S.

independent institution fulfilling important political functions. The major news media enjoy such resources as oligopolistic access to mass audiences, the credibility and trust accorded by those audiences, the ability to damage politicians with bad publicity, and the respect accorded in liberal-democratic law and culture to the idea of freedom of the press. In this view, the media's relationships with the state and other political institutions, which obviously have their own power base and resources, are variable and contingent, with the edge shifting back and forth from one side to the other (Hackett and Hissey, 1991, pp. 46–47).

However, liberal-pluralists concede that during national crises, the media may slide too snugly into the embrace of the State, to the detriment of their (presumed) normal function as a "watchdog" on government (Everette Dennis, quoted in Ruffini, 1992, p. 287). Retrospectively considering their own profession's role in covering the Gulf conflict, some prominent American journalists have reached a similar conclusion: the news media acted more like patriotic cheerleaders than detached, objective observers, and thus failed to get the whole story. Often, such criticism has focussed on external constraints, such as the Pentagon's media pool system and its consequent control and selective use of information and images from the Gulf (see, e.g., The media and the Gulf, 1991; LaMay, Fitzsimon, & Sahadi, 1991, pp. 8–33, 65–76; Smith, 1992). However, the media's own collusion in the nation's yellow ribbon fever and militarist machismo has also been noted (see, e.g. Kalb, 1994). But in this pluralist tradition, the press's cheerleading role has rarely been analyzed as something deeper than a regrettable aberration.

Second, a politically influential conservative variant of this conventional pluralist view sees news media as not just independent, but as power-seeking institutions populated by left-liberal journalists who are hostile to business and authority. In this vein, right-wing ideologues like broadcaster Rush Limbaugh and Reed Irvine of the media watchdog Accuracy in Media, as well as several conservative politicians—then Vice-President Dan Quayle, Senator Alan Simpson—accused some U.S. media of acting as virtual conduits for Iraqi propaganda during the Gulf War. Reporting for CNN from Baghdad, Peter Arnett was a lightning rod for this kind of criticism (see e.g. Smith, 1992, pp. 339–347). But on the whole, the conservative critique of Gulf War media coverage has been undermined by the back-slapping of satisfied generals, politicians and officials. Pete Williams, the Pentagon's top media handler, dismissed as a "myth" the notion that the press "somehow didn't do a good job in covering Operation Desert Storm" (Williams, 1992, pp. 168–70).

Third, and quite by contrast with the conservative critique, a radical school in media theory regards the media as indirectly but systematically subordinate to capital and the state. In this view, far from being adversarial or even independent, the media tend ideologically to legitimize (or even to help constitute) established institutions and social relations, and to marginalize fundamental alternatives. Within the peace movement itself, probably no media research has commanded more influence than one version of this radical critique, namely the "propaganda model" advanced by Herman and Chomsky (1988, Ch. 1). In their view, news is fundamentally shaped by the following five "filters": concentrated, corporate, profit-oriented ownership; dependence on advertising revenue; media reliance on information sources employed, funded, or sanctioned by government and business; right-wing pressure campaigns against the media; and finally, the ideological control mechanism of anti-Communism. Given these filters, dominant media act virtually as extensions of state propaganda, framing, emphasizing or ignoring events in accordance with elite interests. In this model, the press offers sustained debate over foreign policy options only when elites are themselves divided.

Press coverage of Gulf War dissent suggests that to differing degrees, all three of these views need to be qualified. In the next two sections, I summarize the ways that the press framed, and hierarchically structured, antiwar protest. Then, I seek to explain press framing in terms of the political landscape at the time of the Gulf War. Finally, I look beyond that specific conjuncture to relate the press coverage to broader cultural narratives which help both to provide and to restrict opportunities for opposition to the state's most fundamental foreign policy decision—the waging of war.

PRESS FRAMING OF OPPOSITION TO THE GULF WAR

How did the U.S. and Canadian press portray domestic protest against their respective governments' decision to use military force against Iraq? The following conclusions are summarized from a detailed analysis of two collections of newspaper clippings focussing on expressions of protest or opposition. The first comprised 1471 news articles, letters and columns published in 537 small and medium-market papers around the U.S., mainly during the crucial period between January 15—the U.N. deadline for Iraqi withdrawal—and January 31, 1991—when the Iraqi defeat was fairly obvious, and antiwar protests were abating. (This archive was made available to the author by the Center for War, Peace and the News Media at New York University.) The second collection comprised some 400 articles published between January 15 and February 28, 1991 in three Canadian daily papers—the *Toronto Globe* and *Mail*, anglo-Canada's leading prestige daily, and two regional papers, the *Vancouver Sun*—the leading paper in the Pacific coast province of British Columbia—and the *Province*—a Vancouver tabloid.

The Gulf confrontation can be divided into three phases (Dorman and Livingston, 1994, p. 63). The first "establishing" phase lasted from Iraq's August 1990 invasion of Kuwait to President Bush's November 8 announcement of a large U.S. troop increase to the Gulf to provide an offensive option. The second "nominal debate phase" lasted from November 9 until the Congressional decision to authorize force and the U.N. deadline of January 15, 1991. This chapter focusses on the third phase, the actual war when presumably elite consensus and wartime popular nationalism would most constrain the opportunities for oppositional discourse.

Several main points emerge from this analysis of news coverage. (For details, see Hackett [1993a, 1993b] and Hackett and Zhao [1994].)

Considering the U.S. press first, portrayal of antiwar dissent revealed several different frames—"persistent patterns of cognition, interpretation, and presentation, of selection, emphasis, and exclusion, by which symbol-handlers routinely organize discourse" (Gitlin, 1980, p. 7). No single frame predominated to the exclusion of others. The "enemy within" frame positioned antiwar protest as a violent and/or treasonous internal threat to the war effort and even to basic American values and interests. This frame was very evident not only in the op/ed pages, but also in the news agenda. About one-fifth of all news items on antiwar dissent essentially marginalized it by posing it as a problem of law and order: violence, disruption, symbolic defiance of authority, and controls and punishments imposed by the authorities.

Another frame also cast antiwar protest into, or at least to the edge of, the pit of deviance by representing it not so much as treasonous, dangerous or violent, as irrelevant and marginal—outside America's social and political mainstream. This "marginal oddity" frame generally conceded the democratic right of dissent and avoided the insistence on political conformity characteristic of the "enemy within" frame; but it dismissed the substantive validity of protest by characterizing it as outdated or out of touch with reality, as a predictable, non-rational, emotional and ill-informed response, confined to marginal or ignorant groups in the population. Stereotypes of Vietnam-era protest as a youthful and counter-cultural phenomenon abounded, along with trivialization of the movement's composition, dress, motives and behavior.

By contrast, a third approach took a more detached, balanced, or neutral posture— one corresponding to journalism's self-image as an open forum, a mirror of the community, or objective observer, but one which is still a choice, an interpretive frame. In this "legitimate controversy" frame, the movement was portrayed as part of the social and political mainstream, rather than as a criminal, deviant or juvenile phenomenon. Journalists and commentators taking this approach did not necessarily endorse or sympathize with opposition to the war, but they did treat it as part of a legitimate debate and/or a voice in the community with a right to be heard. Such treatment took different forms: news reports which balanced anti- and pro-war rallies and views as equivalent counterparts; editorials which supported the right of dissent, albeit without endorsing the movement's position on the war; small-town weeklies which used the rhetoric of community spirit to try to avoid antagonizing portions of the audience; human interest portrayals or interviews of individual peace activists; and respectful news reports of vigils and other thoughtful, legal rational, discursive expressions of opposition to the war.

Nevertheless, the openings to dissent that were available in the U.S. press had definite limits. Peace protests apparently did not trigger broader analysis of the motives and consequences of U.S. intervention in the Gulf, or of the historical precedents for the antiwar movement. There was near total silence on the internal politics of the movement. The movement's efforts to draw links between the war and other issues—the environment, poverty, racial injustice—were misunderstood or dismissed, even by journalists who otherwise wrote respectfully. With a few exceptions, the commercial press provided little space for the movement's own voices; usually at most, it offered respectful reports from journalists who, however sympathetic, were outsiders.

On the whole, the U.S. antiwar movement spent as much energy defending its own legitimacy as advancing substantive arguments against the war policy. "We support the troops too," declared protesters quoted in news reports, and "we too are patriots." Renunciation and denunciation of violent protest, and references to the right of free expression were other common themes in quotes attributed to protesters. Much the same pattern was evident in the op/ed pages. Editorial endorsements of the antiwar movement were scarce, and positive descriptions far more muted than the robust vilification characteristic of the enemy within and marginal oddity frames. Only a minority of editorials went beyond simply recognizing the right of dissent to speak of the movement in sympathetic terms, applauding its restraint, its responsibility, its contribution to the health of democracy, and its support for the troops (by presumed but problematic contrast with the Vietnam era). Such modest editorial sympathy did not extend to actual editorial disapproval of the war as unjust or unwise, and still less to calls for Americans to actively oppose it. Bitter contestation over the right to claim the symbols of the flag, patriotism and support for the troops were indications that the terms of debate were being set by opponents of the peace movement, which struggled mightily to assert its own legitimacy. Though partly successful, that effort was often at the cost of advancing a case against the war itself.

While neither the samples nor the methods of the U.S. and Canadian studies were exactly comparable, it appears impressionistically that the Canadian press paid more respectful attention to antiwar dissent. The enemy within and marginal oddity frames were certainly present, but not as dominant. Some fundamental critiques of the war policy appeared in columns and features, not just letters to the editor which can be dismissed as mere personal opinion with dubious credibility. Some reports of mass protests were reported respectfully, and included the views of peace organizations, as did several "soft news" or feature items. Local peace activists or organizations were profiled sympathetically in features and, on occasion, were granted access as expert sources. In an analysis of the military-industrial complex, for example, one journalist used local peace activists, environmentalists, and unnamed peace groups to reveal how military spending could be used more fruitfully to address social, economic, and environmental problems. The Vancouver *Province*, one of the three Canadian dailies analyzed, even took a clearcut stand against the war in its own editorials, appealing to universal principles of human solidarity and respect for all life: "So now we must stand up in face of this indignity against our fellow human beings and say that we could have turned the other cheek, that we cannot tout peace and democracy and civilization and then slaughter innocent civilians" (Jan. 17, 1991).

While far from dominating the coverage, such critical distancing from official policy was less rare in the Canadian than in the U.S. papers studied, and it was subtly paralleled in reporting of the war itself. Canadian journalists were less likely to refer to their own country's military forces as "our" troops, for example.

Nevertheless, neither Canadian/U.S. press differences, nor the relative openness of the Canadian press to dissent, should be exaggerated. Even with a generous definition of "dissent" news, it comprised just 19.2 per cent of our sample of Canadian press items about the Gulf War. More importantly, Canadian newspapers probably framed the Gulf crisis in much the same terms as their U.S. counterparts during the crucial "establishing phase" period leading up to the war itself. English-language Canadian media have long been dependent on American-based news agencies for reportage of overseas events (Hackett, 1991, pp. 101–104), and that dependence was increased during the Gulf crisis: Washington was the wellspring of politicial initiative, Canada's military contribution was relatively quite small, and Canadian journalists were shut out of the media pools covering the huge U.S. war effort in the Gulf region.

A HIERARCHY OF DISSENT

A complicating factor in media/movement relations is the reality that contemporary antiwar movements rarely speak with a single voice. They typically contain diverse, even contradictory strands, which are treated differentially by the media. Once opposition to the Vietnam war gained popular momentum by 1968, for example, the press began to distinguish between its "moderate" and radical wings, and to privilege the former over the latter (Gitlin, 1980, Ch. 7).

Case studies of Canadian press coverage of the 1986 U.S. bombing of Libya, and of Vancouver's annual Walk for Peace in the 1980s, suggested that the press amplified and indeed helped to construct a hierarchy of access and legitimacy within the protest movement (Hackett, 1991, pp. 199–268). Some kinds of antiwar speakers, actions and arguments were privileged over others, as assessed by these criteria: the frequency and variety of each discourse's repetition; the relative space it was given for extended explanation; its expression in several different "genres" of news articles—e.g., op/ed pieces as well as hard news reports; whether it was embedded in journalists' own language and reality judgments without attribution to a source; whether it framed news coverage as a whole; and whether it avoided hostile commentary or rhetorical distancing devices such as quotation marks used to bracket suspect concepts.

According to these criteria, political violence labeled as "terrorist," along with the statements of anti-Western governments, ranked on the lowest rungs of the discursive ladder in the 1986 case. Somewhat higher up were radical socio-economic critiques, and at the top were utilitarian cost-benefit analyses and universal moral arguments. Their characteristics are discussed below.

Was a similar hierachy of antiwar speakers and arguments evident during the Gulf War? An analysis of the op/ed pages and the sources quoted in hard news reports in the U.S. press archive suggests that such was the case. When the antiwar movement could move beyond defending its own legitimacy to advancing substantive criticisms of the war in the press—primarily in quotes in news reports, guest columns, and letters to the editor—these arguments were of several types.

Relatively prominent were rejections of war on moral grounds held to be universally applicable, a position which asserts the unity of humankind against the dichotomization of Us versus Them. Examples of such arguments included humanitarian concern with casualties on all sides, and general denunciations of war and affirmations of peace and non-violence. The strength of this kind of position is its moral and mobilizing force, but it is vulnerable to charges of utopianism, idealism, and of playing into the hands of the "enemy"—charges made by those who reject the concept of human solidarity in favour of the real-politik of state power in an international arena seen as inherently conflictual. Thus, moral universalism has had little impact on state policy in general (Walker, 1984, p. 306), and in the Gulf War too, it was insufficient to build a convincing case against the war. For that, the movement would have needed to use media access to articulate a clear analysis of the war's origins and consequences, proposals for alternatives, and an effective answer to the question, "What do you do with bullies like Saddam Hussein?"

A second kind of position was utilitarian, cost-benefit analysis which accepts the State's war objectives, but criticizes the means as disproportionate to the end sought. Much of the "moderate" opposition to the U.S. intervention in Vietnam was of this kind, accepting the benevolence of U.S. intentions while rejecting the war because of its excessive costs—particularly to America itself. Because it shares important assumptions with the warmakers' own discourse, and because it is often articulated within the foreign policy establishment, this kind of critique is relatively privileged. For the same reasons, it is "essentially a very conservative position," although it may have radical implications (Walker, 1984, p. 307).

Although not as dominant as they had been during the Vietnam and Libya conflicts, utilitarian arguments were still relatively well represented during the Gulf War in the U.S. press, especially the op/ed pages. Essentially, critics in this school argued that the war would have negative consequences—especially to the U.S.—which outweighed its benefits, and sanctions or diplomacy should have been given more time and effort.

Radical socio-economic critiques are a third strand of antiwar dissent. These interpret militarism as an outgrowth of vested institutional interests linked with such dominant—and arguably repressive—social forces as patriarchy, capitalism, or imperialism. The strengths of such systemic critiques include their grasp of social and global realities, and their ability to merge with "related critiques made by progressivist social forces about a wide range of issues" (Walker, 1984, p. 306). But this kind of position is difficult to communicate simply, and its holistic radicalism brings it into conflict with powerful forces favoring the status quo—including, arguably, the major mass media.

During the Gulf War, oppositional claims that oil consumption or oil company interests were the real cause of the war were reported in one-third of U.S. news reports of protest, but less often in the op/ed columns—where the slogan "no blood for oil" most frequently appeared as an easy rhetorical target in articles hostile to the peace movement. Otherwise, only fragments of a radical political critique of the war were on tap in the U.S. press. In the pages of the U.S. papers, opponents of the war typically criticized it in a depoliticized and ahistorical way, presenting it as an isolated case, without much reference to the connections between U.S. foreign policy and domestic political and economic power relationships. When historical context was offered, it was by way of analogies with the Vietnam war—an analogy wrought with ambiguity. For some, Vietnam summons images of the unnecessary devastation of a Third World country or the horrors of war in general; but for many others, it is a spectre of primarily American casualties and costs disproportionate to the laudable objectives pursued.

The press's scanting of radical critiques of the Gulf War was paralleled by related blindspots. Press reports quoted demonstration organizers and participants, but few experts. Notwithstanding their availability articulate and knowledgeable opponents of the war who could have most effectively challenged the Bush administration's definition of the Gulf crisis were rarely quoted. The connections between the war and other issues—e.g. racial inequality, poverty, the environment and energy policies—which the movement was articulating in an effort both to critique the war and to build alliances, were ignored or trivialized. There was little attention to the movement's history, internal politics, composition or alliances—in other words, precisely those elements which made it a movement rather than simply reactive protest. There were few quotes from antiwar trade unionists, gay or AIDS activists, environmentalists or ethnic minorities—an array of constituencies which made the antiwar coalition a unique and potentially rich one. Instead, press reports simplified the political context into pro-versus anti-war camps. The press appeared to assume that those groups coming out of the predominantly white, middle-class anti-nuclear movement of the 1980s were the real, legitimate peace movement; other groups were treated as opportunistic adjuncts, or simply ignored altogether. Likewise, little attention was paid to opposition to the war in other countries, or to the Iraqi opposition in exile, which opposed both Saddam Hussein's regime and the war.

In the Canadian press, a broadly similar hierarchy of antiwar dissent was evident. Potential terrorist retaliation and Iraqi government statements were at the bottom of the totem pole, followed by opposition from other non-Western governments, which received little elaboration. In contrast, and compared with previous Middle East conflicts, the Soviet Union was given relatively respectful attention when it opposed aspects of the coalition policy, such as the timing of the ground war. The waning Cold War, the importance of Soviet support in the U.N., and Soviet acceptance of the coalition's overall goals help account for why its position was treated as "news of talk" rather than "news of riot" (cf. Knight, 1983).

The next rung up the ladder included fundamental critiques of the war from within North America. To be sure, these were infrequent—22 of 400 items—and were usually expressed in letters to the editor, and thus framed as merely personal opinion with dubious credibility. But apparently more so than in the U.S. press, the op/ed pages of Canadian dailies did provide space for dissident interpretations of the war as an outgrowth of patriarchal politics, Western business and political interests, or Eurocentric cultural stereotypes.

As in the U.S. press, arguments appealing to universal moral principles, such as human solidarity, non-violence and respect for all life, were treated relatively respectfully in the Canadian dailies, as were more utilitarian arguments weighing the costs and benefits of the war. In the Canadian press, there were far fewer references to Vietnam. On the other hand, two antiwar arguments appeared in the Canadian but not U.S. papers. One argument attacked Canada's military involvement in the Gulf as a departure from, if not betrayal of, Canada's cherished tradition of international peacekeeping. Another suggested that Canada's Mulroney government was too closely following the lead of the Bush administration in its handling of the Gulf crisis.

The analysis of press coverage in the above two sections suggests several questions. Why was the antiwar movement placed on the defensive during the Gulf War? Was the media scanting of dissent inevitable, or could the movement or the press have behaved differently? On the other hand, when both Canada and the U.S. were effectively at war with Iraq, and nationalist emotions were presumably at fever pitch, why did press discourse provide any space at all for the expression of dissent? And what accounts for the modestly greater space for dissent in the Canadian press, by comparison with the U.S.? These questions inform the rest of this chapter.

EXPLAINING THE NEWS:
THE CONJUNCTURE OF THE GULF WAR

The above analysis suggests that even during a moment of profound political closure, with the country at war, tensions and emotions at a fever pitch, and Congressional opposition nowhere to be found, the American press afforded certain opportunities for antiwar dissent to find expression. These openings were in significant measure a legacy of the Vietnam war: in light of that experience, the media could not dismiss the possibilities that the government would mislead the public, and that the war would spawn domestic division and high American casualties. On the eve of Congressional approval for the use of force, U.S. public opinion was still evenly split between war and sanctions. To be sure, as the bombs began to fall, the national networks turned away from the debate over whether to go to war to focus on the "military matchup". But by contrast, local television news found it "harder to set aside the doubts that ordinary people far from the action still had about going to war;" coverage of protest "was quite extensive in the early days of the war, and never entirely disappeared" (Hallin & Gitlin, 1992, p. 14). The same can be said of our archive of local news clippings.

The openings for dissent were also evidence that the anti-nuclear and anti-interventionist movements of the 1980s had managed to insert themselves into political discourse, at least indirectly influencing both foreign policy and the media even during the darkest days of the Reagan era. Gestures towards arms control negotiations, however superficial, and the avoidance of a full-scale invasion of Nicaragua, were concessions that the Reagan administration had to make to such anti-militarist sentiment. A media system whose professional ethics and public credibility revolve around the ethos of objectivity had to take some notice of significant antiwar dissent even during wartime. Such openings may be taken as qualifications to Herman and Chomsky's "propaganda model," discussed above, which views the U.S. media as closely wedded to elite interests.

The greater space for antiwar dissent in the Canadian press is not difficult to explain. Canada's political elites did not close ranks behind the war policy as much as did their American counterparts. On the eve of the war, Jean Chretien, as national leader of the largest opposition party at the time, called for Canadian forces to be pulled back within 48 hours of a war being launched. After the bombing started, he reversed himself, expressing support for Canadian troops in the Gulf, but continuing to criticize the government's "hasty" resort to force. Pledging to continue speaking against "the madness of war," the leader of the second opposition party, the left-leaning New Democratic Party, told Canadians who had expressed concern about going to war that "We are with you." Even more forcefully, the NDP premier of Ontario, Canada's largest province, condemned the American attack and said that sanctions should have been given more time. "Is this a cause for which I would be willing to go to the desert and fight?" he said, as quoted on national television news. "The answer is 'no'."

Similarly, while a majority of Canadians clearly supported the use of force once it began, public opinion was much less one-sided than the 80 percent approval in the U.S. (American Enterprise, 1991, pp. 74–87). In Canada, about 30 percent of poll respondents continued to disapprove of the government's actions, and wanted Canadian military involvement to be reduced or ended; about 40 percent felt the world had made a "big mistake getting into this war" (MacDermid, 1992). Such views were particularly strong in the mainly French-speaking province of Quebec, with its historically isolationist sentiment.

The Canadian press reflected such ambivalence, which was reinforced by broader political and cultural factors. Compared to its massive U.S. counterpart, the Canadian military is a proportionately much smaller and socially isolated institution, with less resonance in popular culture. As a minor player in the anti-Iraq coalition, Canada had much less directly at stake in the Gulf conflict. Lacking great power status, and with strong internal linguistic and regional differences, Canadian nationalism is far more muted. A plurality of Canadians perceived that the U.S. was calling the shots in the Gulf, and this may have tempered support for the war: Canada's nationhood was uniquely founded upon a historical rejection of absorption into the U.S., and there is a long-standing strain of anti-Americanism—as well as enormous American cultural influence!—in English-speaking Canada. Finally, Canada's record of bridge-building diplomacy and of participation in U.N. peacekeeping operations are cherished national myths. Although the Gulf intervention was technically under the U.N. rubric, as the government was at pains to stress in its support-building strategies, it rest uneasily with the Canadian self-image.

The above factors help explain openness for dissent in Canada, but I have argued that these, albeit to a lesser extent, existed in the U.S. press too. The propaganda model of the media thus needs to be qualified as an explanation of the press's role during the Gulf War. But the liberal-pluralist conception of the press as an independent critic of government—and even more so, the conservative thesis of media adversarialism—are more seriously called into question by the Gulf War case. Arguably, the antiwar protests deserved to have received better and more coverage than they actually did. Writing in the New York Times, sociologist Harvey Molotch argued that the protests met the news criteria of novelty and significance: They were spontaneous rather than institutionally staged events, often led by idealistic and politically inexperienced young people; by contrast with Vietnam, they occurred during a very early phase of the war and at a time when oppositional culture was in abeyance (Cited by Gitlin, 1992, pp. 46–47). And they included a rainbow coalition of groups and issues—AIDS, the environment, women's equality, gay and lesbian rights—some of which were absent during the 1960s but prominent in the news agenda of the 1980s. The movement's activities included sizable demonstrations in various American cities, particularly in the first several weeks of the war, including on January 26, one of the largest demonstrations in Washington since the Vietnam era.

Yet press discourse was clearly structured in dominance. When it was not ignored altogether, the peace movement was placed on the defensive, compelled to react to the powerfully positioned enemy within and marginal oddity frames, and forced to defend its own legitimacy more than advance substantive critiques of the war.

The nature of the dominant news frames, and the peace movement's concomitant defensiveness, were partly related to the specific strategies and actions of the media, the protest movement and military and political elites during the specific conjuncture of the Gulf crisis. The Pentagon's control of images and information during the war has been much discussed. More important, though less noticed, was the Bush administration's success in imposing its own definition of the crisis during the "establishing phase" long before the actual war. Bush portrayed Saddam Hussein as "Hitler revisited," as a relentless threat to his neighbours and to world peace, a brutal dictator with whom no compromise was possible. Dubiously equating Iraq with Nazi Germany's hegemonic military and economic power, this definition of the situation worked to exclude other potential frames: the Gulf crisis could have been defined as an intra-Arab regional conflict, and Saddam Hussein as a creature of American and Allied policy, given Western support for him during his eight-year war with Iran. As Dorman and Livingston (1994) have shown, the policy outcome of war was implicit in the historical metaphor of Saddam-as-Hitler: any option short of his unconditional surrender could be dismissed as "appeasement." And indeed, as if on cue, the press's op/ed pages resounded with World War II metaphors, including the description of protesters as "appeasers." The *New Republic* magazine even retouched a cover photo of Hussein to give him a more Hitlerian moustache (FAIR, 1991, p. 10)! To be sure, Saddam Hussein played his own brutal role as designated Foreign Devil almost to perfection.

Sophisticated public relations also played a role in focusing and narrowing public perceptions and the range of policy options. The Canadian and U.S. governments engaged in intensive media monitoring and polling during the entire crisis, scanning public opinion for areas of doubt and opposition, and feeding this information back into their communication strategies (see, e.g. MacDermid, 1992). Through a front group, the Kuwaiti government hired the PR giant Hill and Knowlton for a massive image-making campaign in the U.S., highlighted by the story, later discredited, of Iraqi troops tearing Kuwaiti babies from incubators (Manheim, 1994).

The U.S. media's own general lack of coverage of Hussein and the consequent lack of alternative perceptual frames in public opinion prior to 1990 (Lang and Lang, 1994) no doubt helped Bush to establish the Hitler metaphor, which resonated with Canada's as well as America's World War II experience. So too did the routine organization of political newswork around beats anchored in powerful bureaucratic institutions, with a consequent "indexing" of news coverage to the decision-schedules and reality definitions of top officials and political leaders (Bennett, 1994, pp. 23–29). When division within the U.S. political elite finally did occur for two months prior to the war, editorial opinion largely reflected the boundaries of that debate: linkage with other Middle Eastern issues was rejected, previous U.S. support for Hussein not really examined, and the options reduced to sanctions versus war. Patterns of news coverage of both the crisis and the war, summarized briefly in the next section, also tended to reinforce the selective demonization of the Iraqi dictator. Some journalists interviewed for this study argued that domestic debate ceased to be newsworthy once Congress—and in Canada, Parliament—had approved the use of force. For better or worse, said one, the democratic process had yielded this result. Instead, the story became the war itself, an event so huge it virtually monopolized the news.

For its part, the peace movement did not play its own cards well. With many of its organizations caught in the mid-summer doldrums or still fixated on the fading Cold War, it was slow to mobilize following Hussein's blatant aggression against Kuwait in August 1990, and many on the Left did not initially oppose what they saw as a defensive and internationally sanctioned response by the U.S. (Gitlin, 1991a). The movement was further hindered by its historical reluctance to address Middle East issues, and by serious cross-pressures, political differences and organizational divisions. Actions and positions adopted by some quarters of the movement—anti-Semitism, a casual dismissal of Iraq's transgressions, incidents of violence and disruption—were almost tailor-made for self-marginalization (Gitlin, 1991b). Such difficulties help to account for the judgments of journalists from elite media interviewed for this study: the movement was "minuscule," led by "fringe people," fundamentally failed to provide effective opposition, and thus deserved no better than the coverage it received. Ignoring evidence that the media's own selective coverage may have contributed to ignorance about the war's causes and support for its prosecution (Morgan, Lewis and Jhally, 1992), one columnist argued that anti-war demonstrations, however large, did not influence journalists nearly as much as did the polls showing huge pro-war majorities.

But for the most part, the peace movement was trapped by factors not of its own making. Simply to blame the movement's problems either on its own shortcomings or on the media's propagandistic role would be seriously inadequate. Viewers and readers too are part of the media system. Partly due to the commercial imperatives of attracting audiences whose attention can be sold to advertisers, commercial media organizations are terrified of antagonizing economically significant sections of the audience. As Hallin and Gitlin (1994, p. 157) note, "Journalists were clearly responding to strong sentiments at the grass-roots level, and had relationships at this level just as complex and significant as [their] relationships with elite sources."

Canadian national myths, suggested above, help account for Canadian ambivalence about the war. Similarly, the seemingly spontaneous outburst of hostility to dissent expressed by many American journalists and readers alike suggests that the peace movement was running against a cultural template by which Americans interpret the experience of war—a template generally reinforced by, but not simply reducible to, the power of the state and of political and economic elites. The importance of this template (Keen, 1991, p. 19), or archetype (Galtung, 1987, p. 1), or master narrative (Beeman, 1991, p. 41) becomes clearer if we first sketch it, and then consider the three main strands of antiwar discourse in relation to it.

AMERICA'S MASTER NARRATIVE OF WAR

The master narrative can be sketched very broadly indeed, as rooted in Judaic/Christian/Islamic myths of a chosen people in exile, a special relationship or covenant with God, a New Beginning in a Promised Land. These myths, "so deeply internalized in the culture as to be taken for granted," constitute "the raw material out of which the social cosmology of a people is made, the assumptions built into deep ideology and deep structure, never to be questioned" (Galtung, 1987, p. 1). A version of this archetype, defining the U.S. as the promised land next to God, has become integral to America's definition of itself as a nation. By comparison with other advanced capitalist countries, "Americanism" as a national identity is less rooted in shared ethnicity, history or culture, and conversely more rooted in ideology—the ethic of rugged, possessive or competitive individualism; the myth of the hero; conceptions of the "American founding," or the U.S. as moral and democratic exemplar, "the nation that sits on the hill, the righteous nation, the one that will bring democracy to the world and light to the nations" (Keen, 1991; Darnovsky, Kauffman and Robinson, 1991, p. 483).

What are the implications of this cultural archetype for Americans' conceptions of the geopolitical world? For Galtung, the archetype suggests a manichean construction of world space, with the U.S. at the Center as the epitome of Good, defined by the values and institutions of the free market economy, competitive elections, and faith in the Judeo-Christian God. Next on the scale of moral legitimacy are the western, democratic, capitalist allies of the U.S. followed by the moral periphery of the Third World. At the other end of the moral scale, next to Satan, lies America's antitheses: countries which are hostile to the West, and which abjure capitalism, God and elections (Galtung, 1987, pp. 5–9). For four decades of Cold War, of course, the Soviets' "evil empire" constituted precisely this nemesis.

From this construction of world space flow other associated beliefs. The U.S. has not only a right but a duty to take on godlike characteristics, of omniscience, omnipotence, beneficence. No other nation or supra-national body can be allowed to take on that godlike role in place of the U.S., which is the ultimate decision-maker not accountable to anyone else. Given the moral hierarchy, it is only natural that other countries become Americanized. U.S. foreign policy can be correctly understood as a choice between global responsibility and isolation. Alternative models for U.S. foreign policy must be compatible with the covenant, which is implicit: making it explicit—as Galtung does— renders it ludicrous and thereby weakens it (Galtung, 1987, pp. 9–10, 13–19).

If Americanism implies a special moral responsibility in the world, then America must have the means to exercise that responsibility—namely, hegemonic military power. Perhaps also, in the absence of an alternative ethos of public service such as one would find in Britain, for example, and in light of the popular North American denigration of politics as self-serving and corrupt, the U.S. military functions as the main repository of the civic ideal of service to the republic. In any event, the archetype of America as chosen land does indeed slide easily into a master narrative of America's experience of war. The story begins with a villain who gratuitously, indefensibly and without provocation attacks an innocent victim, thereby challenging the moral order of which the U.S. is the Center. The U.S. is reluctant to resort to war, and tries to persuade the transgressor to return to the paths of righteousness. But the villain may be inherently evil and monstrous, so that the use of reason is out of the question. Then the U.S. may be compelled to take on the role of hero, and swoop down and destroy the enemy, skillfully and surgically employing the technological superiority of American weapons, and then go home again. Unlike lesser countries, the American motive in going to war is not self-aggrandizement or revenge, as it might be in a conflict between equals; rather, the motive is punishment of evil, meted out from above, just as God may punish sinners, and parents may punish their children. So motivated, the American people overcome their initial reluctance to go to war, and unite to support the action, even at the cost of making sacrifices and undergoing difficulties, because it is just and moral to do so. In that struggle against unmitigated evil, the only acceptable outcome is the unqualified triumph of good, and the unconditional surrender of evil (Galtung, 1987, pp. 10–13; Beeman, 1991; Lakoff, 1992, pp. 4–5). The demon is exorcised, the moral order restored, and the troops, as instruments of that order, go home to victory parades.

The war in living memory best matching that master narrative was World War II, from the "sneak attack" on Pearl Harbor to the surrender of Germany and Japan, followed by the judicial punishment of some of the wartime leaders and the restoration of democratic capitalism in those two countries. Small wonder that George Bush and his supporters sought implicitly to evoke the master narrative by explicitly comparing the Gulf conflict with World War II, and Saddam with Hitler, as we have seen.

Vietnam, of course, was an entirely different story, one that Bush promised not to repeat in the Persian Gulf. Why did the Vietnam war cause so much pain to the American psyche? It was not simply the tragedy of 60,000 U.S. troops killed and many more wounded. After all, comparable carnage occurs on America's highways without denting the nation's automobile fetishism. Nor have the devastation of Vietnam's economy and the hundreds of thousands of civilian casualties of U.S. bombing generated much soul-searching in dominant American political discourse. Rather, the Vietnam war caused a national identity crisis because it threw into question the benevolence of U.S. intentions, the morality of its actions, the wisdom of its leaders, the omnipotence of its military forces, and the unity of its people to such an extent that it threatened the master narrative itself. Indeed, during the 1960s, many young people did lose faith in the master narrative entirely, in some cases permanently, while sometimes remaining ironically within its spell by inverting its terms, casting the U.S. and all its works into the role of demon. That anti-American inversion of the master narrative was manifest-ed in some of the actions and positions of some corners of the Gulf War protest move-ment, which helps to account for its self-marginalization.

The lingering "Vietnam syndrome" is only partly to blame for the crisis of American identity. Other factors include prolonged economic stagnation, the econom-ic ascendancy of Germany and Japan, signs of serious social and moral decay at home—and the collapse of the Soviet empire, the Other against which Americanism had defined itself for so long. Deprived of their erstwhile enemy, it has been suggest-ed, Americans may well face a collapse of collective moral purpose and self-identity (Wright, 1989).

Faced with the threatened unravelling of a very useful master narrative, America's political elites have invested enormous ideological labor in trying to restore it. As one aspect of this restoration, other political concepts were thrust forward to fill the "threat vaccuum" created by the collapse of the Red Menace (Hackett, 1991, p. 293). International terrorism, Islamic fundamentalism, the drug trade, were all presented as targets for potential moral crusades. Until Saddam Hussein made himself a candidate by invading a neighbor without Washington's approval, none of them quite worked. For Bush, the metaphor of Hussein as another Hitler played into:

> ...the long-standing ideological rationale of U.S. imperial ambition: the Americanist quest for a moral identity through virtuous conquest of evil, the sense of a people pursu-ing its self-interest while collectively embodying some transcendent ideal. (Darnovsky, Kauffman, and Robinson, 1991, p. 484)

Restoring the master narrative has also required dispelling the Vietnam syndrome. One approach has been to dismiss the Vietnam intervention as an isolated tragedy, a huge but discrete mistake resulting from particular circumstances and decisions from which we have learned and that will not be repeated. That approach has an Achilles' heel, though: it tells the millions of Vietnam veterans and their families that their sac-rifice was pointless.

Consequently, there is fertile ground for a second interpretation, a right-wing revi-sionist reconstruction of the Vietnam war more in accordance with the precepts of the master narrative. In this reconstruction, the intervention was a "noble crusade", as Ronald Reagan called it. It failed, but not because the American military lacked omnipotence and met battlefield defeat; rather, the troops were betrayed by media, politicians and protesters at home who demoralized them and made the U.S. forces—which in reality unleashed more tons of bombs in the Vietnam war than did all the com-batants in World War II combined (Herman, 1982, p. 167; Sivard, 1985, p. 49)—fight "with one hand tied behind their backs". In this ideological reconstruction, Vietnam is cast as villain and the U.S. as victim; one device for achieving this remarkable inver-sion was to focus intense attention on the handful of U.S. "missing in action" prison-ers still allegedly being held by Hanoi, an effort popularized by Hollywood's Rambo films. The revisionist Vietnam myth has disturbing parallels—wounded national pride, betrayal from within, our nation as victim—with widespread sentiment in pre-Nazi

Germany regarding the German defeat in World War I. It is a mindset which implicitly calls for another, successful war as an act of national redemption. But one need not
accept the conspiracy theory that U.S. elites actually sought such a redemptive blood-
letting to recognize that the Gulf War could not have been better designed and packaged to "kick the Vietnam syndrome once and for all," as Bush put it, and restore the
original master narrative.

Assuming that news coverage of the Gulf confrontation was indeed scripted according to the master narrative, what patterns of emphasis and exclusion would we expect?
We would expect coverage to emphasize U.S. efforts during the crisis to find a peaceful solution without allowing unprovoked aggression to be rewarded; evidence of the
inherently evil nature of the enemy; the preparedness of U.S. troops and the efficiency
and precision of their weapons. Conversely, information contradicting the master narrative would tend to be filtered out, if not by journalists, then by their audiences whose
sense of patriotism would be outraged: previous U.S. support for Saddam Hussein; the
notions that the Bush administration might have been "shopping for a war," and/or had
given Iraq a "green light" to invade, and/or had snubbed Iraqi overtures to settle the crisis peacefully; the tarnished human rights record of the victim, Kuwait, and especially
of some U.S. allies—Syria, Turkey—in the crusade against Iraq; the possibility that
Kuwait was not a blameless victim, that Iraq had plausible historical claims and economic grievances; U.S. violations of international law, as alleged by Ramsay Clark's
war crimes tribunal; the imprecision of many U.S. weapons, only a minority of which
were "smart"; Iraqi civilian casualties; U.S. motives for intervention in the Middle East
apart from reversing aggression. To a considerable extent, mainstream press coverage
of the Gulf crisis and the subsequent war indeed followed this model (see Kellner,
1992; Chomsky, 1992).

And there is a good deal of evidence from the U.S. press clipping archive that the
master narrative influenced coverage of the peace movement too. In particular, the
enemy within and marginal oddity interpretations of dissent fit most closely with the
master narrative of war, and with the right-wing revisionist myth of Vietnam. Even
much of the op/ed commentary which accepted the legitimacy of protest interpreted it
as an affirmation of American values like free speech.

At the same time, the experience of Vietnam, and lingering social and economic
problems, have blunted the power of the master narrative. They have also contributed
to a sense of frustration and powerlessness felt by many ordinary Americans, and a
malaise if not crisis of national identity. Those factors, along with the political work of
critical social movements, created a certain space for the expression of antiwar dissent
during the Gulf War, both within and without the media. Those very same factors, however, also help account for the vehemence of hostility to antiwar dissent, the vigorous,
almost desperate reassertion of the master narrative, and "the intense nationalism,
racism, glorification of violence, and militarism" evident during the Gulf conflict
(Kellner, 1992, p. 255, citing Carl Boggs, unpublished paper). Through pro-war rituals, people found experiences, however temporary, of community and empowerment
denied them in everyday life.

Our analysis of how and why the press framed the antiwar movement can be refined by considering each of the three strands of antiwar discourse in relation to the master narrative.

1. Cost/Benefit, Utilitarian Analysis.

Asserting that the costs of war—to Americans—are too great relative to the objectives sought, this kind of argument normally finds it easy to gain a respectful hearing in the media; it operates within the terms of State policy discourse, and offers no fundamental challenge to the master narrative. But in the case of the Gulf War, it was not as dominant as it had been in press coverage of the conflict with Libya (Hackett, 1991: Chap. 10), or the later years of the Vietnam war (Gitlin, 1980: Chap. 7). Several reasons for this difference can be speculatively suggested. Bush had succeeded in convincing many of his potential critics that the main alternative avenues proposed by the utilitarian critique—namely, economic sanctions and diplomacy—had been exhaustively tried but did not work. Once the Congressional decision to authorize force had been made, many of the critics who had argued for sanctions, especially congressional Democrats who would normally find ready access in the media, simply fell silent. Their silence, and the momentum of the war itself, meant that there were no concrete "realistic" alternatives that could be taken seriously by "responsible" participants in policy discourse. Finally, one variant of the utilitarian argument focussed on the potential cost of war in American lives. This "body-bag" argument, along with fear of the reintroduction of a Vietnam-type draft, undoubtedly spurred initial opposition to the war. But when the war went much according to the Pentagon plan, with relatively few U.S. casualties, and with Germany and Japan paying many of the economic bills for U.S. taxpayers, this critique lost credibility. Given substantial changes in military doctrine (low-intensity conflict through proxies, or else massive and overwhelming deployment) and technology (the electronic battlefield), it may be that future U.S. interventions will not result in high American death counts, whatever its other costs to the target countries, the global economy and environment, and to American society itself. So the "body bag" argument may have less impact as a means of mobilizing popular resistance to war.

2. Universalist/moral critique

This kind of critique, exemplified by pacifism, also commands a certain respect in American political culture, though more as a statement of individual conscience than as a practical political option. It has an ambiguous relationship with the master narrative. On the one hand, it shares its concern to find and take the moral high ground, and perhaps also, the notion that America has a special moral role in the world. On the other hand, it directly challenges the master narrative's identification of the military as an instrument of moral purpose. It also finds it difficult to establish itself as a "realistic" way to deal with tyrants who appear as impervious to moral pressure as Saddam Hussein.

3. Radical political critiques

While offering a coherent re-interpretation of U.S. motives, it not only threatens the legitimacy of dominant elites, but offends many "ordinary" people who believe, or want to believe, in the master narrative. It also challenges the worldview of journalists themselves, and the credibility of the sources on whom they routinely rely for information.

Not surprisingly, this kind of critique—apart from the slogan No blood for oil—was pushed to the margins in the mainstream press, and found much better expression in alternative papers. Only there did one find police harassment of protesters as a significant news topic—reversing the Enemy Within frame—or extended discussion of the internal politics of the antiwar coalition as a movement with traditions and complexity. Alternative media were more likely to seek a broader context which departed from the master narrative, and to access voices otherwise marginalized. For example, Sandy Close, executive editor of Pacific News Service, described three principles of her medium's coverage of the Gulf crisis: cultivating Arab and Muslim voices to provide a broader perspective on the Middle East; exploring the logic of domestic opposition to the war; and monitoring the motives and reality of U.S. intervention (San Francisco Media Alliance, 1991, p. 6).

For the peace movement, this analysis of press framing implies the need to name and identify militarism as a cultural problem, and to take into account the politics of national identity and the influence of the culture's master narrative of war. A long-term task for those advocating a less militarized foreign policy, then, would be either to propose alternative foreign policies which are consistent with a recognizable version of the cultural archetype, or to challenge and replace the archetype itself, a formidable project tantamount to transforming the political culture. In either case, the movement would need to continue building coalitions which transcend purely reactive, negative politics, towards proposing a compelling alternative vision of what America could be.

For journalism, this study implies the need to acknowledge the influence of the master narrative, and of dubious stereotypes of the Vietnam era, on reporting of domestic debates about U.S. foreign and military policy. And for students of international politics, it indicates, as Hallin and Gitlin (1994) suggest, the fruitfulness of analyzing the meanings of war in popular culture as an important part of the landscape within which media and policymakers operate.

REFERENCES

American opinion on the Gulf. (1991, March/April). *The American Enterprise*, 74–87.

Beeman, W. (1991). Renewed debate: covering the aftermath of victory. In Graduate School of Journalism, University of California, Berkeley, The media and the Gulf: A closer look (Conference proceedings, May 3–4, pp. 41–42).

Bennett, W. L. (1994). The news about foreign policy, in W.L. Bennett, & D. L. Paletz, (Eds.), *Taken by storm: The media, public opinion, and U.S. foreign policy in the Gulf War.* Chicago: University of Chicago Press.

Chomsky, N. (1992). The media and the war: What war? In H. Mowlana, G. Gerbner & H. I. Schiller (Eds.), *Triumph of the image: The media's war in the Persian Gulf—a global perspective* (pp. 51–63). Boulder, CO: Westview Press.

Darnovsky, M., Kauffman, L. A., & Robinson, B. (1991). What will this war mean? In M. L. Sifry & C. Cerf (Eds.), *The Gulf War reader* (pp. 480–86). New York: Times Books/Random House.

Dorman, W.A., & Livingston, S. (1994) The establishing phase of the Persian Gulf policy debate. In W.L. Bennett & D.L. Paletz (Eds.), *Taken by storm: The media, public opinion, and U.S. foreign policy in the Gulf War* (pp. 63–81). Chicago: University of Chicago Press.

FAIR [Fairness and Accuracy in Reporting]. (1991). Who appeased Saddam Hitler? *Extra!* 4(3), 10.

Galtung, J. (1987). *United States foreign policy: As manifest theology*. La Jolla, CA: Institute on Global Conflict and Cooperation, University of California at San Diego.

Gitlin, T. (1980). *The whole world is watching: Mass media in the making and unmaking of the New Left*. Berkeley, CA: University of California Press.

Gitlin, T. (1991a, January/February). Dissent crosses the threshold. *Deadline, 6*(1), 7–8.

Gitlin, T. (1991b). Toward a difficult peace movement. In M. L. Sifry & C. Cerf (Eds.), *The Gulf War Reader* (pp. 320–22). New York: Times Books/Random House.

Gitlin, T. (1992). The peace movement, the war movement, the media and democracy. In H. Kreisler (Ed.), *Confrontation in the Gulf: University of California professors talk about the war* (pp. 35–48). Berkeley: University of California, Institute of International Studies.

Hackett, R. A. (1991). *News and dissent: The press and the politics of peace in Canada*. Norwood, NJ: Ablex Publishing Corporation.

Hackett, R. A. (1993a). Structuring the hierarchy of dissent. *Peace Review* 5(1): 19–26.

Hackett, R. A. (1993b). *Engulfed: Peace protest and America's press during the Gulf War*. New York: NYU Center for War, Peace, and the News Media.

Hackett, R. A. & Hissey, L. (1991). Who sets the agenda? Perspectives on media and party politics in Canada. In H.G. Thorburn (Ed.), *Party politics in Canada* (6th ed.). (pp. 42–52). Scarborough, Ontario: Prentice-Hall.

Hackett, R. A. & Zhao, Y. (1994). Challenging a master narrative: peace protest and opinion/editorial discourse in the U.S. press during the Gulf War. *Discourse & Society 5*(4), 509–541.

Hallin, D. & Gitlin, T. (1992, May). Prowess and community: the Gulf War as popular culture and as television drama. Paper presented to International Communication Association, Miami, FL.

Hallin, D. & Gitlin, T. (1994). The Gulf War as popular culture and television drama. In W. L. Bennett & D. L. Paletz (Eds.), *Taken by storm: The media, public opinion, and U.S. foreign policy in the Gulf War* (pp. 149–163). Chicago: University of Chicago Press.

Herman, E.S. (1982). *The real terror network: Terrorism in fact and propaganda*. Boston, MA: South End Press.

Herman, E.S. & Chomsky, N. (1988). *Manufacturing consent: The political economy of the mass media*. New York: Pantheon.

Kalb, M. (1994). A view from the press. In W.L. Bennett & D.L. Paletz (Eds.) *Taken by storm: The media, public opinion, and U.S. foreign policy in the Gulf War* (pp. 3–7). Chicago: University of Chicago Press.

Keen, S., interviewed by Cox, R. (1991). *Propaganda Review, 7*, 19–21.

Kellner, D. (1992). *The Persian Gulf TV war*. Boulder, CO: Westview Press.

Knight, G. (1983, March 24–26). *News of talk, news of riot.* Paper presented to Fifth International conference on Culture and Communication, Philadelphia.

Lakoff, G. (1992). Metaphor and war: The metaphor system used to justify war in the Gulf. In H. Kreisler (Ed.), *Confrontation in the Gulf: University of California professors talk about the war* (pp. 1–19). Berkeley, CA: University of California, Institute of International Studies.

LaMay, C., Fitzsimon, M. & Sahadi, J. (Eds.) (1991). *The media at war: The press and the Persian Gulf conflict.* New York: Gannett Foundation Media Center [now The Freedom Forum].

Lang, G.E. & Lang, K. (1994). Media coverage of Saddam's Iraq, 1979–1990. In W.L. Bennett & D.L. Paletz (Eds.), *Taken by storm: The media, public opinion, and U.S. foreign policy in the Gulf War* (pp. 43–62). Chicago: University of Chicago Press.

MacDermid, R.H. (1992, June 2). Public opinion polling and Canadian involvement in the Gulf War. Paper presented to Canadian Political Science Association, Charlottetown, Prince Edward Island, Canada.

Manheim, J.B. (1994). Managing Kuwait's image during the Gulf conflict. In W.L. Bennett & D.L. Paletz (Eds.), *Taken by storm: The media, public opinion, and U.S. foreign policy in the Gulf War* (pp. 131–148). Chicago: University of Chicago Press.

The media and the Gulf: A closer look. (1991, May 3–4) (Conference proceedings).Graduate School of Journalism, University of California, Berkeley, CA.

Morgan, M., Lewis, J., & Jhally, S. (1992). More viewing, less knowledge. In H. Mowlana, G. Gerbner, & H.I. Schiller (eds.), *Triumph of the image: The media's war in the Persian Gulf—a global perspective* (pp. 216–233). Boulder, CO: Westview Press.

Ruffini, G. (1992). Press failed to challenge the rush to war. In H. Smith (Ed.), *The media and the Gulf War* (pp. 282–287). Washington, D.C.: Foreign Policy Institute of the School of Advanced International Studies, John Hopkins University/Seven Locks Press.

San Francisco Media Alliance. (1991). Covering the war: A MediaFile roundtable. *Media File, 12*(1): 6.

Sivard, R.L. (1985). *World military and social expenditures 1985.* Washington, D.C.: World Priorities.

Smith, H. (1992). *The media and the Gulf War.* Washington, D.C.: Foreign Policy Institute of the School of Advanced International Studies, John Hopkins University/Seven Locks Press.

Walker, R.B.J. (1984). Contemporary militarism and the discourse of dissent. In R.B.J. Walker (Ed.), *Culture, ideology and world order* (pp. 302–322). Boulder, CO: Westview Press.

Williams, P. (1992). Excerpts from remarks to the National Press Club. In H. Smith (Ed.), *The media and the Gulf War.* Washington, DC: Foreign Policy Institute of the School of Advanced International Studies, Johns Hopkins University/Seven Locks Press.

Wright, L. (1989). Peace: Living without enemies. *Rolling Stone,* (560), 54–65, 82–88.

chapter 9

presidential initiatives and foreign news: the Carter human rights policy and coverage of central and South America

Catherine Cassara
Bowling Green State University

INTRODUCTION

W hen President Jimmy Carter took office in January 1977, many U.S. newspapers covered all of Central and South America with one bureau (Lent, 1977; Rosenblum, 1981). The *Washington Post* was no exception. *Post* reporter Karen DeYoung covered all of Central and South America from her paper's bureau in Buenos Aires. By 1978, however, Carter's policy of tying U.S. aid and assistance to the observance of individual human rights had begun to focus particular attention on Latin America, and the *Post* and other news organizations allocated more resources to the region and created new bureaus. For DeYoung it meant the chance to choose her post (K. DeYoung, personal communication, August 6, 1986). She chose to cover Central America, where she made a name for herself as a foreign correspondent.

DeYoung's story highlights an important aspect of the relationship between American foreign policy and foreign news coverage by the major U.S. media—how changes in policy influence coverage. It also suggests an opportunity to look at how one major foreign policy initiative affected coverage of one particular region of the world. Media researchers have frequently looked at the role the media play in setting the public affairs agenda of their audiences, but less attention has been paid to how the media's own agendas are shaped (Rogers, Dearing, and Bregman, 1993).

The topic examined in this chapter offers an opportunity media researchers rarely get—to isolate a particular force and study its effects on coverage. To accomplish that goal, the project studied the coverage of the region in the major papers read by policy makers that are noted for their coverage of foreign events—the *New York Times*, the *Washington Post*, the *Christian Science Monitor*, and the *Los Angeles Times*. The newspapers' content was analyzed to assess the impact of the Carter human rights policy on coverage of Central and South America.

Before those findings are explored, the chapter reviews the contexts in which they can be understood. The first section looks at the theoretical context of the research, while the second reviews the development of the human rights policies—internationally and as an ingredient of U.S. policy. The third section explores some of the challenges and problems facing correspondents who write about human rights. The fourth section briefly reviews the study's research methods. The fifth section looks at the findings of the content analysis and then explores their implications.

THEORETICAL FRAMEWORK

At the heart of the American political system lie two assumptions that provide the underpinnings for the both the role of the press in the process of foreign policy formulation and the role of human rights in that policy. Those assumptions are: the voting public is both capable and worthy of determining the course of U.S. actions and involvements; and, it is the purpose of government to protect the rights of individual citizens, not to abuse them (Cohen, 1963). It is the role of the press to provide the information the public needs in order that it may judge its government's actions, as well as the officials who implement them (Cohen, 1963).

Critics have charged that the press of the First World over-emphasizes coups and earthquakes in its coverage of the Third World (Shanor & Johnston, 1983). This could, in part, result from the pressures on newspaper managers reviewing their commitment of resources to gathering international news coverage. With limited resources to keep correspondents in the field, traditional news criteria would demand the coverage of such obvious news events first. Latin American coups and earthquakes would be enough to fill the limited newshole available for the traditionally under-covered region, which has traditionally received erratic coverage in the U.S. press (Bolling, 1985; McAnany, 1983). Critics have charged that where there was coverage the issues have frequently been misunderstood and misreported (Geyer, 1969–1970). Lippmann (1946) long ago criticized the tendency of the press to spotlight issues with fleeting illumination that does not provide the context Americans need to understand what is really happening.

This research project is part of what McCombs and Shaw identify as agenda setting's fourth phase—research concerned with the sources of the media agenda

(McCombs & Shaw, 1993). It is what Rogers et al (1993) identify as "media agenda setting" as opposed to the more familiar idea that the media shape what people think about—identified as "public agenda setting." A third part of the process, "policy agenda setting," is concerned with the forces that shape policy.

Media agenda setting "includes those studies that conceptualize the mass media news agenda as the main dependent variable of the study" (Rogers et al., 1993). Researchers suggest that the media agenda is shaped by a process of interactions between the news media and their sources. These interactions are shaped by competition between news organizations, by the news handling practices and routines, and the influence of issue interest groups (Rogers, 1993; Shoemaker & Reese, 1991). Certainly, the results of this research project fit neatly into that description.

DEVELOPMENT OF HUMAN RIGHTS POLICIES

The first international effort to protect human rights occurred in the mid-1860s as an attempt to protect people caught up in war. All of the early international efforts concerned themselves with human rights in war time. Each new initiative to expand the protection of those rights generally followed a war (Forsythe, 1983).

If wartime conduct generated the early efforts to protect individual rights, perhaps it is not surprising that the first concerted efforts to protect human rights as they are now understood came at the end of World War II. Those efforts grew out of the Allied belief that Nazi aggression and genocide represented atrocities against the human being and against the international political system itself (Forsythe, 1983, p. 8). As a result, the charter that founded the United Nations in 1945 raised the subject of human rights, and in 1948 the U.N. General Assembly adopted the Universal Declaration of Human Rights. In the years since its adoption, the declaration has been reaffirmed numerous times. By 1980 more than 20 treaties addressed the rights of individuals and groups.

American Foreign Policy and Human Rights

From Jefferson to Lincoln to Wilson, Kirkpatrick (1986) argues, American presidents have concerned themselves with the larger world or withdrawn from it as alliances served or impeded the moral purpose of the underlying democratic principles. Though some presidents and policy makers have tried to combine ethics and power, at other times the concern has been almost exclusively with power and stability (Forsythe, 1983).

Entering the Second World War, President Franklin D. Roosevelt pledged a commitment abroad to four freedoms—freedom of speech, freedom of religion, freedom from want, and freedom from fear. Those freedoms became the cornerstones of the Atlantic Charter, which Britain and the United States signed on Aug. 14, 1941, and laid the foundation for the United Nations War Crimes Commission, which brought Nazi and Japanese leaders to trial for war crimes and crimes against humanity (Frankel & Saideman, 1989).

After the war ended in 1945, President Truman tried to combine ethics and power. The United States was active in the establishment of the United Nations and played a major role in writing the Universal Declaration of Human Rights. Under the leadership of U.S. Ambassador to the United Nations Eleanor Roosevelt and her delegation, the U.N. Commission on Human Rights labored for two years to produce the Universal Declaration, but it took twenty years before human rights surfaced again in U.S. policy. As the horrors of the war faded and the Cold War heated up, international differences arose over human rights definitions. Human rights concerns were dragged out for their propaganda value when it was convenient, but the few activists who pushed for human rights protections were considered unrealistic utopians.

It was not until the 1960s that the situation began to change. Opposition to the Vietnam war focused on U.S. support for the South Vietnamese government, which showed little respect for the human rights of either its prisoners or of its subjects (Schoultz, 1982). And the civil rights movement and the anti-war movement both offered examples of how interest groups could be mobilized, a lesson human rights activists learned.

By 1976, liberal congressmen were concerned about the activities of right-wing dictatorships and conservative congressmen were concerned about Soviet activities (Muravchik, 1986). However, if there was interest in human rights on Capitol Hill, there was next to no interest at the White House. The Nixon-Ford administration foreign policy focused on power and the few State Department diplomats designated as human rights officers were chosen not for their ability to do anything about the problem but rather for their ability to counter criticism from the public and Congress (Schoultz, 1982, p. 307).

The Carter Administration

Human rights became a serious issue in domestic politics for the first time in the 1976 presidential campaign. The human rights issue provided Carter with a popular cause that echoed his strongly-held feelings about the need for renewed commitment to morality and ethics in foreign policy. Even after the election, polls continued to show the strong public approval for his stand (Muravchik, 1986). In his inaugural address, Carter stressed that human rights would be the "soul" of his foreign policy.

It was now clear to American diplomats that human rights had become an issue they must consider. It took six months or more before an implementation pattern began to emerge and, when it did, critics charged it was inconsistent and frequently less than effective (Muravchik, 1986). However they felt about the policy, experts agreed that human rights had for the first time assumed an unparalleled prominence in foreign policy. This shift in national policy had side effects, particularly for the non-profit groups pressing for human rights protections. Amnesty International, the Washington Office for Latin America, and the myriad of labor, religious and other groups monitoring rights abuses became valid and valued sources of information and publicity for rights efforts (Forsythe, 1983).

Carter's appointments to human rights positions were one of the strongest indications that his policy was meant to have teeth. His appointees became a formidable force in policy implementation, overseeing all aid proposals for countries with records of rights violations. The most significant appointment Carter made was naming Patricia Derian to head the State Department's newly-formed Bureau of Human Rights and Humanitarian Affairs. A strong willed, civil rights activist, she set the tone of the bureau's activities. Under her leadership, the bureau focused on building its staff and expanding its expertise in specific policy areas such as foreign aid, but also persisted in its pursuit of direct bilateral diplomacy on behalf of human rights—both inside the State Department bureaucracy and directly with leaders of repressive governments (Schoultz, 1981). Once established within the bureaucratic network, Derian's bureau was an insistent and dreaded opponent of agencies pushing for aid free of human rights considerations.

The early focus of the administration's human rights concerns was the Soviet Union. Shortly after he took office, President Carter made a series of statements about Soviet denial of human rights. The Soviet response suggested that the Soviet leadership did not take kindly to public chastisement over its internal affairs, particularly in the area of alleged human rights abuses. Thus, it became clear early on that if the administration sought any productive relationship with the Soviets, its lobbying for Russian Jews and dissidents would have to occur out of the public view. As a result, the administration quickly learned that where major strategic relations with large powers were concerned human rights might not always be the most important policy consideration (Muravchik, 1986). Latin America was a very different story, however.

With the exceptions of Brazil and Panama, the region had never been of particular concern to large numbers of Americans. When Carter assumed the presidency, U.S. strategic interests in the area were at an all time low (Schoultz, 1981). But if there was no overwhelming strategic interest at stake in Latin America, there was a moral interest. Reports of U.S. involvement in the Allende overthrow in Chile and support for the repressive Pinochet regime in Argentina upset many Americans (Schoultz, 1981).

Many countries in Latin America had traditions of human rights violations. American policy makers before Carter acknowledged this, but took no action. Instead, they often viewed human rights violations in the region as an inherent shortcoming of Hispanic political culture or as regrettable excesses that responsible Latin American officials were powerless to halt (Schoultz, 1981, p. 6). It was clear by the mid-1970s, however, that the repressive regimes developed in response to growing political participation by populist interests, which threatened the supremacy of the ruling elites. Faced with repression and the loss of power and self-determination, the populists fought back with strikes, slowdowns, and demonstrations, which the regimes countered with more repression (Schoultz, 1982).

Argentina and Uruguay were among the countries which suffered the first Carter aid cuts in 1977 because of their human rights records. Carter's secretary of state went to a meeting of the Organization of American States to rebut the contention that human rights abuses are a necessary by-product of the war against terrorism

(Muravchik, 1986). The level of human rights violations accompanying political repression had risen so dramatically that Congress acted to limit the types of aid that could be provided.

The administration used four principal foreign policy tools to reduce levels of human rights violations: military aid, economic aid, multilateral development bank loans, and private economic transactions. Requests for military assistance worldwide remained level between federal fiscal years 1977 and 1979, but Latin America's share of the total dropped from 8.1 percent to 2.3 percent (Schoultz, 1981). By the end of 1978, aid reductions affected many countries in the region, and some chose not to request aid and thus avoid censure. In other cases, the agencies within the U.S. government stopped asking for aid when they thought either Derian's bureau or the liberal members of Congress would put up a fight (Schoultz, 1982).

In 1977, the State Department delayed the release of funds to the Somoza government in Nicaragua because of its human rights violations, and in 1978 placed a complete ban on military aid to that country. By 1978, Congress and the administration had reached agreement that bilateral economic assistance to Latin American countries was to be halted or reduced to countries with bad human rights records, unless the aid could be shown to directly benefit needy people. U.S. economic assistance to Chile fell from $93.7 million in 1975 to $5.8 million in 1978, and by the end most of that aid was in the form of Food For Peace funding (Schoultz, 1981). From the Ford administration's $220,000 assistance to Uruguay in 1977, the Carter administration cut its aid request to $25,000 for 1978 (Schoultz, 1981).

By the 1979 federal fiscal year—the first budget request for which the Carter administration could be held fully responsible—the distribution pattern of U.S. economic aid to Latin America had changed dramatically. Aid programs to nations with relatively repressive regimes like those of Bolivia, Guatemala and Haiti had been cut and been redesigned to reach only the neediest social sectors in these countries. Aid to Chile and Nicaragua had dropped precipitously and substantial increases had been recommended for relatively non-repressive governments (Schoultz, 1981).

As aid was reduced, the U.S. government's influence over offending nations was also reduced, which led to a change of policy philosophy. Begun as an effort to dissuade offending governments from human rights violations, the aid reductions came to be seen as a means of disassociating the American government from the offenses (Muravchik, 1986). By 1978, aid was being given to showcase countries like Costa Rica and Jamaica, and bilateral aid had become a minor instrument of U.S. policy toward Latin America.

The administration was less adamant in its stand against repressive nations when it came to the multilateral development banks. It nonetheless adopted a policy of using its influence to promote greater respect for fundamental human rights in the banks and, if nothing else, served to deter loan applications by Latin America's most repressive governments (Schoultz, 1982). In the private sector, the Carter administration exercised little clout. Business interests in good investments meant that the most stable governments, most likely to facilitate repayment on investments, were the most attractive to business interests. In Latin America this generally meant the most repressive countries. In several Latin American countries, the 1970s ended with a somewhat improved human rights picture. The overthrow of Somoza in Nicaragua, encouraged if not facilitated by American aid cuts, and improved conditions in Brazil were the most hopeful signs. Incidents of torture, political arrests, harassment of returning exiles, kidnapping and disappearances of Argentinean and Uruguayan exiles in Brazil continued, but were viewed as exceptions to a larger trend toward greater respect for human rights (Schoultz, 1981). In the Dominican Republic about 200 political prisoners were granted amnesty by a new government, though Amnesty International reported in late 1979 that some were still being held.

For a brief period in late 1979 both the U.S. State Department and Amnesty International agreed that for the first time in living memory there were no political prisoners in Bolivian jails. States of siege, special security measures or similar legislation were in force in Argentina, Brazil, Chile, Colombia, Paraguay, Uruguay, and periodically in El Salvador and Peru. Political murder and torture, sometimes by security forces or paramilitary death squads, were widespread (Amnesty International, 1980, 1979).

The situation got worse, not better, in Argentina. Torture, disappearances, and kidnapping continued. In 1979 Amnesty International accused the Videla government of the disappearances—or political murder—of 15,000 to 20,000 citizens and of the detainment of 3,000 political prisoners. Other estimates of the number of disappeared by 1979 ranged from 6,500 to 10,000 (Amnesty International, 1979; Schoultz, 1981). The end of the decade saw little significant change in Chile. Uruguay still had the highest number of political prisoners per capita in the Western Hemisphere. In Guatemala there were few political prisoners, but few prisoners were taken alive (Schoultz, 1981).

The Reagan Administration

Under Ronald Reagan human rights concerns were no longer the "soul" of American foreign policy. The Reagan policy makers saw their goals as fighting terrorism and fighting Soviet-led communism. Ernest Lefever, Reagan's first nominee to replace Derian, made clear in his testimony to the Senate Foreign Relations Committee that he conceived of human rights as a weapon against communism (Forsythe, 1990). He noted that authoritarian regimes on the right would be dealt with differently because they were anti-communist. In part because of opposition to his views and in part because of ethical issues raised by money he had taken from Nestle and the South African government, Lefever's nomination was withdrawn. The administration eventually nominated Elliott Abrams, whose stance was simply a more polished version of Lefever's.

At the United Nations, the administration was outspoken in its attacks on human rights violations by communist nations, and equally outspoken in its defense of authoritarian allies like Chile, Argentina and Guatemala. The double standard on human rights guided policy between 1981 and 1985. Not only did the Reagan administration not reduce aid to non-communist countries with bad human rights records, it worked as closely as possible with countries like South Africa, Chile, and Argentina.

The Reagan policies were frequently challenged at home and abroad. The administration's policies on South Africa's activities against Angola were challenged by Western European nations. Mexico and France challenged U.S. policies supporting the regime in El Salvador and instead recognized the legitimacy of opposition. With other countries, Mexico and France also called attention to the long history of Salvadorian human rights violations and refused to sweep them under the rug. At home, Congress fought a running series of battles with the administration over human rights, from the Lefever nomination to the administration's policies regarding specific nations and international agreements on human rights (Forsythe, 1990). The bipartisan majority in Congress not only objected to administration policy, it went further to pass general and specific legislation that addressed human rights issues abroad, forcing the administration's compliance, this in spite of Republican control of Congress and the president's undoubted popularity.

HUMAN RIGHTS REPORTING

Atrocities and other rights violations have been the stuff of foreign coverage since its early days, but according to Rosenblum (1979) by the mid-1970s the reporting of human rights had become a distinct genre of its own. Rosenblum's story and an update shed light on the many difficulties facing a journalist covering human rights issues (Rosenblum, 1993).

As an Associated Press reporter based in Buenos Aires, Rosenblum got his own introduction to human rights reporting in 1975 when he had a luncheon meeting with the FBI agent who served as the legal attache at the American Embassy. The agent told Rosenblum that Argentine security agents dumped suspected guerrillas into the sea from helicopters. He said they preferred to drop their victims alive because on impact they would breathe in water and sink like stones (Rosenblum, 1979). The agent also connected the secret police with the kidnapping and torture deaths of Uruguayan dissidents and guerrillas in Argentina. He said he had been offered a Uruguayan child, because the security police didn't know what do with the two they had orphaned.

Coming from a trusted source and just after the 1976 military coup, the information was big news for Rosenblum. For the first time, it connected Argentine officials to the "right-wing terrorists" who had been systematically eliminating leftists since before the overthrow of Isabel Peron. With the information the first source gave him, Rosenblum (1979) got other sources to talk, but none wanted to be quoted. In the end, he got most of the information on the AP wire one way or another. However, because it had to be couched so carefully with qualifiers and ritual government denials, only experienced readers would have been able to decipher its real impact. Other correspondents had their own sources, but the same problems. The result was vague allegations of terrorism by the police and military attributed to mysterious outsiders denounced by the government as an embarrassment to the country. The upshot was that "for long afterward, the Argentine military government retained its moderate image" (Rosenblum, 1979, p. 195).

One of the major challenges facing reporters covering human rights issues is verifying their stories. "When reporters accuse officials of mass murder, torture or flagrant violation of their constitutions, it is not enough for them to be sure in their own minds. They must back up their assertions with specific attribution and supporting detail" (Rosenblum, 1979). But the facts of the story are not easy to come by since the people who commit the torture or murder are hardly willing to discuss their activities with reporters. Victims are good sources, but the reporter has to be sure that such testimony is not faked. And while people with access to information about rights violations can be valuable sources, to protect their own lives they are nearly always anonymous.

And sources are not the only people who can be threatened. A *New York Times* correspondent who began to investigate discreetly when the Argentine death squads first appeared, received a call warning him that pursuing the story would be dangerous for him. Conferring with his editors, the reporter concluded that writing the story would mean he would have to leave Argentina, so he waited until he was leaving anyway and then ran the story.

Publish and be damned is an admirable credo for societies in which disputes are settled with libel suits and negotiations, but it is hardly practical in a country where letters to the editors are often in the form of car bombs and machine-gun bursts (Rosenblum, 1979, 196).

Sometimes correspondents encounter problems at home. Raymond Bonner's promising career as a reporter with the *New York Times* was cut short by the reaction to a story he wrote about a 1981 massacre in the Salvadorian village of El Mozote. The massacre was committed by government troops trained by American military advisors, who entered the village, opened fire on its residents, and then torched the homes. Estimates of the casualties range between 733 and 926. Bonner and Alma Guillermoprieto, of the *Washington Post*, independently traveled to the village, interviewed survivors, and gathered corroborating evidence and filed their stories.

At home their stories met harsh criticism from U.S. government officials and from other American media—particularly, the *Wall Street Journal*. Bonner was charged with letting his personal ideology govern his writing rather than the facts and it was suggested that perhaps his coverage gave more credence to communists than American officials (Rosenblum, 1993). The furor hurt both reporters personally and professionally—even their own editors questioned the credibility of their work. In 1992, forensic archaeologists working near the village found evidence that confirmed that the reporters' stories had been accurate.

Sometimes heated disagreements arise because there is no general agreement on what should be covered, and for what purpose. Some newspeople feel it is a social responsibility to draw attention to abuses, particularly in countries which receive American aid. Others suggest that human rights violations are par for the course in developing countries and covering them is "belaboring the obvious"(Rosenblum, 1979).

Patterns of interest in human rights are even more spotty than coverage of foreign news in general. A high profile case involving one or two people may get more attention than systematic problems that affect thousands. As a result, few Americans have any real idea of how a particular government abuses human rights, or how widespread the violations are (Rosenblum, 1979).

One of the major problems is the terminology itself. "Human rights" by itself means little, as do torture or arrest, and it falls to the correspondent to provide the context. Every police force in the world may at one time or another handle suspects roughly, but "a sharp elbow in the ribs hardly compares with the systematic use of dental drills on good teeth or alternately gang raping and electroshocking women prisoners chained to an iron bed-frame" (Rosenblum, 1979). The constant use of such words and phrases such as "torture," "human rights abuses," and "arbitrary arrest" may blur the subject and numb readers.

When they file stories based on government reports, correspondents may some-times be aware that it is unlikely that things happened exactly the way they are report-ed. A questionable domestic police account in a U.S. paper could be balanced by challenges from defense attorneys or witnesses. The same is not true of accounts of events in countries where a witness would be crazy to talk and there is no one repre-senting the "guerrillas" (Rosenblum, 1979). Frequently, correspondents are powerless to do anything short of including enough of the erroneous detail so as to shed doubt on the story. For those details to mean anything to a reader, however, they have to survive trimming and make it into the paper.

Governments seeking to deflect attention from their human rights records are quick to find and call attention to the slightest errors or discrepancies in reporting, so reporters must check every detail they use. The loss of credibility that results from a reporting error hurts not only the correspondent and his or her news organization, but also all successive attempts to cover the rights abuses. Certainly reporters writing about human rights after accusations against Bonner found the going harder.

The problems aside, Rosenblum says more—and better—human rights reporting in the mid-1970s had a snowball effect, creating more interest in the subject and more space for coverage. It had its drawbacks, however. Security forces learned from others' mistakes and made a point of leaving fewer victims around to talk. On the other side, increased coverage meant reporters and editors were paying more attention to the inter-national organizations monitoring rights violations (Rosenblum, 1979).

The change of administrations from Ford to Carter had significant impact on human rights coverage. At the insistence of Congress and President Carter, the U.S. State Department revealed more information about human rights abuses abroad. Embassies were ordered to pay close attention to the subject, and desk officers in Washington made new contacts with experts in the field. "Administration officials at times were brutally forthright in criticizing abuses, giving reporters legitimate pegs to write at length on the subject" (Rosenblum, 1979, p. 202).

RESEARCH METHODS

The study set out to assess the impact of the Carter policy on foreign news coverage. While there was anecdotal evidence of an impact from DeYoung and others, the goal of the research was to see what effect that impact had on the paper's coverage. The research centered on a content analysis—a systematic study of specific characteristics of news coverage. For this study, the relevant content was the coverage of Central and South America in newspapers relied on by decision makers and journalists alike as the standard for foreign coverage—the *New York Times*, the *Washington Post*, *Christian Science Monitor*, and the *Los Angeles Times* (Cohen, 1963; Henry, 1984).

Since the purpose of the study was to look at the impact of the Carter policy, it was important to look not only at the coverage during his presidency but also before and after. Therefore, the study looks at coverage over an eight-year period—from 1975 before Carter's election through 1982—Reagan's second year in office. Because it would be very difficult to look at every story during that time, the study adopted an approach used by researchers studying newspaper content, which provides a small sample of coverage that is representative of the whole (Riffe et al., 1993; Stempel, 1955).

The result was a sample of 641 stories from eight years. Those stories were analyzed and note was made of a number of things, including their origin, length, author, topic, how prominently the newspaper ran them, and whether they had a human rights theme or mentioned human rights. Once the data was gathered it was analyzed in an attempt to answer the questions raised by the research hypotheses that the policy produced increases in coverage and increase depth in the coverage of the region.

FINDINGS

The results of the study support the suggestion that the Carter policy initiative had an impact on the coverage of Central and South America. Over the years of the study the number of stories written about the region increased. And the number of stories and the amount of space given to stories that dealt with human rights issues also increased. In addition, the stories devoted to human rights issues tended to be longer than stories about non-human rights subjects.

While the number of stories about the region and the amount of space given to its coverage increased, they did not increase in a straight line. There was an early peak in coverage of the region in 1976 and then the number of stories about the region dropped a bit and hit a plateau in 1977 and 1978. By 1979, however, the number of stories had begun to increase and it increased again in 1980, dropped slightly in 1981 and took off again in 1982. Equally important, however, is how much space coverage was given— the number of square inches devoted to coverage. Those figures tell a slightly different story. They also show an early peak in 1976 and a slight dip in 1977, but from 1978 on they show a steady increase over the rest of the study.

But it is not enough to address whether coverage of the region increased. For the research to find an impact of the Carter policy, there must also be changes in coverage of human rights, and there are, though again there are some peaks and dips. This time there is a peak in the number of human rights stories in 1977 and a dip in 1978 an increase in 1979 and a peak again in 1980 followed by another peak in 1982. This time, the peaks in the number of stories mirror the peaks in the space given to coverage.

Breaking the coverage down by short, medium and long stories, there are also interesting differences between coverage that deals with human rights and coverage that doesn't—differences that suggest better reporting. Over the years covered by the study, the length of the stories written about the region increased, as did the number of sources the reporters cited in their stories. In addition, human rights stories tended to run longer and to use more sources than did other stories. They were also more likely to originate with the newspapers' own staff writers than they were to come from the wire services. These are important characteristics. Better coverage of a subject tends to be coverage that is longer, has more depth, cites more sources and provides the reader with more information.

If coverage of the region increased over the period in question, coverage focused on human rights increased, and the space devoted to coverage increased, then the research findings support the research hypothesis. The results support the conclusion that Carter policy initiative focused more attention on the region, cleared the way for more coverage of human rights, and with that attention came measurable changes in the caliber of the reporting from the region. All of the relationships—longer coverage for human rights subjects, the increased use of sources in stories about the region, the use of more sources for reporting about human rights—are confirmed by statistical tests, which were significant at the level of p=.000.

The findings suggest no significant difference in how the papers covered human rights subjects. The patterns of their coverage devoted to human rights were similar. Even the average lengths of the stories the papers ran were similar. There were larger coverage differences, however. The *New York Times* devoted more effort to covering the region. In the study sample, the *Times* ran 230 stories about the region and devoted the most space to that coverage, in all 4,424 square inches. The *Times* also sent out more correspondents. Over years of the study, the number of *Times* correspondent names found in bylines on the stories from the region ranged from 2 to 8 and averaged 5.5.

The *Washington Post* came next, both in the number of stories about Central and South America—186—and in space given over to the region—3,602 square inches. The *Post* had from 1 to 7 different staff bylines during the years of the study and averaged 3.1 correspondents. The *Los Angeles Times* was next, with 151 stories, 3,001 square inches and an average of 2.5 correspondents. The *Christian Science Monitor*, which published only five days a week in contrast to the others' seven-day publishing schedule, had 74 stories, 2,063 square inches and averaged 1.7 correspondents. It should be noted, that all four papers had fewer correspondents in the region in 1975 than were there by the last years of the study.

DISCUSSION

The story of the dips, plateaus and peaks of the graphs that chart the relationships between the study's variables are facets of the complex relationships between news coverage and foreign policy that lend credence to the study results. Carter administration officials ran into some problems as they tried to implement their policies. Reporters covering human rights also ran into trouble. In both cases, the forces behind the problems were the countries subjected to the spotlight of the government and media attention. As noted earlier, faced with aid cuts for human rights violations, some countries cut themselves off from U.S. help, thus also cutting the U.S. government's leverage over their affairs. And, faced with reporters covering their human rights abuses, governments fought back on that front. Rather than allow reporters to interview survivors of human rights abuses, some governments started making sure there were no survivors. They also mounted publicity campaigns aimed at discrediting the reporters or the reports of abuses and or threatened correspondents. Both the government and the correspondents adapted and found new ways to address their concerns, but the result was fluctuations in policy implementation and coverage.

While events occurring in Central and South America during the period obviously play a role in coverage fluctuations, the important thing to remember is that human rights violations and political unrest were ongoing in the region before during and after the Carter presidency, but the increases in coverage of human rights came only after the administration focused media attention in that direction.

Systematic research often finds results the researcher was not expecting and answering the questions raised by those unexplained results often points researchers toward another project. That is certainly the case here. The literature, theoretical context and history explained why the coverage of human rights should have increased over the course of the Carter presidency. They also explain why coverage of the region and the subject of human rights would persist after Carter left office, but they may not so readily explain the occurrence of an all time high in human rights coverage during the second year of the Reagan presidency, since as the earlier section pointed out the Reagan administration did its best to put human rights issues on a back burner when it came to foreign policy. By 1982, events in Central America were heating up again and, while Reagan was not a great proponent of human rights enforcement, perhaps the Carter policies had legitimized the subject and made rights-monitoring groups routine sources for the reporters and editors.

CONCLUSIONS

While the purpose of this study was to explore the connection between the Carter human rights policy and newspaper coverage of Central and South America, the larger goal was to examine one aspect of the interaction of presidential foreign policy initiatives and American press coverage of foreign news. Thus, while the findings support the idea that the Carter policy influenced newspapers' coverage of the region, they also suggest dynamics and interactions in the relationship that might be considered in other studies of the relationship between foreign policy and coverage.

Both the anecdotal accounts of the correspondents working in the region and the results of the quantitative study highlight the interdependence of the correspondents and bureaucrats involved in the development of the policy and its ramifications. Not only were human rights violations common occurrences in Latin America, reporters were trying to cover them with limited success before Carter took office. After he took office, U.S. policy was concerned with human rights and the government offices concerned with oversight were beefed up. Bureaucrats were available and interested in talking about rights concerns, government officials would go on the record. And, in a climate of concern, non-governmental groups concerned with human rights took on new importance. So, reporters had sources for their stories, editors believed those stories were newsworthy, and human rights sources in and out of government became "routinized."

Thus, while reporters may have been interested in human rights before the president's initiative, the initiative itself cleared the way for increased coverage. In addition, once there were more correspondents covering the area there were more opportunities to do in depth reporting of the kind involved in human rights coverage because there were more people to share the burden of covering breaking news. Increased resources meant increased coverage of all kinds, though particular attention was paid to human rights. This highlights the importance of understanding how foreign policy affects foreign coverage, particularly because it suggests that some of the most important impacts may be how policy affects the newsgathering process itself.

REFERENCES

Amnesty International. (1979). *Amnesty International Report 1979*. Amnesty International. (1980, January). Newsletter.

Bolling, L. R. (Ed.). (1985). *Reporters under fire: U.S. media coverage of conflicts in Lebanon and Central America*. Boulder: Westview.

Cohen, B. C. (1963). *The press and foreign policy*. Princeton, NJ: Princeton.

Forsythe, D. P. (1983). *Human rights and world politics*. Lincoln, NE: University of Nebraska.

Forsythe, D. P. (1990). Human rights in U.S. foreign policy: Retrospect and prospect. *Political Science Quarterly, 104*(3), 435–454.

Frankel, M. E. & Saideman, E. (1989). *Out of the shadows of night: The struggle for international human rights*. New York: Delacorte.

Geyer, G. A. (1969-1970, Winter). Latin America: The making of an uncontinent. *Columbia Journalism Review,* 49–53.

Henry, W. A. (1984, 30 April). The ten best U.S. dailies. *Time,* pp. 58–63.

Kirkpatrick, J. (1986) Introduction. In J. Muravchik, *The uncertain crusade: Jimmy Carter and the dilemmas of humn rights policy*. Lanham, MD: Hamilton.

Lent, J. A. (1977, Winter). Foreign news in American media. *Journal of Communication, 27,* 46–51.

Lippmann, W. (1946). *Public opinion*. New York: Pelican Books.

McAnany, E. (1983). Television and crisis: Ten years of network coverage of Central America. *Media, Culture and Society, 5,* 199–212.

McCombs, M. E. & Shaw, D. L. (1993, Spring). The evolution of agenda-setting research: Twenty-five years in the marketplace of ideas. *Journal of Communication, 43*(2), 58–67.

Muravchik, J. (1986). *The uncertain crusade*. Lanham, M.D.: Hamilton Press.

Riffe, D., Aust, C.F. & Lacy, S.R. (1993, Spring). The effectiveness of random, consecutive day and constructive week sampling in newspaper content analysis. *Journalism Quarterly*, 70, 133–139.

Rogers, E. M., Dearing, J.W. & Bregman, D. (1993, Spring). The anatomy of agenda-setting research. *Journal of Communication, 43*(2) 68–84.

Rosenblum, M. (1979). *Coups and earthquakes: Reporting the world for America*. New York: Harper & Row.

Rosenblum, M. (1981). Reporting from the Third World. In J. Richstad & M. Anderson (Eds.), *Crisis in international news: Policies and prospects*. New York: Columbia University.

Rosenblum, M. (1993). *Who stole the news? Why we can't keep up with what happens in the world and what we can do about it*. New York: John Wiley & Sons.

Schoultz, L. (1981). *Human rights and United States policy toward Latin America*. Princeton, N.J.: Princeton University.

Schoultz, L. (1982). The Carter administration and human rights in Latin America. In M. Crahan (Eds.), *Human rights and basic needs in the Americas*. Washington, D.C.: Georgetown University.

Shanor, D. & Johnston, D.H. (Ed.). (1983). *Third World news in American media: Experience and prospects*. New York: Columbia University.

Shoemaker, P. J. & Reese, S. (1991). *Mediating the message: Theories of influence on mass media content*. New York: Longman.

Stempel, G. H. III. (1955, Winter). Sample size for classifying subject matter in dailies. *Journalism Quarterly*, 60, 449–455.

chapter 10

global news and domestic needs: reflections and adaptations of world information to fit national policies and audience needs

Rebecca Carrier
East Carolina University

I n the last four decades, scholars, journalists, and international policy-makers have debated the dangers and merits of the global news system. Painted in the broadest strokes, this debate champions on one side the advantages of a global system where news is supplied by multiple agencies to a network of satellites which, in turn, make vast amounts of information available to every national broadcaster in the world. This position assumes national broadcasters are capable of and responsible for selecting and repackaging information to best suit their conceptions of domestic needs (Gurevitch, 1991). However, on the other side of the debate are arguments about control and regulation of the network of satellites, equality in and access to the global information system, as well as national control of news production. Those who argue against the advantages of the global system (e.g., Mowlana, 1993; Pavlic & Hamelink, 1985; Schiller, 1976) assert Western powers monopolize this information system and damage the development plans and cultures of nations that wield less power in the global information system.

Although the two sides disagree on the effects of the global information system, they both agree that news is culturally dependent (Larson, 1984; McPhail, 1987; Nimmo & Combs, 1990; Sussman & Lent, 1991). As such, news is both product and producer of the culture in which it is consumed. Media scholars such as Altheide and

Snow (1979), Blumbler (1989), Nimmo and Combs (1985) explain that through topic selection, amount of coverage, and narrative interpretation news reflects social, professional, and political conditions.

However, despite this agreement about the interdependency of news and culture, there is much disagreement about which culture global news reflects. Such disagreement is born out of two separate domains of research; the first involves theories of globalization and is reflected in the work of the MacBride roundtables. The second is news content research that postulates how news is adapted to domestic audiences.

GLOBALIZATION THEORY AND DOMESTICATION THEORY

In the first domain, the thesis of globalization is maintained through three important lines of work exemplified in the MacBride roundtables. First is the economic analysis that explains why lesser developed countries are dependent upon the global system, despite Western domination of that system (Pavlic & Hamelink, 1985). Second is the technological analysis that describes how lesser developed nations not only have to rely upon the global system, but also have little input because they lack the technologies to compete with more sophisticated Western media products (Golding & Murdock, 1991). And third is the culturally based analysis that asserts those who control the media exert unfair influence to shape and define the societies of those most dependent upon international media products (Schiller, 1976). This influence, globalization theorists claim, harms the development plans of smaller nations because it constructs these nations in terms of coups and earthquakes, ignoring the rich cultures of their societies. These three lines of work in globalization theory generally ignore the content of news messages in favor of economic, technological, and cultural critiques of news production.

In direct opposition to the domain of globalization scholarship are the researchers who compare news content across countries. Agreeing with globalization theorists that news is culturally dependent and that the world information system is largely controlled by Western powers, these researchers are interested in how news is adapted to local cultures despite these conditions. Scholars who focus upon comparisons of international news content generally argue that there are differences in national broadcasts of world news, and these differences exist because broadcasters do not act merely as relay stations. Instead, they recreate and restructure information to fit national cultures. This view stands in direct opposition to that of globalization because it asserts that news content differs from country to country, despite the Western domination of the world information system and the interdependence of news and culture.

These competing research domains give rise to the central question of this chapter: To what extent are national policies and local audience needs reflected or obscured by use and adaptation of stories and pictures about the Gulf War from the global news system? Because news and culture are interdependent, national newscasts should reflect local institutional and social practices. When national broadcasts fail to reflect local interests and especially when they emphasize news that conflicts with local culture, then worrisome effects of globalization may be discerned.

GULF WAR NEWS AS A UNIQUE RESEARCH OPPORTUNITY

The Gulf War presents a unique opportunity to observe the tensions between globalization and domestication of news because it allows researchers to compare national newscasts about a single world event. As other scholars have found, news agendas vary widely from country to country on any given day. Hence, direct comparison of news across national boundaries is often impossible. However, the Gulf War was a universally important story. Marked as the lead story and receiving detailed coverage, the Gulf War was covered in nearly every nation as the most important story during each newscast during the first week of the conflict (Swanson & Smith, 1993). As a result, pictures and scripts received from the global news system were available and important to nearly every national broadcast system. Because of its universal coverage, the Gulf War allows direct, detailed comparison of news content across nations to test the hypotheses of globalization in the content of international news.

In addition to its saturation coverage, the Gulf War, unlike other newsworthy events such as natural disasters, allows researchers to observe how national sentiments may be obscured or reflected by use of the global news system. The nature of war places nations in conflict with one another, and their national interests can be contrasted with those of countries they oppose. The Gulf War presents a unique opportunity to observe how supporters of the coalition forces might construct national newscasts differently than those produced by the news systems from nations that supported Iraq during the war. If such differences are found, then they will provide evidence that news is adapted from the global system to fit local needs. However, if newscasts are much the same despite the differences in national positions in the war, then the case for globalization is strengthened.

METHODS

Broadcasts from seven different national news organizations were compared in a three-step process. First a micro level analysis was conducted to describe news agendas, source attribution, and video usage. Second, a macro level analysis was used to generate a grand narrative that described in the most general terms what each broadcaster presented as the overall story the first week of the war. And third, exemplary stories were chosen to illustrate how similarities and differences between broadcasters best illustrate the tensions of producing local news from a global information system.

In the first step, a micro level analysis was conducted to determine the degree to which each broadcaster relied upon the global system to generate its news. Each newscast was divided into story units, and an agenda-setting study was conducted to determine which stories dominated each newscast. A source analysis revealed the degree to which each broadcaster relied upon foreign versus domestic news informants to corroborate stories. Third, the amount of internally versus externally produced video was compared to determine how much each broadcaster relied upon globally disseminated video to produce its stories. The results of these procedures were used to substantiate and check the reliability of the following macro level analysis.

The macro level analysis was created by synthesizing stories about the war in each national broadcast into a grand narrative about the first week of the Gulf War. First, stories were summarized into single topic sentences. Second, these summaries were taken together to generalize an entire day's newscast. And third, each day's story about the war was combined so that a grand narrative would describe, in the most general terms, what each broadcaster presented as the story about what happened during the first week of the conflict. The grand narrative was then tested against each individual story to assure no contradictions occurred.

While the overall story each broadcaster told about the first week of the war produces some evidence for the tensions between globalization and domestication, observing particular differences in the way each nation treated individual stories provides an even clearer illustration of the effects of the global system on producing national news. Hence, two stories were selected to best represent more specific content differences and similarities among national broadcasters. Stories about Iraqi missile attacks on Israel and stories about Iraqi treatment of POW's were selected to give more specific insight to the similarities and differences in national broadcasts. Although space limitations prevent a detailed narrative analysis of these stories, comparing even their largest story elements lends important insight to how national policy is or is not reflected in the content.

Seven National Broadcasters and Their Stories

Broadcasters from the United States, United Kingdom, Germany, Chile, Malaysia, India, and Jordan were chosen for this analysis because they differ in both their broadcast systems and their national representation in the Gulf War. CBS (U.S.), BBC (U.K.), and ZDF (Germany) represent broadcast systems that play important roles in global information system. Television Nacional (Chile), TV3 (Malaysia), Doordarshan (India), and Jordan Radio and T.V. all represent developing nations that relied heavily upon the global system for their news about the Gulf War. In addition, these broadcasters represent nations that varied in their degree of participation and cultural interests in the war. While the U.S. and U.K. represented the strongest coalition interest and support in the Gulf, Jordan clearly sided with the Iraqis. Germany officially supported the coalition efforts, but German public opinion was much more mixed than public opinion in the U.S. or U.K. Both Malaysia and India had mixed cultural interests in the Gulf War because each has significant Muslim populations, though the official national position was to side with the coalition.

These differences are important to both the claims of globalization scholars and news content researchers. The following analysis uses the Gulf War as an opportunity to examine how national news differs and degree to which cultural and social institutions are reflected or obscured by use of global stories as they were used in the U.S., U.K., Germany, Chile, Malaysia, India, and Jordan.

United States CBS

The United States CBS broadcast was selected because it represents national news from a highly developed country with a media system that operates in a very competitive commercial market. The importance of television as an information source is marked by the large number of television sets owned by the population. Americans own one set for every 1.3 citizens, and 98% of all U.S. households own at least one television, compared to two radios per person and a newspaper circulation of 255 per 1000 population (*World Almanac*, 1994).

The media are privately owned and operate under minimal government regulation. There are three major terrestrial national broadcasters: CBS, ABC, and NBC. These national broadcasters are supported by advertising and offer daily national newscasts. Additionally, there are national direct news broadcasters such as C-Span and CNN offered through national cable television, which are not a part of the free broadcast system and are supported by cable fees. Supplementing the national broadcasters and cable networks is public television, which is supported by grants and contributions. Public television offers news programs and commentaries such as *The MacNeil/Lehrer News Hour*. Together, national broadcasters, cable, and public television are the foundation of U.S. television news.

The CBS broadcast was selected because it is a dominant producer of news in the global information system, and as such, it is expected to help guide the global definition of Gulf War stories. If the globalization view is demonstrated, then other nations should mimic CBS's interpretation of Gulf events and few differences between other national broadcasts and CBS news should exist. However, if domestication theorists are correct, then important differences between the U.S. position and other national roles in the war might influence CBS content in ways not reflected in other national newscasts. The U.S. held the unique position of being the leader in the coalition efforts. Domestication theorists would argue that this unique leadership position should be reflected in news content by having more coverage of the war, topics that favor U.S. leadership in the coalition efforts, and greater use of U.S. sources.

CBS's war narrative.   In CBS's war story, the United States is supported by the coalition of United Nations forces in its efforts to free Kuwait from Iraq's wrongful control. This narrative is supported in a complex mix of stories that both reflect the duality of conflict as well as the tradition of war news coverage. On one hand, the United States as the leader of coalition forces is undertaking the noble mission of freeing Kuwait, and together the coalition of nations is succeeding against the Iraqis in this effort. On the other hand, Iraq is a formidable opponent who makes this a dangerous and complicated mission for U.S. and coalition fighting forces. The injustice of Iraq's control of Kuwait coupled with its military power make this a righteous and heroic duty for the

U.S. as a leader and protector of the "new world order." Additionally, worldwide support for this mission insures its popularity despite the misguided protests and demonstrations of a small minority of citizens who mistake this effort with that in Vietnam.

In fact, CBS uses elements of Vietnam in contrast with the Gulf War to corroborate its narrative that this is a noble mission. The Gulf military personnel soon to become veterans are heroes, and the U.S. government officials have justly and carefully undertaken this mission. This is contrasted with the failures in Vietnam and public opinion against the outcast military personnel. Vietnam film footage, Vietnam veterans, and old military strategies are used to show just how different the Gulf War is. Gulf War veterans will not become victims of public opinion against the war, the mission in the Gulf will be won in just a few short months, and coalition casualties will be minimized because ground battles are being replaced by bombing raids. In contrasting the Gulf to Vietnam, CBS again emphasizes the importance of the U.S. role by casting it in terms of U.S. military history.

CBS's ability to independently cover the Gulf War is evident in its narrative. U.S. officials are most often the sources of information about the war, internally produced video of the Gulf is mixed with pool video, and the news agenda is dominated by how the war is affecting the U.S. As a result, the CBS narrative clearly places the U.S. at the center of action and as the pivotal decision maker in the Gulf. If the media are in fact American, then this is the story that should dominate the global agenda as well.

United Kingdom BBC

Similar to the U.S. networks, the BBC operates in a highly competitive media market. However, the BBC is a quasi-public service broadcaster, funded by licensing fees paid by viewers (Hollstein, 1983). The BBC competes against commercial program providers similar to those in the U.S., and television in the U.K. serves as an equally important source of information, which is evident in television set ownership (Euromedia Research Group, 1992). In the U.K. there is one television set for every 3 citizens, compared to one radio per person and a newspaper circulation of 388 per 1,000 population (*World Almanac*, 1994).

Similar to CBS, the BBC is a powerful shaper of the global information system because it has both the economic resources and technology to cover stories independently and contribute them to the global news system. Similar to the U.S., the U.K. played a very important role in the war. Its contribution of troops and financial support of the war was exceeded only by the U.S.

If globalization theorists are correct, then very little difference should appear between the U.K. and U.S. broadcasts because both were consumers and producers of global news about the Gulf War. However, if domestication theorists are correct, then the BBC should focus upon the British role in the conflict by concentrating upon U.K. political officials' comments about coalition efforts and extensive coverage of British troops' activities in the Gulf.

BBC's war narrative. The grand narrative in the BBC is much like that of CBS, except the United Kingdom is portrayed as having an important leadership role in the coalition's efforts to free Kuwait from the wrongful hold of the Iraqis. In the BBC narrative, the U.S. relies upon the U.K. to make leadership decisions. As both an important ally of the U.S. and a leader of Europe, the U.K. is represented in the BBC broadcasts as the most important supporter of coalition efforts. In this way, the BBC places its own nation at the center of the war effort, and nearly all reports are presented with information about how the U.K. is affected by the events in the Gulf.

Unlike the CBS broadcast, the BBC did not emphasize Iraq's worthiness as an opponent in the war. Instead, the BBC's narrative placed Saddam Hussein as the underdog in this war, and from the very beginning made it clear that the coalition forces would win. There was little attempt balancing coverage between coalition and Iraq efforts in the war. The few reports on Iraq were always contextualized with information about coalition superiority. Additionally, Saddam Hussein was neither characterized as a military expert nor a man with a cause. He was instead a villain who unjustly seized Kuwait, failed to understand the sophistication of coalition technologies or power, and would not act reasonably to end this war through peaceful means.

Use of British sources often replaces U.S. sources when the same type of information can be obtained from local informants. British government officials, military personnel, and citizens provide much of the on-camera source information. When external sources are used, they either provide information that could not be gotten from British sources, or they provided color to a story. Interviews with American pilots include romantic or flamboyant quotes that were not included in CBS's presentation of the same pool video interview. Similarly, use of internally produced video dominates the BBC broadcast. Though some CNN and pool video is used, it is nearly always augmented with internally produced video to complete packaged reports. Additionally, when externally produced video is used, it is always accompanied by domestically created audio and local interpretation.

Germany ZDF

ZDF is Germany's second national network (the first is ARD, Arbeitsgemeinshaft der Rundfunkanstalten Deutschlands). Similar to the BBC's funding, ZDF is financed primarily by licensing fees paid by citizens. Like the U.S. and U.K. networks, ZDF operates in a highly competitive media market as is evident in the high number of cabled households. Among larger European countries, Germany has the highest percentage of cabled households (Euromedia Research Group, 1992). Additionally, the importance of television as a source of information is reflected in the number of sets in that nation, with an average of one set for every 2.6 citizens, compared to one radio per 2.3 persons and newspaper circulation of 401 per 1000 population (*World Almanac*, 1994).

Although Germany is a developed, Western nation and has significant influence over the global broadcast system, it is unlike the U.S. and U.K. because it did not play as crucial a role in the coalition efforts. The U.S. criticized Germany for failing to contribute a greater share to the effort. Also, German public opinion about the war was more mixed than in the U.S. or U.K. Germany wished to continue its post-World War II policy of not sending German troops abroad and feared being drawn into a combat role by its treaty obligations to defend fellow NATO member Turkey if Turkey were attacked by Iraq. Hence, Germany hoped to confine its participation in the coalition to financial contributions.

While globalization theory would argue that mixed public opinion and Germany's reluctance to send troops to the Gulf would be overruled in favor of the global story, domestication theorists would expect news from ZDF to differ substantially from other Western broadcasters. Because the mainstream opinion was not as unified in Germany as it was in the U.S. and U.K., domestication theorists would expect ZDF to give more coverage to topics such as war protests that reflect the mix of public opinion. Further, while the global story championed the use of troops abroad, content researchers would expect evidence of German policy to avoid sending troops abroad in the ZDF broadcasts.

ZDF's war narrative.   Like the other two national broadcasters, ZDF emphasizes Iraq's wrongful hold on Kuwait and features coalition successes. Unlike narratives from CBS and BBC, the story ZDF presents does not represent Germany in a Gulf War leadership role. Instead, ZDF emphasized Germany's important relationships with both Turkey and Israel. In ZDF's grand narrative, the Gulf War potentially involves German leadership only if it must exercise its NATO obligation to defend Turkey. Turkey risks Iraqi attack because it has allowed the coalition air force to use Incirlik air base, and this becomes a major theme of the ZDF story. While NATO is of only minor concern in the other two Western broadcasters' stories, it is central to ZDF's telling of the Gulf War tale.

Additionally, ZDF emphasizes its unique relationship with Israel in this conflict. German companies have illegally sold arms to Iraq. These are the same arms used to attack Israel, and ZDF includes, as part of its Gulf War story, the important diplomatic efforts Germany must make to assuage Israel. As a result, though ZDF does not cast Germany as either a manipulator or an instigator of the Gulf actions, it does tell the Gulf War story from the view of German interests in Turkey and Israel.

Additionally, ZDF provided detailed coverage of anti-war protests, though these protests were always contextualized with German officials condemning the demonstrations and calling for support of the coalition. The official German position was clearly in support of coalition forces, however, mixed German public opinion was also reflected in these broadcasts more than it was in other Western nations.

Much of ZDF's coverage is a mix of externally produced video that is reorganized and narrated by ZDF journalists. However, nearly one fourth of ZDF's war coverage contains independently produced video. Like CBS and BBC, ZDF relied primarily upon German sources whenever a local source could provide similar information to substantiate stories. Though ZDF used more external video than either CBS or BBC, they were not entirely dependent upon the global news system for Gulf War information.

Chile Television Nacional

Unlike the other Western nations selected, Chile is both a developed and developing nation. Until 1961, Chile had no television broadcasts, and the first television station was created as a experiment by technicians at the University of Chile. Two university channels continue to operate with a combination of university, government, and advertising funds to finance broadcasts. Competing with these networks is Television Nacional, which is selected for this study because it represents the greatest reach and prominence for the Chilean audience. Television Nacional is a government owned and operated channel that began with the Christian Democrats' rule in the mid-1960s (Catalan, 1988). A law was passed in 1970 to guarantee at least 40% of the national television budget to Television Nacional (Catalan, 1988).

Similar to that of other Western nations in this sample, television in Chile operates as an important source of information. There are approximately two million sets in the country, with an average distribution of one set for every 4.1 citizens, compared to one radio per 3.3 persons (*World Almanac,* 1994).

The main reason for including Chile in the sample is to compare a nation that was both less involved in the war and highly dependent upon the global system for its news, with developed countries that were more committed to the conflict and less dependent upon the world information system for news about the war. Chile's participation in the Gulf was much less than the United States' and European countries' roles. Chile's primary involvement was in the form of contributing medical supplies, and their most important interest was in the effect the war had on oil prices, since Chile is also an oil producing nation. Partly as a result of this smaller interest, and partly due to technological and economic reasons, Chile was more dependent upon the global news system for stories and pictures about the war.

Globalization theorists would argue that Chile's dependence upon the world information system should result in its transmission of a global story that is much the same as stories found in CBS and BBC broadcasts, despite the differences in national interest in the war. Domestication theorists, however, would suggest TN's news content should reflect both Chile's comparatively lower involvement in the conflict through less coverage of the war, and its attempts to make the war of greater audience interest by using local sources to represent the importance of the war to Chile.

TN's war narrative. Television Nacional's grand narrative presents the war as an important story but does little to emphasize Chile's national role in the event. Instead, the view of the Gulf War is offered from a distant observer position in which care is given to tell both sides of the story, though distinctly favoring the coalition view that Kuwait is unfairly held by Iraq. Often, Television Nacional's broadcast emphasizes the need to present both views, and when information to represent a balanced view is unavailable, the broadcaster apologizes for the shortcoming.

Though unlike other broadcasters who tried to cast their nation in a central role in the Gulf, Chile did attempt to make the war interesting to its local audience by augmenting information from the global system with local stories but did emphasize sources of cultural interest. Native Chilean's fighting in the war were featured along with detailed coverage of the Catholic Pope's opinions on the war. The Pope's views are understandably important to Television Nacional's war narrative because Catholicism is a dominant cultural feature in Chile, where 89% of the population are Catholics (*World Almanac,* 1995).

Though TN relied upon pool and CNN video for much of its presentation of Gulf events, it provided a substantial amount of internally produced reports from correspondents in Washington, DC and Jordan. Additionally, other Spanish language broadcasters used reports and packaged interviews from TN, indicating TN's ability to both supply and consume information from the global news system. Unlike other developing nations in this sample, TN displayed more independence from the global system and more ability to enter its news products for distribution to other broadcasters.

Malaysia

Unlike Chilean Television Nacional, the Malaysian TV3 service is privately owned and commercially financed (Lent, 1991). Malaysian media operate in an environment "moderately unfree" from government control (Stephens, 1991). Restricted to broadcasting which does not harm the security or well-being of the state, Malaysian media are more controlled by the government than media in the U.S. or U.K. (Nam, 1983; Stephens, 1991). Similar to the other nations in this sample, television plays an important role in providing information. There is approximately one television for every nine Malaysians, compared to one radio for every 2.4 persons and a newspaper circulation of 145 per 1000 population (*World Almanac*, 1994).

Like Chile, Malaysia is a developing nation, but its interests in the Gulf conflict were more complex, and this is the most important reason for including TV3's broadcast in the sample. Because Malaysia has a significant Muslim population and had a number of Malaysian citizens in Iraq, its cultural interests in the war were much greater than those of other national broadcasts in the sample (Lent, 1991; Nain, 1992). Additionally, Malaysia has complex economic and cultural ties to U.K., U.S. and Japan. Caught between a large Muslim population who would sympathize with Hussein's jihad, and the colonial and economic interests of the U.K. and other coalition nations, Malaysia had a much more delicate position on the war.

Including Malaysia in the sample provides an opportunity to observe the globalization theory that colonial interests and Western media powers are able to suppress the cultural concerns of developing nations (McPhail, 1987). If these claims hold true, then Malaysian national news should focus on coalition efforts while ignoring the concerns of the Muslim population. However, if domestication theorists are correct, then at least some attention to Muslim interests should appear in Malaysia's adaptation of the story.

TV3's war narrative.   The overall narrative for TV3 is more fragmented than that of any other national broadcaster, and this may reflect the variety of interests Malaysia held in the war (Swanson & Smith, 1993). TV3's grand narrative is that war is always bad, and everything possible must be done to end the conflict peacefully. Malaysia is portrayed in TV3's narrative as a nation saddened by the war and calling for Iraq to leave Kuwait to avoid further disaster. There is no nobility to the conflict; there are no heroes.

Like Chile's Television Nacional's narrative, TV3's emphasizes the coalition successes but simultaneously concentrates upon providing a balanced view. The need for balance is so great that the shortage of pro-Iraqi information may have resulted in TV3's unique interpretation of world opinion. The best example of this is on January 17 when

UN Secretary General Perez de Cuellar's expression of sorrow is framed in a story about negative world opinion that includes statements from Iran, Libya, and China.

Unlike Chile's TN, Malaysia's TV3 was much more dependent upon the global system for its news about the war. Video was mostly produced externally and narrated by TV3's anchor, and sources of information were generally international. Though several on-camera interviews with local officials are included, they provide little information about the war. Hence, TV3's dependence upon the global system is evident in both its content and use of video and sources of information. This dependence however, does not render a global story or reflect a narrative similar to CBS's as might be expected. Instead, TV3's broadcast reflects the fragmentation of cultural interests in the war. National sentiments that supported the UN while maintaining Arab relations are reflected in TV3's presentation of the Gulf War in ways that are not reflected in the global story.

India Doordarshan

Doordarshan developed in 1976 from AIR (All India Radio) as a function of reorganizing the Indian broadcast system (Chatterji, 1991). Similar to the German and Chilean stations represented in this sample, Doordarshan is financed and regulated by the government. Ten percent of the total channel output can be devoted to advertising to fund the network (Chatterji, 1991). However, India is unique in this sample because of its relatively small number of television sets, and this may indicate a lesser dependence on television because fewer people have access to sets. Indian populations are the least media involved of any nation in the sample. In India, there is only one television for every 44 citizens, compared to 15 persons per radio and a newspaper circulation of 21 per 1,000 population (*World Almanac*, 1994).

Like Chile and Malaysia, India is a developing nation, and its cultural ties to coalition leaders are much like Malaysia's. News flow scholars have cited colonial ties between India and the U.K. as being strong determinants of how much and what type of foreign news is covered in national broadcasts (International Association for Mass Communication Research [IAMCR], 1985). Compounding this issue is the absence of Indian journalists from the reporter pools, leaving India completely dependent upon the global system for its news from the Gulf (Sainath, 1992). Indian news offers a stronger test of the hypothesis that post-colonial influences persist and affect how nations construct and interpret stories about world events.

Doordarshan's war narrative.   Doordarshan's grand narrative is similar to TV3's in Malaysia. The same fragmentation occurs as each emphasizes a balanced presentation of both sides in the conflict. Unlike TV3 however, Doordarshan's narrative does not emphasize the coalition's success but instead subtly supports Iraq by presenting Iraqi information in its best light. Iraqi civilian casualties are reported, while Iraqi attacks upon Israel and Saudi Arabia are presented as successful and strategic military endeavors. The general theme of the war presented by Doordarshan is one of wanton destruction of Iraq where coalition forces are indiscriminately bombing civilian and cultural centers. In this narrative, the Iraqi military has sustained little damage, and

Saddam Hussein is saving his resources for a powerful ground battle. Additionally, Doordarshan emphasized worldwide protests against the war and features demonstrations in the United States. Clearly these broadcasts present the war as a catastrophe for which the U.S. led coalition must shoulder most of the blame.

As in other countries, the war received detailed coverage and led the newscasts for the first week of fighting, however India's role in the conflict is a minor one. Doordarshan's narrative includes little information about the war's relationship to India. India's most important role as missionaries of peace associates India with both the former Soviet Union and Libya in efforts to stop the bombing and enter peace talks. This theme is not central to this narrative and serves only as a detail about the war.

Doordarshan is nearly entirely dependent upon the global system for both information and video about the war. Few local sources are used for substantiation of Gulf stories, and nearly all video was externally produced. Despite Doordarshan's use of global information, no clear global story emerged from Doordarshan's broadcasts. Though India officially supports the UN efforts in the Gulf, Doordarshan uses information retrieved from the global system to emphasize the protests against the war, Saddam Hussein's strengths, and the coalition's faults in bombing civilian areas.

Jordan Radio and Television

The newscast from Jordan comes from the second of two channels in that country and operates in the least competitive media market of any in this sample. Jordan began television broadcasting in 1968 (Boyd, 1993). Financed and regulated by the government, Jordanian television is ranked as the "least free" press from government control in this sample (Stephens, 1991). In addition to government funding are advertising dollars, which Boyd (1993) claims influence a heavy reliance on foreign programming as a way of gaining foreign advertising investments. The nightly news is broadcast in English, French, and Hebrew (Boyd, 1993); the news used in this sample is the English version. While the other nations in this sample all operate in a relatively competitive market, Jordanian broadcasts do not. Though there are two channels operating in the nation, they have simultaneous transmission of the main nightly Arabic news to increase coverage and prevent alternative viewing (Boyd, 1993).

Although Jordanian broadcasting is the most restricted of those included in the sample, it remains an important source of information for its citizens. There is nearly one television set for every 12 persons, compared to one radio for every 4.5 persons and a newspaper circulation of 73 per 1,000 population (*World Almanac*, 1994).

Jordanian Radio and Television's war narrative.   The war narrative presented by Jordanian Radio and Television is the most pro-Iraqi broadcast in this sample. In this story, Iraq looks forward to the beginning of ground offensive, for which the U.S. led coalition is poorly equipped and prepared. Iraq has been surprisingly successful in avoiding military damage from coalition bombing raids, and U.S. technological superiority has failed to accomplish coalition goals. The bombing raids primarily are hitting cultural and civilian targets, killing innocent Iraqi citizens and destroying mosques and other historical buildings. Coalition sources are not to be believed. They are reported to have launched a propaganda campaign against Iraq in claiming Iraqi treatment of P.O.W.'s is against the Geneva conventions, they refuse to admit to their losses caused by Iraqi military success, and they lie about hitting civilian targets. Additionally, Jordanian Radio and Television emphasizes the uneven application of Geneva rules during the war, explaining the bombing of civilians in Iraq must be investigated by the international community.

Jordan's role in the conflict is more complicated than that of other developing nations in this sample. Sharing a border with Iraq and an important relationship with Saddam Hussein, combined with a dense Muslim population, Jordan had a much greater interest than either Malaysia or India in the Gulf War. Officially, Jordan's most significant involvement came in the form of refugee camps set up to receive fleeing Iraqis. However, cultural and political ties presented Jordan with a much more difficult row to hoe. Recognizing that Iraq was fighting against a much more powerful force, and not wanting to be drawn into the battle, Jordan made great efforts to make it's official position clear: They would not become involved militarily, would not sanction either side flying over Jordanian airspace, and would only provide humanitarian aid in the conflict. As a result, though Jordanian Radio and Television favored the Iraqi side of the conflict, the role of Jordan was cast as official neutrality but in moral support of Iraq.

Jordanian Radio and Television relied heavily upon its own sources for information about the war. When external sources were used, they were contextualized into the story to make the information consistent with the Jordanian position in the war. For example, President Bush is presented on the second day of the war stating that Iraq is a powerful military machine, and the war will take some time. This statement is contextualized by the anchor who explains that the president gave a brief statement that allied losses would be terrible, despite the president's earlier belief that the war would be short and decisive. This is a consistent pattern Jordanian Radio and Television uses of external video and sources. Most externally produced material is used to show how surprised coalition officials are at the success of Iraq and the difficulty of the war mission. Corroborating this context is a significant amount of internally produced video and domestic sources. Jordanian Radio and Television often used interviews with Jordanian ambassadors in other nations to substantiate its war story. As a result, although these broadcasts employed video and information from the global system, they were able to reinterpret this information and contextualize it with domestic sources and video to present an entirely unique war narrative.

COMPARISON OF TWO EXEMPLARY STORIES

From each of the grand narratives, it is clear that no universal global story was presented by all of the broadcasters in this sample. While the general description of the overall war narrative in each country indicates important national differences, it does not illustrate just how these differences are played out in terms of particular story events.

On the side of globalization, the agendas for each nation in the sample were remarkably similar. On any given day, most nations presented the same set of events to describe what had happened in the Gulf since their last broadcast. Though the story events were closely related across national broadcasts, they varied in the order of their presentation, the length of time each broadcaster dedicated to coverage, and most importantly the context and interpretation each event was given by national broadcasters. Whether broadcasters selected nearly the same war events is due to the limitations of what actually happened in the Gulf on a particular day, or due to the limitations globally available information, cannot be determined from this study. However, this similarity in story events provides an excellent opportunity to observe specific differences in how events were cast from one national broadcaster to the next. For this part of the analysis, stories about the Iraqi attacks upon Israel and stories about prisoners of war taken by Iraq were selected because they received the significant attention in each national broadcast.

News interpretations of the Iraqi attacks upon Israel

By the seventh day of fighting, Iraq had attempted multiple missile attacks on Israel, with two different attacks resulting in damage. The first came on the night of January 18, when 12 missiles landed in Tel Aviv and Haifa. The second came on January 22, when three missiles fell on Tel Aviv (Hiro, 1992). Though few deaths or injuries resulted from the attacks, they had political significance for nearly every nation involved in the war. Coalition nations were angered by the attacks because they believed that Iraq's strategy was to inflame Arab nations, thereby destroying coalition unity by restructuring the war in terms of Arab-Israeli issues. Pro-Iraqi nations viewed these attacks as not only fair, but evidence of Saddam Hussein's preservation of military power and strategic genius, as well as a failure of U.S. technologies. Hence, stories about these attacks received attention in every nation in this sample, but the interpretation and framing of the story varied significantly.

In coalition nations, the most important consideration was whether or not Israel would choose to retaliate against Iraq independent of the coalition. CBS, BBC, and ZDF stories about Iraq's attacks sympathize with the Israelis, praise them for restraining the urge to retaliate, contextualize the attacks in terms of Saddam Hussein's desperation, and emphasize the speed with which the U.S. is implementing patriot missiles that will guarantee Israeli protection. As a sidebar to this, CBS and BBC report during the second day of fighting that scud missile launchers are nearly eliminated, thereby removing the possibility of attacks. When it becomes clear from additional Iraqi attacks that the coalition has not eliminated the missile launchers, these stories are modified to explain how difficult it is to spot the launchers, and more emphasis is placed on the success of the patriot missiles in shooting scuds out of the sky.

ZDF has an addition to the Israeli attack story that does not appear in either CBS or BBC broadcasts. Along with the reports on scud missile damage to Israel, ZDF covers the German government's apology for their nation's role in these attacks. Multiple stories on German envoys sent to Israel to offer financial aid and emotional support, as well as stories about how German officials will crack-down on illegal arms sales of the type that provided Iraq with part of the means to attack Israel receive domanant attention in ZDF's broadcasts.

Though CBS, BBC, and ZDF clearly present the Iraqi attacks upon Israel as desperate attempts by Saddam Hussein, this story receives an entirely different interpretation in India's Doordarshan and Jordan's Radio and Television broadcasts. In each of these nations, attacking Israel is not presented as an act of military desperation. Instead, it is represented as a superior strategic act on the part of Hussein. In Doordarshan's broadcasts these attacks are presented as U.S. and United Nations failures. From their view, the American bombing raids have done little but kill civilians and damage historical buildings, and the U.N. is helpless to resolve the Gulf crisis or protect Israel.

Even stronger than Doordarshan's narrative in pointing out the failures of the coalition is Jordan's news about the attacks upon Israel. In Jordan's story, not only is this a superior military strategy for Iraq, but it is also a divine mission that proves Iraq is on the honorable side of this holy mission. One news commentator explains that the scud missiles are so accurate that they only damage the non-Muslim populations in Israel. He claims it is divine intervention that protects the Muslim populations in Israel, and it is divine intervention that causes the rich, technological war horse of the Western nations to fail. Both Doordarshan's and Jordan's stories emphasize the difficulties the coalition is facing in protecting Israel, and the superior military strategies of Saddam Hussein.

News interpretations of Iraqi treatment of POW's

During the first week of the war, most news services presented stories on Iraq's treatment of coalition POW's. On January 20, Iraq showed seven captured airmen on television. The airmen were video taped giving their names, ranks, missions, an explanation of how their aircrafts were downed, and a statement that they did not support the coalition bombing missions or the war against Iraq. This video tape was made available to national broadcasters around the world, and each of the news services in this sample carried parts of that video. In addition to the video tapes, Saddam Hussein released a statement that the POW's would be used as human shields and distributed to militarily strategic sites to inhibit coalition bombing raids.

The threat of using POW's as human shields angered leaders in both the U.S. and U.K., but the video of the airmen's statements received the most news attention. Explanations of the POW's statements accompanied the video in both the CBS and BBC broadcasts. In both cases, the journalists and several domestic on-camera sources interpreted the video as evidence of Saddam Hussein's desperate attempt at propaganda. The statements the airmen made against the war were interpreted as forced statements that were generated through threats of torture. Vietnam veterans were called upon in both CBS and BBC broadcasts to explain that the statements could not be believed and should be disregarded as the result of shock from the plane crash, threats of coercion, and sleep deprivation. The POW's in these broadcasts were presented as brave but tormented soldiers who were doing their best for their nation and their personal survival under difficult and unfair circumstances.

In contrast, Saddam Hussein was presented as an evil and unethical antagonist who failed to uphold the promise he had made as a national leader when he signed the Geneva Conventions. CBS and BBC emphasized that world opinion was on their side, and Iraq's treatment of POW's was just more evidence of the unjust and unethical behavior displayed by Saddam Hussein. The conclusion of both CBS and BBC was that Hussein was not to be trusted.

Although the story about Iraqi treatment of POW's was a prominent story for CBS and BBC, it received far less attention in Chile, India, Malaysia, and Germany. In these nations, this story was treated as just another facet of war and reported as a form of keeping score between the Iraqis and the coalition. Although the story was used in CBS and the BBC to feature Saddam Hussein's evil and unethical character, it was used in Chile, India, Malaysia and Germany as a balance to reporting the number of bombing raids. The video of the captured airmen in these services was not used to portray Hussein as a propagandist, but instead as a form of verifying that Iraq had succeeded at capturing coalition pilots. Importantly, while the U.S. and U.K. both had pilots among those captured, these nations did not. Hence the use of human shields and treatment of POW's was not a domestic issue for these countries.

Although it also was not a domestic issue for Jordan, the Iraqi treatment of POW's was still an important story. Jordanian Radio and Television began the story by stating Americans are worried about prisoners after Iraqi forces shot down more than 160 hostile aircraft. In this story, the Iraqis were merely protecting themselves against the overwhelming and unjustified aggression of the United States. Using the pilots as human shields was not an unethical behavior but rather a strategic one to protect Iraqi economic, scientific, and military sites. Additionally, this use of human shields is expected to have an "effect on the morale of enemy pilots who have been facing the terrifying resistance of Iraqi forces, despite the intensive raids."

Unlike the interpretation of the video in CBS's and BBC's broadcasts, the Jordanian broadcast explains that the hesitant speech and mumbles of the pilots indicate low morale among the POW's. The tapes are not a means of Iraqi propaganda in this broadcast. Instead, they are evidence against the coalition propaganda campaigns that claim there have been few if any coalition military losses. In all, these tapes serve as evidence in the Jordanian broadcast that the U.S. is not telling the truth about the morale of its troops, its military losses, or ability to overtake Saddam Hussein.

CONCLUSION

The effects of globalization and domestication are both present in this research. Though no global story about the Gulf War dominated the seven national broadcasters in this sample, the agendas for what features of the war should be covered were remarkably similar. The similarities between agendas from each of these nations provides a preliminary indicator that the strongest effect of the global information system may be one of agenda-setting, at least in the case of the Gulf War. In this case, the global information system may have dictated what features of the war were salient for each broadcaster, though this system cannot be held accountable for how those features should be interpreted and contextualized by each national broadcaster.

Clearly from this study, national news broadcasts do, to some extent, reflect national policies, cultures, and institutional interests in news about the Gulf War. Though the source of information about the war was often restricted to the global news system, scripts and pictures of the war were often contextualized in terms of domestic news pegs. Nations that did not have independent access to Gulf War news were able to obtain local source commentary or additional information from correspondents they had available in other nations. This commentary was used to interpret, add detail to, and contextualize information so that it was better suited to their national audiences.

REFERENCES

Altheide, D. & Snow, R. (1979). *Media logic.* Beverly Hills, CA: Sage.

Blumbler, J. (1989). *The internationalization of communication.*Paper presented to College of Communication, University of Texas, Austin.

Boyd, D. (1993). *Broadcasting in the Arab world: A survey of the electronic media in the Middle East* (2nd ed., rev.). Ames, IA: Iowa State University Press.

Catalan, C. (1988). Mass media and the collapse of the democratic tradition in Chile. In E. Fox (Ed.), *Media and politics in Latin America: The struggle for Democracy* (pp. 45–55). London: Sage.

Chatterji, P. (1991). *Broadcasting in India* (2nd ed., rev.). New Delhi: Sage.

Euromedia Research Group. (1992). *The media in western Europe: The Euromedia handbook.* London: Sage Publications.

Golding, P. & Murdock, G. (1991). Culture, communications and political economy. In J. Curran & M. Gurevitch (Eds.), *Mass media and society* (pp. 15–32). London: Edward Arnold.

Gurevitch, M. (1991). The globalization of electronic journalism. In J. Curran & M. Gurevitch (Eds.), *Mass media and society* (pp. 178–193). London: Edward Arnold.

Gurevitch, M., Levy, M. R. & Roeh, I. (1991). The global newsroom: Convergences and diversities in the globalization of television news. In P. Dahlgren & C. Sparks (Eds.), *Communication and citizenship: Journalism and the public sphere in the new media age* (pp. 195–219). London: Routledge.

Hiro, D. (1992). *Desert shield to desert storm.* New York: Routledge.

Hollstein, M. (1983). Media economics in western Europe. In L. Martin & A. Chaudhary (Eds.), *Comparative mass media systems* (pp. 241–264). White Plains, NY: Longman.

Hollstein, M. (1983). Media economics in western Europe. In L. Martin & A. Chaudhary (Eds.), *Comparative mass media systems* (pp. 241–264). White Plains, NY: Longman.

International Association for Mass Communication Research, (1985). *Foreign news in the media: International reporting in 29 countries* (Report No. 99). Paris: Unesco.

Larson, J. (1984). *Television's window on the world: International affairs coverage on the U.S, networks.* Norwood, NJ: Ablex Publishing Corporation.

Lent, J. (1991) Telematics in Malaysia: Room at the top for a selected few. In G. Sussman & J. Lent (Eds.), *Transnational communications: Wiring the third world* (pp. 165–199). Newbury Park, CA: Sage.

McPhail, T. (1987). *Electronic colonialism: The future of international broadcasting and communication* (2nd ed., rev.). Newbury Park, CA: Sage.

Mowlana, H. (1993). From technology to culture. In G. Gerbner, H. Mowlana, & K. Nordenstreng (Eds.), *The global media debate: Its rise, fall, and renewal* (pp. 161–166). Norwood, NJ: Ablex Publishing Corporation.

Nain, Z. (1992). The state, the Malaysian press, and the war in West Asia. In H. Mowlana, G. Gerbner, & H. Schiller (Eds.), *Triumph of the image: The media's war in the Persian Gulf—A global perspective* (pp. 75–95). Boulder, CO: Westview Press.

Nam, S. (1983). Press freedom in the third world. In L. Martin & A. Chaudhary (Eds.), *Comparative mass media systems* (pp. 309–326). White Plains, NY: Longman.

Nimmo, D., & Combs, J. (1985). *Nightly horrors: Crisis coverage in television network news.* Knoxville, TN: University of Tennessee Press.

Nimmo, D. & Combs, J. (1990). *Mediated political realities* (2nd ed.) Boulder, CO: Westview Press.

Pavlic, B. & Hamelink, C. (1985). *The new international economic order: Links between economics and communications* (Report No. 98). Paris: United Nations Educational, Scientific and Cultural Organization.

Sainath, P. (1992). The new world odour: The Indian Experience. In H. Mowlana, G. Gerbner, & H. Schiller (Eds.), *Triumph of the image: The media's war in the Persian Gulf—A global perspective* (pp. 67–74). Boulder, CO: Westview Press.

Schiller, H. (1976). *Communication and cultural domination.* White Plains, NY: M.E. Sharpe.

Stephens, L. (1991). The world's media systems: An overview. In J. Merrill (Ed.), *Global journalism: Survey of international communication* (2nd ed. rev., pp. 51–71). New York: Longman.

Sussman, G. & Lent, A. (1991). Introduction: Critical perspectives on communication and third world development. In G. Sussman & A. Lent (Eds.), *Transnational communications: Wiring the third world.* Newbury Park, CA: Sage.

Swanson, D. & Smith, L. (1993). War in the global village: A seven-country comparison of television news coverage of the beginning of the Gulf War. In R. Denton (Ed.), *The media and the Persian Gulf War.* Westport, CT: Praeger.

Word almanac and book of facts (1994). New York: Press Pub.

Word almanac and book of facts (1995). New York: Press Pub.

chapter 11

the impact of media and images on foreign policy: elite U.S. newspaper editorial coverage of surviving communist countries in the post-cold war era

Paul Grosswiler
University of Maine

INTRODUCTION

For almost half a century the Cold War provided an ideology for the U.S. media to frame international events and foreign policy issues. Now that the Cold War has ended, the loss of this ideology, its symbols and images may affect the relationship of the media and government in the foreign policy process. With the fall of "communism" and the end of a bipolar superpower global system, the loss of the Cold War ideology may have a greater impact on U.S. media coverage of surviving communist and socialist countries, most of which are in the Third World, such as two countries with high national interest in the United States, Cuba and Vietnam, as well as other small states more tangential to U.S. interests, such as Tanzania, Mozambique and Zimbabwe in East and Southern Africa.

More than a dozen studies of countries before the breakup of the Soviet Union and the East Bloc in the late 1980s and early 1990s, including China, Cuba, India, Iran, Japan, Korea, Laos, the Soviet Union, Vietnam, and countries in Central and South

America, lead to some general conclusions about the media's role in the foreign policy process (Chang, 1993, p. 33). First, the media are mostly supportive of U.S. foreign policy; second, editorial coverage of foreign policy reflects the views held by policy makers; and third, U.S. foreign policy goals have a significant impact on how foreign policy news is reported. In summary, the media are marginal players in foreign policy decision-making.

The media's role in creating and sustaining symbolic associations and positive or negative images of other countries was a central element in Chang's study (1988, 1993) of U.S. media coverage and foreign policy toward China from the beginning of the Cold War in 1950 until the mid-1980s. For most U.S. residents, knowledge and perceptions of international events depend on how those events and issues are symbolized in the media (1993, pp. 101–102). Removed from direct experience, the U.S. public relies on symbols as a means of public understanding and participation in political life. Symbolism also appeals to politicians as a means of engaging the "popular imagination" in a way that may yield public support or opposition to a policy (Chang, 1993, citing Bennett, 1988, p. 79).

This process is especially problematic in realms of experience either substantially different from or inaccessible to the public, either culturally, politically, or economically. Trade embargoes have been in effect against Cuba from 1963 until the present, and against Vietnam from 1975 until 1994. As a result, Americans have been prohibited by U.S. law from traveling to Cuba and Vietnam except under the most restrictive conditions. The African socialist countries, while accessible legally, are psychologically distant, with little contact from Americans and little interest among U.S. policy makers. The U.S. media, especially in cases of countries like these, become the sole arbiter of reality for both the public and policy makers through news coverage and editorializing.

A void of coverage of these three African countries, Tanzania, Zimbabwe and Mozambique, as with the rest of Africa's 50 countries with the exception of South Africa and several others, results in what Larry Gross calls "symbolic annihilation" (1991, p. 21), which leaves groups that are at the bottom of power hierarchies in their place through invisibility. Michael Parenti (1993, p. 191) offers "deliberate omission" as one of seven ways the media misrepresent public life through packaging and presentation. Africa is one of the most underreported regions in the World (Hachten and Beil, 1985, p. 626). Partly, this invisibility results from the difficulty foreign journalists face in reporting within African countries, but many Western media have decided that Africa is no longer newsworthy.

Difficulties stemming from the media themselves in news coverage of countries such as Cuba, Vietnam, Tanzania, Zimbabwe and Mozambique are made clear by the "propaganda model" of Herman and Chomsky (1988), which suggests that the media must systematically propagandize in order to convey to individuals the values and beliefs of the larger society (p. 1). The propaganda model offers a set of five news "filters" through which economic and political elites marginalize dissent and allow the government and private concerns to reach the public. One essential filter has been "anti-communism," which serves as an ideological symbol representing the "ultimate evil," as a control mechanism (pp. 2, 29–31). Among foreign policy issues, the Chinese and Cuban revolutions have been "traumas" to Western elites.

An analogy may be offered by the analysis of U.S. media coverage of Islam (Said, 1981, pp. 106–107). Said argues that the editorial sector of the media responded to the 1979 Iranian revolution with incredulous levels of disdain and suspicion. In editorial coverage, the press relied on euphemisms, to create the image that Iran had committed an act of war against the United States. The media ignored the possibility that the U.S. participation in the 1953 coup was an act of war (p. 109). In critiquing the political and media perspectives on Cuba, Fitzgerald (1994) argues that the U.S. policy uses President Fidel Castro as a "lightning rod." Policy makers and commentators refer to "Castro's Cuba," personalizing the revolution and the nation in a way that constructs a powerful elite and a powerless public. This perspective erroneously focuses on Cuba's top leadership and ignores the middle and lower levels of Cuban society (p. 7).

After discussing the theoretical context of the media's role in the foreign policy process, specifically involving surviving communist and socialist countries in the post-Cold War era, this chapter will analyze editorial coverage of five major newspapers, *The New York Times, The Washington Post, Wall Street Journal, Los Angeles Times* and *Christian Science Monitor*, on Cuba, Vietnam, Tanzania, Mozambique and Zimbabwe, published from 1991 through 1994. This chapter will look at editorials in terms of (a) their use of ideological and non-ideological symbols; (b) their position on U.S. policy toward the country, (c) their position on U.S. embargoes against Cuba and Vietnam, and (d) their position on each country's existing political system.

MEDIA: MANIPULATED OR POWERFUL?

Whether the news media are passive participants manipulated by the U.S. government in affirming foreign policy or powerful influences shaping foreign policy has been debated for several decades. Cohen's 1963 study found that the press was a helpful government partner that addressed government elites through editorials as it routinely supported foreign policy goals (O'Heffernan, 1991, p. xi; 1993, p. 187). Cohen found that although journalists neutrally transmitted foreign policy, the press was still a powerful political actor (Berry, 1990, p. xi). Cohen's thesis that the media may not tell audiences what to think, but do tell them what to think about is one example of a powerful-effects theory (Nacos, 1990, p. 4).

According to Nacos, research has linked public opinion preferences to policy making (Page and Shapiro, 1983), and presidents pay attention to popularity polls and adjust policies (Brody and Page, 1975). On the other hand, the impact of the mass media on public opinion has been discounted by some research (Lazarsfeld, Berelson and Gaudet, 1944). Other research suggests the media have a powerful agenda-setting function (Shaw and McCombs, 1977; Iyengar, Peters and Kinder, 1982). Some research also has linked media content with public policy preferences among U.S. citizens (Page, Shapiro and Dempsey,1987). And research suggests the media are public proxies to policy makers awaiting opinion polls (Gans, 1980).

Nacos believes the press has significant impact on political elites (Linsky, 1986; Graber, 1989). She points to a study that government officials are strongly influenced by the media (Linsky, 1986). Presidents, she asserts, presume the media have great power (p. 4), and act accordingly to attempt to control the messages about their policies. How successful the foreign policy makers are in managing the media is supported by research. Berry (p. xii) points to a study that identifies shared ideology as the reason the press agreed with the U.S. government in reporting on Iran (Dorman and Farhang, 1987). Reliance of the press on official sources for political reporting has been identified as a reason that the media are deferential to authority (Sigal, 1973, Davison, 1974).

Berry offers an alternative hypothesis: The media's role in foreign policy is minimal and the government's control of the media is also minimal (p. xii). Excluding the editorial function of the press, Berry finds that in two of the three stages of foreign policy, its formulation and execution, the press is unable to report foreign policy critically and accepts the consensus of the foreign policy makers. The press is only able to become critical when foreign policy is at the outcome stage, and it has failed (p. xiii). Criticism is possible at the outcome stage because the story itself develops depth and includes foreign perspectives and expert criticism (p. 140). Thus the press embodies both roles at different stages in the foreign policy process, acquiescing in the formulation and execution stages, and actively criticizing in the outcome stage (pp. 143–44). Because of this pattern, Berry advocates that scholars and commentators expand their analysis early in the foreign policy process in order to "help avoid future Bay of Pigs or other brainless interventions" (p. 146).

Addressing the relationship between news coverage and editorial positions, Nacos concludes that political views expressed in newspapers' editorials influenced their news coverage (p. 188). Nacos studied 24 phases comprising six crisis case studies, including the Cuban missile crisis, and she found a relationship between editorials and news reporting in 18 of the phases. Only one phase showed news coverage contrary to editorial positions. Nacos also suggests that one reason presidents are dissatisfied with the press is the weight they place on editorials, especially in *The Washington Post* and *The New York Times*. Editorials tend to be more critical of presidential actions and policies than news stories (p. 189).

Combining news and editorials, Chang (1988, 1993) traces the relationship between the United States, China and Taiwan by measuring the symbols used to denote China and Taiwan in *The New York Times* and *The Washington Post*. Chang argues that the climate of opinion in the United States regarding the policy toward both Chinas was set by the U.S. government. This policy was reflected in the use of "referential" and "condensational" symbols in the newspaper coverage and in government documents (Bennett, 1988, pp. 178–180). Referential symbols are neutral, including geographic and legal symbols, such as Peking or Taiwan, for the former, and People's Republic of China and Republic of China. Condensational symbols are those that suggest emotional associations, including ideological symbols such as Communist China, Red China, Chinese Communist regime, Nationalist China and Free China.

Measuring the frequency of these image-laden condensational symbols and neutral referential symbols in newspaper articles and editorials from 1950 to 1984, Chang finds the coverage shifted sharply from ideological symbols in the first two decades to referential symbols after 1971, following closely the change of U.S. policy toward China and Taiwan, and change in the use of symbols in presidential documents. U.S. media coverage of U.S.–China policy since 1972 clearly agreed with the official U.S. stand on the changing status of the two Chinas.

Another characteristic of foreign policy coverage is its geographic focus on specific areas and neglect of larger regions. In 1990 elite press coverage of foreign affairs issues during the congressional campaigns, Wells and King (1994) found that almost half the editorial coverage of foreign affairs in the prestige press, including *The New York Times, The Washington Post, Los Angeles Times* and *Chicago Tribune*, was devoted to the Persian Gulf War and the Middle East. Another 11 percent of the editorial coverage focused on the Soviet Union and Eastern Europe, and 11 percent on general foreign policy. Only 6 percent of the editorial coverage dealt with Latin America, 6 percent with Asia, and slightly more than 2 percent with Africa (pp. 656–657). A study of U.S. news magazine strategic and tactical critiques of the U.S. invasion of Panama in 1989 (Gutierrez-Villalobos, Hertog and Rush, 1994) found that two news magazines predominantly supported the U.S. policy toward Panama. A fair amount of "tactical" opposition—which accepts the basic ideology but questions the techniques used to carry out the foreign policy goal—was found, but no strategic opposition that would oppose the world view within which the policy was framed (p. 625). As in other studies over time, the media opposition decreased in moving toward the Panama crisis and increased in the outcome phase of the policy (p. 624).

THE PRESS AND CUBA AND VIETNAM

Analyzing coverage of Cuba, Berry's study of the Bay of Pigs found the press was not a major, autonomous participant in policy formulation or execution, but neither was it successfully manipulated by the government when the policy outcome was negative (p. 24). Nacos's analysis of editorial positions during four crisis periods of the Cuban Missile crisis revealed a pattern of editorial responses. In the pre-crisis period, almost all *The Washington Post* editorials were supportive of President Kennedy's policy to avoid rash military action (p. 21). Similarly, *The New York Times* was in favor of the administration in three-fourths of its editorials. In the acute crisis period, all *Times* editorials and all *Post* editorials supported Kennedy. Even a more critical paper, the *Chicago Tribune* made an about-face, shifting from criticism to support of Kennedy in all editorials (p. 27). In the lingering crisis period, all *The Washington Post* editorials supported the Kennedy Cuba position, as did more than 80% of editorials in the *Times*. (p. 34). In the post-crisis period, the *Times* remained supportive of Kennedy in 75% of its editorials. The *Post* continued its unanimous support, while the *Tribune* resumed its criticism of Kennedy's policy.

In coverage of the Vietnam War, Berry found that *The New York Times* reported the U.S. Vietnam policy consistently with the administration's point of view during the formulation and execution stages of the policy, but as with Cuba, the media became critical when the outcome of the policy was evident (p. 52). Hallin (1986) argues that the media are constrained by both ideology and journalistic routines that tied Vietnam War news coverage to Washington perspectives and excluded discussion in the news agenda of other policy options based on a moderate view of the Vietnamese Communists (p. 214). The media's coverage is closely related to the unity and clarity of the government as well as the degree of consensus in society, Hallin suggests. The opposition to Vietnam policy grew in the media largely as a result of political divisions within the United States and within the government itself, and Hallin doubts the controversy surrounding Vietnam could have been contained longer by the government (p. 213–214).

THE PRESS AND TANZANIA, MOZAMBIQUE AND ZIMBABWE

Unlike Cuba and Vietnam, the African socialist countries of Tanzania, Mozambique and Zimbabwe have little in common historically, geographically, politically, economically or culturally with the United States. Research suggests Africa is one of the least covered regions (Fair, 1993). For example, analysis of coverage of Tanzania and Ghana from 1965 to 1982 found a precipitous drop in coverage by 1970 that then leveled off for the remaining decade (Hachten and Beil, 1985, pp. 627–628). Fair notes that U.S. media coverage of any foreign country is dependent on its social, cultural, economic, geographic and political ties with the United States (p. 128). Countries with weak ties will receive little coverage, as media editors sift through news based on personal and organizational values.

Fair attributes several causes, such as the media's demand for corporate profits, the routines of pack journalism, crisis orientation, "parachute" journalism and capital city reportage, to the media system in which reporters knowing little about Africa must cover news using a narrative form that represents cultural conventions, rules and codes. Ultimately, it is this contextless journalistic form that limits the boundaries of meaning and creates media representations of Africa as the "Other" (Fair, pp. 129–130). After centuries of Africa's unequal relationship with the West through slavery, colonialism and neo-colonialism, Africa's history of domination is expressed in images and representations produced by and for Europeans and Americans using race as an organizing principle. The negative stereotypic cultural associations of "savage" and "primitive" become the bases for media representations (pp. 130–133).

The negative, stereotyped or non-existent coverage of Africa has an impact on both policy makers and the public. Fair argues that U.S. legislators and policy makers who mostly have little knowledge or direct experience of Africa rely largely on the media for information about Africa (Wiley, 1991, p. 45). The media, however, generally report on Africa's problems, deepening political and public pessimism about the continent and providing a negative context for consideration of African policy. This ignorance and stereotyping of Africa also affect the media, the public and policy makers. Albritton and Manheim (1983) found a dramatic effect in media images after the former illegal white minority government in then-Rhodesia hired a U.S. public relations firm in 1976. The effect of public relations on editorial commentary in *The New York Times* was "highly significant," with the public relations contract alone accounting for 42% of the variance in all editorial commentary in the two-year study period (p. 626). Albritton and Manheim note that in foreign policy the public and policy leaders tend to perceive and react to the same information and images at the same time. This is true, in part, because policy makers are more dependent for their information on the media, as is the public. What the media report can become the source of public perception and foreign policy (p. 622). With information being manipulated by public relations efforts for what may be the sole source of public and policy-maker information, policy itself is more susceptible to manipulation (p. 628).

In many case studies of U.S. media coverage of Africa (Hawk, 1992), events and issues are filtered through both a U.S. foreign policy filter and a Cold War frame. The U.S. media have presented news stories shaped by public relations campaigns of other African governments. In South Africa, for example, the African National Congress was portrayed for U.S. media as a communist front. South Africa also promoted a positive image of Jonas Savimbi, leader of a non-communist faction in Angola's civil war in the 1980s. This packaging of Savimbi, embraced by the Reagan administration as a "freedom fighter," however, failed to gain the backing of most of the country's newspaper editorials, including *The New York Times, The Washington Post, Los Angeles Times,* and *Christian Science Monitor* (Windrich, 1992, p. 199–200).

In another case, U.S. policy toward Libya also affected media coverage of the bombing of Libya in 1986 (Ebo, 1992, p. 19). In coverage of the Algerian national liberation movement in the 1950s, media and U.S. foreign policy perceptions of North African leaders affected coverage, so that praise was given to "pro-Western" leaders and criticism given to "extremists." This symbolic labeling framed the Algerian War in purely Western terms that ignored political realities and obscured real issues of the war (Bookmiller & Bookmiller, 1992, pp. 69, 73). Looking at *The New York Times* (1992) coverage of food aid in the 1980s, Fair found that a Cold War framework was used to report and interpret information about U.S. food aid policy in Africa (p. 113). As a backdrop for all international coverage, Fair argues, food aid also became a struggle between the "free world" and communism. Television coverage of Africa also was congruent with U.S. foreign policy, with Cold War rhetoric used in reports on Mozambique as a "Marxist-Leninist government." In another example, changing U.S. policy toward Zimbabwe from negative to supportive in the late 1980s led to a series of positive network stories on that Marxist country (Patterson, 1992, p. 189).

By contrast, an analysis of coverage of the Nigerian civil war in the late 1960s in *Time* magazine, found scarcely any evidence of a Cold War fixation, although Cold War ideology was not an issue in the war, which U.S. public opinion polls found to be the second most pressing foreign issue in 1968, following Vietnam (Ibelema, 1992, p. 89). Investigating Cold War references in *Newsweek* coverage of domestic violence in

Africa from 1957 until 1987, Govea (1992, pp. 104–105) found that coverage did not appear to be affected by U.S.–Soviet relations and that references to Soviet influence declined in the 1980s as Cold War themes became less prevalent in the media in the 1970s and 1980s. Govea also found that *Newsweek*'s approach was often at odds with the official U.S. stance on East–West relations.

For the most part, however, the dominant U.S. media image of Africa is no image at all. A study of *The New York Times* coverage of the continent from 1976 to 1990, selecting a sample of issues, found about 50 stories on Africa per year. Yet during the decade from 1975–1985, only 25 of the 51 countries received any coverage, and only a few high-profile countries received more than one story. In 1990, with South Africa, Tunisia, Liberia and Libya receiving more than five stories apiece, only Ethiopia, Morocco, Uganda and Zimbabwe also were covered, receiving one story each (El Zein & Cooper, 1992, p. 139–141). In the entire time, Mozambique was the topic of one story. No stories were published on Tanzania.

EDITORIAL IMAGES AND FOREIGN POLICIES

To evaluate U.S. media images and their impact on foreign policy, editorials from Jan. 1, 1991, through Dec. 31, 1994, in *The New York Times, The Washington Post, Wall Street Journal, Los Angeles Times*, and *Christian Science Monitor* about Cuba and Vietnam will be discussed. Editorials and columns about Mozambique and Zimbabwe, as well as news articles about Tanzania also will be reviewed. These newspapers were selected as those that provide extensive foreign policy coverage and that function as foreign affairs gatekeepers and agenda setters for other U.S. media and government policy makers (Graber, 1989; Rubin, 1979; Read, 1975). The editorials were selected for analysis as direct institutional attempts by the prestige press to portray and influence foreign policy regarding these surviving communist and social-ist countries. Columns and news articles on the African countries are included because of the dearth of editorials.

The amount of editorial and news coverage of Cuba and Vietnam was nearly iden-tical in the 1991–1994 time frame. In all, 53 editorials were published about Cuba, representing 4.4 percent of the 1,185 total number of articles about Cuba published in these five newspapers. Together with 191 columns and letters to the editor, the total editorial-opinion coverage of Cuba represented 20% of the total item coverage of Cuba. In the same time period, 55 editorials were published about Vietnam, repre-senting 5.3% of all 1,031 articles about Vietnam. Together with 91 columns and let-ters to the editor, the total editorial-opinion coverage represented 14% of the total news coverage of Vietnam.

Only a small fraction of the coverage given to Cuba and Vietnam were given to Tanzania, Mozambique and Zimbabwe. Over the four-year span, only 45 articles were published about Tanzania, including no editorials and only four columns. Only one edi-torial was published in four years about each of the other two countries, Mozambique and Zimbabwe. Of 68 articles about Zimbabwe, there were one editorial, four columns and two letters. Of the 92 articles about Mozambique, one editorial, 10 columns and one letter to the editor were printed.

MEDIA IMAGES OF CUBA AND VIETNAM

The United States began its trade embargo against Cuba in 1960, shortly after the Cuban Revolution, and consolidated the embargo in 1963 with the Trading with the Enemy Act. In the United States, the embargo was seen as way to discourage Soviet expansion in the Western Hemisphere, as well as a way to prevent Cuba from building a successful socialist economy and to provoke internal political dissent (Fitzgerald, 1994, pp. 4–5). As it evolved over time, the embargo always included efforts to keep other countries from trading with Cuba. Originally, it kept U.S. businesses and citizens from trading with Cuba at all. As the Cold War ended with the collapse of the Soviet Union, Cuba's economy by 1990 was reeling with the loss of its Eastern European trading partners. As Cuba's economy weakened, in 1992 the United States enacted the Cuban Democracy Act, which tightened restrictions on travel to Cuba, made it illegal for foreign subsidiaries of U.S. corporations to trade with Cuba, and made it illegal for any ship to enter U.S. waters within six months after docking in Cuba. In the wake of the 1994 influx of Cuban refugees into Florida, the embargo was tightened even more.

The United States began its economic embargo against Vietnam at the end of the war in 1975, as U.S. policy sought to cut off reparations, aid and trade with Vietnam, as well as block assistance from other sources (Herman & Chomsky, 1988, p. 184). Talks in early 1977 between U.S. officials and Vietnamese officials to explore U.S. recognition of Vietnam ended in 1978 when the U.S. postponed plans to normalize relations with Vietnam (Karnow, 1983, pp. 28, 685–686). The plans were abandoned because of hostile U.S. public opinion toward Vietnam and concerns about protecting U.S. relations with China, as well as the problem of Vietnam's refugees and intelligence reports of Vietnam's immanent invasion of Cambodia (p. 28). These plans gathered dust until September 1990, when U.S. and Vietnamese officials first met to discuss normalization. In 1991, the U.S. government moved toward normalization, and the October 1991 Cambodian peace treaty called for eventual normalization of relations with full trade with Vietnam. In 1992, U.S. businesses asked the State Department to eliminate the trade embargo, and President Clinton, after several intermediate steps, lifted the trade embargo in February 1994.

These two communist countries were both objects of U.S. trade embargoes, but with contrasting experiences since the end of the Cold War as U.S. foreign policy makers moved to end the embargo against Vietnam while they intensified the embargo against Cuba. These contrasting experiences offer an opportunity to look at media images and perceptions as U.S. policy moves in conflicting directions. More than 100 editorials were analyzed in terms of (a) their use of condensational, or ideological, symbols and referential, or geographic and legal symbols, (b) their negative, neutral or positive position on U.S. policy toward the country, (c) their position on U.S. embargoes against Cuba and Vietnam, and (d) their position on each country's existing political system.

1. Condensational and referential images

"Referential" symbols are economical, concrete and emotionless, using specific and precise terms, such as geographic locations. "Condensational" symbols, on the other hand, carry emotional and ideological appeals with them. The word "Communist," for example, carries with it associations of "oppression" and "totalitarianism." In coverage of Cuba, more paragraphs included condensational symbols, either ideological symbols such as "Communist Cuba" or personal negative symbols such as "Castro's Cuba," than referential symbols, including geographic symbols such as "Havana" and legal symbols such as "Cuba." Overall, 54% of all paragraphs in the 53 editorials used condensational symbols, compared to 50% of paragraphs using referential symbols. The use of impersonal ideological symbols, such as "Communist Cuba," or "totalitarian state," and other terms, was much less frequent than terms that personalized the negative symbolism, calling the country "Castro's Cuba" or referring to "Fidel" or "Castro" instead of to the government or political leadership. The *Wall Street Journal* went so far as to refer to Castro as "the bearded one." These personal condensational symbols appeared in 50% of all paragraphs; impersonal ideological symbols appeared in 17% of all paragraphs.

This negative labeling of Cuba was consistent over the four years, as the economic embargo was tightened in 1992, and during the refugee influx to Florida in 1994. Different newspapers followed different strategies in using symbolic labels, however, as the *Wall Street Journal* and *Los Angeles Times* included far more personal references than the other three newspapers. Editorials differed, too, in types of condensational symbols in commenting on Cuba. In all, 91% of the editorials referred to Castro as a symbol, while 60% used at least one impersonal ideological symbol.

This finding is consistent with Chang's that ideological labeling of China did not fall below the level of referential labeling until 1966, when Senate hearings were held on China; after a slow decline, a drastic drop in ideological symbols did not occur until President Nixon announced he would visit China (1988). A change in government policy led the way for a change in media symbolism.

This pattern of changing images is borne out in coverage of Vietnam from 1991 through 1994. During that time, only 16% of all paragraphs used ideological labels, such as "Communist Vietnam," "the old-line Communist government in Vietnam" or "an undemocratic Communist-ruled country." A far higher percentage, 74% of all paragraphs, contained geographic and legal references, such as "Vietnam" and "Hanoi." Because no leader is associated in the media or U.S. foreign policy with Vietnam's government as Castro is in Cuba, there were no personal ideological labels.

The pattern of predominant referential symbols was true in the 1991–1993 period, before the embargo was lifted, as it was in 1994, when the Senate voted to lift the embargo and President Clinton did so. In the first three years, 16% of all paragraphs contained ideological symbols; 76% contained referential symbols. In 1994, 14% of paragraphs used ideological images and 70% referential. Each newspaper's use of ideological symbols also reflected a different strategy. Ideological labeling was far higher in *The Washington Post* and *Wall Street Journal* than in the other newspapers. Far lower, by contrast, was *The Los Angeles Times*, where a sizable Vietnamese American population lives. Only 7% of its editorials used ideological symbols.

This finding also is consistent with Chang's study of China. The United States and Vietnam began discussing normal relations and trade in 1990, with goals set in the fall of 1991. Businesses asked the government to end the embargo in 1992, and, although the business-oriented *Wall Street Journal*'s ideological symbolism was high, total editorial coverage indicated that the government set the symbolic tone for the media to follow in toning down the ideological references to Vietnam to help normalize relations.

2. Position on U.S. Policy

This pattern of symbolic labeling does not reflect the editorial positions expressed about U.S. policy. In criticism dominated by *The New York Times* and *The Washington Post* , the percentage of editorials criticizing U.S. Cuba policy (45%) outweighed those supporting it (30%), with a crescendo of criticism from 1991 (4%) to 1994 (26%). Together, *The New York Times* and *The Washington Post* accounted equally for more than four-fifths of the critical editorial coverage. Each criticized U.S. Cuba policy in more than half of its editorials.

The response to the Vietnam embargo was reversed, with 36% of the editorials favoring U.S. policy and 22% criticizing it. The largest percentage of editorials, 42%, responded neutrally or with mixed criticism and praise. *The Wall Street Journal* and *The New York Times* generated most of the opposition to U.S. policy. *The Washington Post* and *Los Angeles Times* were most in favor of U.S. policy, with the latter approving each policy change that lifted parts of the embargo.

3. Position on the U.S. embargoes

U.S. policy criticism focused in both cases on the U.S. trade embargoes. Criticism of the U.S. embargo dominated opposition to U.S. Cuba policy with 49% of all editorials opposed to either maintaining the embargo at current levels or intensifying it; 13% favored the embargo; and 20% did not mention the embargo. Opposition grew from one editorial in 1991 to 18 in 1994. The *New York Times* was unanimous in its opposition to the embargo, while the last half of *The Washington Post* editorials opposed the embargo.

As U.S. policy was formulated to end the Vietnam embargo over the four-year period, support for the embargo was low, with only 4% percent of editorials—three of four in the *Wall Street Journal*—supporting the embargo. The only other support for the embargo was from a *New York Times* editorial. By contrast, 49% of the editorials were opposed to the embargo, clearly in line with developing U.S. policy. Another 30% were mixed in evaluating the embargo; and 14% discussed other issues, such as missing U.S.

military forces in Vietnam. The strongest opposition to the embargo was in the *Los Angeles Times* and *The New York Times*.

4. Position on the Cuban and Vietnamese political systems

In this atmosphere of increasing disagreement with U.S. foreign policy and the embargo against Cuba, the editorial position toward the Cuban political system itself was an unchanging rejection. Of all 53 editorials, none supported the Cuban government, while 85% opposed the Cuban government and 15% did not pass judgment. Opposition started out unanimous in 1991, then remained relatively constantly high. The *Los Angeles Times* and *Wall Street Journal* were unanimous in opposing the Cuban system.

A less negative stand was taken in assessing the Vietnamese government, with two *New York Times* editorials supporting Vietnam's system without criticism. In all, 69% of the editorials were neutral or mixed in assessing Vietnam's political and economic system. Only 27% were solely critical of the government.

In summary, these findings show that the U.S. media's use of condensational and referential symbols will reflect the direction of U.S. policy, regardless of media support or opposition to that policy. Media criticism of U.S. Cuba policy was substantial, but the ideological symbolism still was higher than referential symbolism, indicating an underlying agreement with U.S. Cuba policy. The overwhelming rejection of the Cuban political system underscores that underlying agreement. The percentage of referential symbols of Vietnam in the 1990s, along with support for the changing U.S. policy toward normalizing relations with Vietnam, indicates that the media are following U.S. policy as it sought to end the embargo. The less negative positions on Vietnam's political system also showed agreement with U.S. moves to end the embargo.

MEDIA IMAGES OF TANZANIA, ZIMBABWE AND MOZAMBIQUE

All three African countries built socialist systems but are undergoing shifts toward liberalization of the economic and political processes in the 1990s, Tanzania, in East Africa, had spent several decades since independence in 1961 developing a system of African socialism under the political leadership of Julius Nyerere. With a worsening economy, in the mid-1980s Nyerere stepped aside and his elected successor reached an agreement with the International Monetary Fund that helped improve the economy. Along with economic privatization, Tanzania began shifting from a one-party state to a multi-party system in 1992, with elections scheduled in October 1995. Zimbabwe won independence in 1980 after a 10-year civil war against a white-minority government. A socialist government was elected then that remains in office in mid-1995. Mozambique also suffered a civil war after winning independence in 1975 from the Portuguese colonizers and electing a Marxist government. An anticommunist military resistance group financed first by white-ruled Rhodesia and later by the white South

African government waged a civil war until a peace accord was reached in 1992 that led to elections in 1994, in which the Marxist government retained power.

Examination of the coverage of these three socialist African countries suggests that the Cold War framework is no longer being applied to African media coverage, but neither does U.S. policy appear as a filter for African news, except in its relative absence. The one finding that emerges from the sheer lack of coverage is the "symbolic annihilation" of Africa in the U.S. media, and, perhaps, among U.S. policy makers. Coverage was minimal to non-existent. In four years, only two editorials were written about these three countries, as well as 21 columns, including several letters to the editor. Of these, only 22% included single ideological references about socialism in these countries or their past relations with the Soviet Union. It seems the anti-communist filter and Cold War framework have dissolved in coverage of socialist Africa.

Only 45 articles were published about Tanzania, including no editorials and four columns, none of which used any ideological symbols about socialism in Tanzania. Only one column touched partially on U.S. foreign policy toward Tanzania by including several paragraphs on the nomination of the U.S. ambassador to Tanzania. Two columns focused on wildlife issues and the third focused on a U.S. couple teaching villagers how to farm. More than half of the articles, 23, were published after the outbreak of the civil war in Rwanda that erupted when the Rwandan and Burundi presidents were killed in a plane crash in April 1994. These focused on that war and only incidentally on Tanzania because of its acceptance of Rwandan refugees. Of these 41 articles, only two used an ideological reference: a *New York Times* article on Tanzania's shift from "one-party African socialism" to a multiparty system and a *Washington Post* article on the use of Kiswahili as the national language mentioned Tanzania's "decades of socialism." Both articles were published in early 1992, when former President Julius Nyerere ushered in discussions of moving toward a multi-party system.

Only one editorial each was published about Mozambique and Zimbabwe, with only one ideological symbol. A *Wall Street Journal* editorial about Zimbabwe included a single ideological reference, reporting that television news used to include a "picture of Marx fading into Lenin." A *Washington Post* editorial on U.N. peacekeeping efforts in various countries, including Mozambique, had no ideological references.

The media published four columns about Zimbabwe, including three about drought and one about wildlife policy. Only one included a reference to "Zimbabwe's former inclination toward socialism." Two letters were written by the Zimbabwean ambassador to the United States. Of the 92 articles about Mozambique, 10 columns and one letter to the editor were printed with three containing single ideological symbols. Of the 10, half dealt with the civil war fought from 1975 until 1990, and the peace process, and two dealt with 1994 elections. None looked at U.S. foreign policy. And only one included an ideological reference to "the nominally Marxist government," while another added that the "Marxist-Leninist Front for the Liberation of Mozambique… has today turned to democracy and a free market economy." A third mentioned that in 1990 "the Soviet Union disengaged" from aiding Mozambique.

DISCUSSION

The media help shape the way that the public perceives political issues, whether those media symbols are real or imagined (Chang, 1993, p. 102). From apathy to arousal, the media use of political symbols offers a serious potential to affect responses to foreign policy issues and could have serious policy impact (p. 103). The symbols provide a link to the world of international events that few people have directly experienced. The editorial coverage of several remaining communist states reinforce some aspects of the relationship between media and U.S. foreign policy and challenge others.

First, the media focus on areas that reflect U.S. foreign policy interests, such as Cuba and Vietnam, while ignoring countries with little foreign policy interest, such as Tanzania, Zimbabwe and Mozambique.

Second, where the media focus their attention, such as in Cuba and Vietnam, they are more likely to follow Berry's theory that formulation and execution of policy is likely to be supported, as the media supported policy initiatives to end the embargo against Vietnam. The media are likely to criticize foreign policy outcomes, with criticism against the Cuba embargo centering on its failure to bring down the Cuban government, an almost universal goal among the U.S. media.

Third, the levels of condensational symbols and referential symbols in the 1990s editorial coverage of Cuba and Vietnam would imply that the media are following U.S. policy even as their editorials criticize it. With substantial ideological symbols applied to Cuba and much fewer to Vietnam, it appears that this rhetorical variable is a good predictor of underlying media support for U.S. foreign policy. Given the U.S.'s continued embargo policy against Cuba and more recent restrictions, Chang's finding would predict that ideological symbols would still outweigh geographic-legal symbols in editorials about Cuba. A change in U.S. policy would be the key to a change in symbolic references to Cuba.

Fourth, the high level of personal ideological symbols and low level of impersonal symbols about Cuba, as well as the low level of ideological symbols about Vietnam, and the near-absence of such symbols about the African countries, suggest a revision of Chomsky's and Herman's propaganda model that anti-communism is an important filter, but these levels support the criticism of Fitzgerald that the U.S. media and government policy have erroneously personalized Cuba, ignoring important professional groups that will be crucial participants in the future of Cuba.

Media images of Cuba as the personal dictatorship of Fidel Castro and of its Communist system reduce the U.S. public's ability to develop a full and multifaceted understanding of Cuba at a time when U.S. policy makes direct experience of Cuba nearly impossible for almost all U.S. citizens. The media, even as they oppose U.S. policy, share the U.S. policy goal of ending the current Cuban system, and the media's images are an important factor in pursuing that U.S. policy goal. Similarly, U.S. policy is shaping the symbolic discourse about Vietnam, as media symbolism changes to concur with U.S. efforts to dismantle the embargo, even as public opinion remains strongly divided, with significant opposition to full normal relations with Vietnam.

Again, the media are following U.S. foreign policy goals.

The media images of Africa, by virtue of their absence, also indicate an adherence to U.S. foreign policy, turning away from a region that is undercovered and that is falling even farther from view as the Cold War recedes. The media's framing of African issues and events in terms of the Cold War has ended, this chapter suggests. But U.S. foreign policy interest in Africa has historically been limited, matched by limited media coverage. As U.S. foreign policy interests shift away from Africa, which is no longer a proxy context for superpower conflict, the media are following U.S. foreign policy interests by removing coverage from Africa.

REFERENCES

Albritton R. & Manheim, J. (1983). News of Rhodesia: The impact of a public relations campaign. *Journalism Quarterly, 60*, 622–628.

Bennett, W. L. (1988). *News: The politics of illusion,* 2nd ed. New York: Longman.

Berry, N. O. (1990). *Foreign policy and the press: An analysis of The New York Times' coverage of U.S. foreign policy* . Westport, CT: Greenwood Press.

Bookmiller, R. J. & Bookmiller, K. N. (1992). Dateline Algeria: U.S. press coverage of the Algerian war of independence 1954–1962. In B. Hawk (Ed.), *Africa's media image.* New York: Praeger.

Brody, R. A. & Page, B. (1975). The impact of events on presidential popularity: The Johnson and Nixon administrations. In A. Wildavsky (Ed.), *Perspectives on the presidency* Boston: Little, Brown and Co., 136–148.

Chang, T. K. (1988). The news and U.S.–China policy: Symbols in newspapers and documents. *Journalism Quarterly, 65*, 320–327.

Chang, T. K. (1993). *The press and China policy: The illusion of Sino-American relations, 1950-1984.* Norwood, NJ: Ablex Publishing Corporation

Cohen, B. C. (1963). *The press and foreign policy,* Princeton, NJ: Princeton University Press.

Davison, W. P. (1974), *Mass communication and conflict resolution* New York: Praeger.

Dorman, W .A. & Farhang, M. (1987). *The U.S. press and Iran* Berkeley, CA: University of California Press.

Ebo, B. (1992). American media and African culture. In B. Hawk (Ed.), *Africa's media image.* New York: Praeger.

El Zein, H. M. & Cooper, A. (1992) *New York Times* coverage of Africa, 1976–1990. In B. Hawk (Ed.), *Africa's media image.* New York: Praeger.

Fair, J. E. (1992). Are we really the world? Coverage of U.S. food aid in Africa, 1980–1989. In B. Hawk (Ed.), *Africa's media image.* New York: Praeger.

Fair, J. E. (1993). War, famine, and poverty: Race in the construction of Africa's media image. In F. Eribo, M. Wubueh, O. Oyediran, L. Zonn (Eds.), *Window on Africa: Democratization and media exposure.* Greenville, NC: East Carolina University.

Fitzgerald, F. T. (1994). *The Cuban revolution in crisis: From managing socialism to managing survival.* New York: Monthly Review Press.

Gans, H. J. (1980). *Deciding what's news.* New York: Vintage Books.

Govea, R. (1992). Reporting African violence: Can America's media forget the Cold War? In B. Hawk (Ed.), *Africa's media image.* New York: Praeger.

Graber, D.A. (1989). *Mass media and American politics* (3rd ed.). Washington, DC: Congressional Quarterly Press.

Gross, L. (1991). Gays, lesbians and popular culture. In M. A. Wolf & A. Kielwasser (Eds.), *Gay people, sex, and the media*. Binghamton, NY: Harrington Park Press.

Gutierrez-Villalobos, S., Hertog, J., & Rush, R. (1994). Press support for the U.S. administration during the Panama invasion: Analyses of strategic and tactical critique in the domestic press. *Journalism Quarterly , 71*, 618–627.

Hachten, W. & Beil, B. (1985). Bad news or no news? Covering Africa, 1965–1982. *Journalism Quarterly, 62 ,* 626–631.

Hallin, D. (1986). *The uncensored war: The media and Vietnam*. Berkeley, CA: University of California Press.

Hawk, B. G. (Ed.) (1992). *Africa's media image*. New York: Praeger.

Herman, E. S. & Chomsky, N. (1988). *Manufacturing consent: The political economy of the mass media* . New York: Pantheon.

Ibelema, M. (1992). Tribes and prejudice: Coverage of the Nigerian civil war. In B. Hawk (Ed.), *Africa's media image*. New York: Praeger.

Iyengar, S., Peters, M. D., & Kinder, D. (1982). Experimental demonstrations of 'not-so-minimal' consequences of television news programs. *American Political Science Review, 76*, 848–858.

Karnow, S. (1983). *Vietnam: A history*. New York: Viking.

Lazarsfeld, P., Berelson B., & Gaudet, H. (1944). *The people's choice*. New York: Columbia University Press.

Linsky, M. (1986). *Impact: How the press affects federal policymaking*. New York: Norton.

Nacos, B.N. (1990). *The press, presidents, and crises*. New York: Columbia University Press.

O'Heffernan, P. (1991). *Mass media and American foreign policy: Insider perspectives on global journalism and the foreign policy process*. Norwood, NJ: Ablex Publishing Corporation.

Page, B. & Shapiro, R. (1993). Effects of public opinion on policy. *American Political Science Review, 87,* 175–190.

Page, B., Shapiro, R., & Dempsey, G. (1987). What moves public opinion? *American Political Science Review, 81,* 23–43).

Parenti, M. (1993). *Inventing reality: The politics of news media*. New York: St. Martins.

Patterson, C. (1992). Television news from the frontline states. In B. Hawk (Ed.), *Africa's media image*. New York: Praeger.

Read, W. H. (1975, Spring). Multinational Media. *Foreign Policy,* 155–167.

Rubin, B. (1979). International news and the American media. In D. B. Fascell (Ed.), *International news: Freedom under attack*. Beverly Hills, CA: Sage.

Said, E.W. (1981). *Covering Islam: How the media and the experts determine how we see the rest of the world*. New York: Pantheon Books.

Shaw, D. & McCombs, M. E. (1977). *The emergence of political issues: The agenda-setting function of the press*. St. Paul: West Publishing.

Sigal, L. (1973). *Reporters and officials* . Lexington, MA: D.C. Heath.

Wells, R. A., & King, E. G. (1994). Prestige newspaper coverage of foreign affairs in the 1990 congressional campaigns. *Journalism Quarterly, 71,* 652–664.

Wiley, D. (1991). Academic analysis and U.S. policy-making on Africa: Reflections and conclusions. *Issue, 19,* 38–48.

Windrich, E. (1992). Savimbi's image in the U.S. media: A case study in propaganda. In B. Hawk (Ed.), *Africa's media image*. New York: Praeger.

chapter 12

African news media and foreign policy: the case of Botswana

James J. Zaffiro
Central College

INTRODUCTION

T
his chapter investigates relationships between news media and foreign policy in the Republic of Botswana, a France-sized, southern African democracy of 1.4 million people. Some broad comparisons with other African states are offered as a commentary on changing dynamics of international political communication in the post-Cold War, African context. Broadly stated, it argues that media influence on foreign policy-making is minimal and that media content tends to reflect the foreign policy agenda of the President and top external affairs elites.

Because so much of the existing research in this area centers on the U.S., it is important to begin on a note of caution. African news media, like African foreign policy systems, are very different from their U.S. counterparts. Scholars of U.S. media and foreign policy fail to acknowledge the unique availability of media access to and information about foreign policy decisions and the process of decision-making here. It is most certainly an inappropriate research perspective to apply it in an African context, even in those few states with a private press, like Botswana. One must be clear about the centralized, regime-controlled nature of virtually all African media when seeking interconnections with foreign policy. Care must be taken not to assume that patterns, trends, even hypothesized relations between news media and foreign policy themselves, will generalize reliably from Washington to Botswana.

American journalist David Lamb writes that "In almost every country of Africa, the prime role of the media is to serve the government, not to inform the people" (Lamb,

1982, pp. 244–245). If this is so, even for Botswana, then how do Botswana news media serve government in foreign affairs?

In his study of the politics of economic reform in Ghana, Herbst (1993, pp. 244–245) argues that "having a press truly able to convey information to members of society" is an important aspect of sustainable economic and political democratization. Accountability cannot be promoted if the public has no idea of what the government is doing and if critics' voices are not heard expressing their doubts. But does—or should—this argument extend to foreign policy?

Political communication in Botswana, as it is worldwide, is fundamentally about influence and control over information flows. African governments work hard to control the versions of news and events which appear in domestic and international media. Much "official" news is intended in some way to serve foreign policy objectives and national interests (Bennett, 1994, pp. 177–178).

Are African governments, even relatively democratic ones like Botswana's, willing to accept criticism of external policies which relate to the vital national interests, state sovereignty, and national security? Botswana's foreign policy elites increasingly convey the impression that maintenance of the country's international reputation as a "showplace of African democracy" is itself a vital foreign policy interest and that press reporting of scandals, corruption, mismanagement, and fraud are seditious because they might tarnish that image.

While far from "typical" in the African context, Botswana offers a revealing case because, in addition to a less heavy-handed government media system, it is probably the only African state which has had both a relatively free private press over the post-independence period and has maintained a highly stable, successful foreign policy strategy. With the end of apartheid and the Cold War, this strategy, the regional economic and geopolitical factors which underpinned it, and external policy structures and processes, are now undergoing rapid change (Zaffiro, 1995).

What are media-regime relations like in this sensitive policy area? Does media content always reflect or echo regime policy priorities or are there instances of opposition to or criticism of foreign policy? What are media-military relations like? Are there significant differences between government and private media? How have post-Cold War international news collection, editing, selection, and impact changed? Do foreign policy elites use media-based sources of information to formulate or implement foreign policy?

In Botswana, as is true for all states, there is a direct link between domestic politics and the making of foreign policy. Vital national interests are inherently economic. Development policy *is* foreign policy, by definition. Paternalistic, "authoritarian" senior-level bureaucrats manage an External Affairs Department housed within the Office of the President—as is the Department of Information and Broadcasting—which views itself as apart from and above other ministries, a kind of elite-of-elites mentality (Zaffiro, 1993, pp. 139–160). Such a worldview does not often nor readily lend itself to an open access policy for release and sharing of information with news media.

To borrow Cohen's description of Washington (1963, pp. 264–267), in the competing demands of diplomacy and democracy on the organization and conduct of foreign policy news flows, "the needs of diplomacy for privacy" win out over "the needs of democracy for publicity and information." The political and administrative challenges of managing a foreign policy establishment, even a small, relatively contained one, "so that it speaks with one voice in support of decisions and actions" encourage senior officials to view media, even state media, as uneducated intruders.

Some African foreign ministers may pay lip service to "the public's right to know," or "promote interaction between foreign policy practitioners and members of the informed public with a special interest in external relations." None, however, are willing or able to actually manage and share information in a way that serves to "encourage opportunities for better understanding of and support for our Administration's foreign policy" (Gambari, 1989, p. 3).

In Botswana, even ruling party MP's and junior Cabinet ministers find themselves locked out of the foreign affairs information loop, with most major decisions in this realm taken by the Head of State and one or two trusted advisors. This is the normal state of affairs in most African states.

MOVING ANALYSIS BEYOND WESTERN MEDIA THEORIES

In the African context it is especially important to consider ruling elite attitudes about acceptable news media roles, management, access, content and effects. Because African foreign affairs are dominated by the head of state and a few top decision-makers, it is also important to focus upon when, how, and why they make use of the media. Government news media pronouncements, to borrow from Sigal (1973, pp. 131, 135–136), help functionaries within the foreign affairs bureaucracy to overcome uncertainty about the world outside, taking their cues from the president or senior ministers, the officials whose preferences matter most. Translating these preferences into government action requires a thorough grasp of the world inside the government.

African media systems were a key brick in the bureaucratic edifice of the authoritarian, centralized, colonial state apparatus bequeathed to nationalist elites at formal independence. They function today as anything but a "Fourth Estate," anything but free, particularly in the area of news collection and reporting. In addition, Cold War-era, North American theories of media-government relations have negatively reinforced African governments' perceptions of the role of mass media in politics and foreign affairs. Ethnocentric attempts by foreign academics and governments to apply inappropriate, culture-specific press models to dozens of post-independence African media systems have badly backfired. "Authoritarian," rather than "Social Responsibility" or "Libertarian" (western-democratic-pluralist) media theories are today reflected in the various "Developmental Journalism" paradigms now underpinning most African media systems, including Botswana's.

Most African leaders simply assume that state-controlled media systems are perks of power and tools for regime perpetuation. Independent *or* official government news media actively seeking and disseminating sensitive foreign and defence information and policy stances is viewed as alien and seditious. Similarly, an unregulated media role in mediating elite or popular foreign affairs debate or influencing public opinion about regime external policies, is perceived as frivolous at best, treasonous at worst. In Botswana, British administrative models and traditions of foreign affairs elitism and official secrecy permeate the contemporary governmental external affairs bureaucracy and strongly influence the official media policy ethos.

The result is an elite-serving style, focus, and content in foreign news reporting by state media. The contrast with the more mass audience-centered, private newspapers' foreign affairs coverage is striking and politically significant. Media style is one of the revealing but little-studied points of political culture contact between old and new world order thinking, agenda-setting, and media philosophies—self-perceptions of mission for media—in the African context.

NEWS MEDIA AND POLITICS IN AN AFRICAN CONTEXT

In the words of a famous Ghanaian journalist and media educator, "in Africa the principle is not generally accepted that the public is entitled to information about government business" (Ansah, 1981). News media serve as an official forum or channel through which government elites communicate with each other across ministries and departments, express their views, and attempt to gain favorable visibility in the eyes of fellow elites country-wide.

Only in a handful of states, notably Nigeria and South Africa (Mytton, 1983), is the media sector large, professional, endowed, and diverse enough to be able to provide its own views—as media elites—while at the same time reporting the main viewpoints of government elites. As of 1989, seven African states had no daily newspaper whatsoever, while most of the rest had only one, usually government-owned, daily paper. Only Kenya, Nigeria, and South Africa had more than two privately-owned dailies (Merrill, 1991, pp. 161–164). Much the same is true of broadcasting.

Unlike radio or television audiences, which need not be literate, African press readership, even today, is still largely an urban-based, educated elite itself. Most papers are published in the ex-colonial European languages, another elite-serving barrier to mass access. National distribution is sparse, erratic, and urban-centered. Given these parameters, press content, under conditions of government information monopoly, or near-monopoly, can be more exclusively elite-serving. This is a large part of the explanation for why so much of African press content and coverage, including foreign affairs news, does not appear to be of interest or relevance to a majority of the population of the state. They are not the intended readership. In this sense, the truly national newspaper in Africa is a rare, almost nonexistent entity.

Foreign news content reflects regime policy preferences, government media use and control policies, limited news gathering resources (Graber, 1993, pp. 360–395) as well as the attitudes and education of media workers, whether state bureaucrats or freelance journalists. This is just as true of the press in African democracies, like Botswana or

Namibia, as it is for more overtly authoritarian regimes like those today in power in Nigeria or Zaire.

Today, in times of shrinking foreign aid allocations from western donors, cut-throat competition for scarce foreign investment, and Africa's steady decline in international visibility *vis-à-vis* the Bosnias and Russias of this world, how can regimes use national media institutions to advance their foreign policy goals and agendas? Again, one must begin with the question of audience: foreign as well as national, rural as well as urban, opposition as well as pro-regime.

In Botswana, where press circulation and English literacy outside of urban areas have traditionally been low, a logical first question to ask about the extensive foreign affairs coverage in the Government's own *Daily News* is: who reads this and why? African governments concerned with formulating successful foreign policies in the difficult, costly, and dangerous world of the 1990s need to pay more attention to media use and control policies in this context than ever before. In the past it may have been enough to simply use foreign news items to fill-up space and give visibility to international comings and goings of top officials. This is no longer the case.

Would a reconsideration of priorities lead to changed news selection criteria? Why devote such a large share of total space to foreign news today? What type of foreign news story deserves coverage, exposure, space? How much private press criticism of regime foreign policy goals and actions should be tolerated? Should *state* media criticize foreign policy? How much foreign news content should be for "public education or information," how much for the exposure and edification of national leaders themselves? Should opposition leaders, especially popularly elected MPs, be allowed to criticize regime foreign policy in the pages of the *Daily News*? Such questions are inseparable from media content, the visible product or "output" of state and private newspapers.

THE BOTSWANA PRESS

Botswana currently has four private weekly newspapers, *The Guardian*, *The Midweek Sun*, *The Gazette*, and *Mmegi wa Dikang*. The government-run *Daily News*, began life as a one to two page intra-governmental, mimeographed, English-language broadsheet during the waning days of British colonial administration. At independence in 1966, it was the only locally produced newspaper in the country. Its official brief has been to interpret government to the people and the people to the government.

Only in the 1980s was there a sufficiently large local commercial economic base to allow for a viable private, national press in Botswana. As Mytton points out, there would probably be no daily newspaper in Botswana had the government not decided to finance one (Mytton, 1983, pp. 63, 67–68).

In 1987, the *Daily News*—Monday through Friday—expanded from four to eight pages, with international, national, and district news sections. By continuing not to charge for the paper—*Mmegi*'s price currently is 1 Pula, about 50 cents—the government puts economic pressure on the private papers. Other key advantages of government owner-ship, besides financial subsidy, include a national distribution potential, via Air Botswana domestic flights and on government road transport vehicles, a country-wide network of reporters and news collection points through local Botswana Press Agency offices, and a new state-of-the-art print facility in Gaborone (Zaffiro, 1989, pp. 51–73).

The most important and viable private paper soon came to be the weekly *Mmegi wa Dikang*—The Reporter of the News. By the 1990s, *Mmegi* had come to be con-sidered the most significant media outlet for alternative news and reporting in the country, with a reputation for hard-hitting critique and analysis of government poli-cies and tough, expose-style investigative reporting of alleged abuses of power and privilege by those in office.

Many readers tend to identify *Mmegi* as a semi-official organ of the political oppo-sition, particularly the Botswana National Front and a mouthpiece of its leaders. Depending on the issues, *Mmegi* can be a critical editorial voice or a supportive team-player for government policy. In the area of foreign and defense policy, however, it rarely directly criticizes the government. Two significant forms which such criticism normally takes are editorials and political cartoons.

FOREIGN POLICY ELITES AND THE MEDIA

The extent to which any regime provides foreign policy information to the private press, or uses the government press to disseminate it, depends heavily on the person-alities and political agendas of elites in power at a particular time. In the case of Botswana today, the three key individuals, to some extent professional bureaucrats in politicians' ministerial clothing, are President Sir Ketumile Masire, External Affairs Minister Lt. Gen. Mompati Merafhe, and Presidential Affairs Minister Ponatshego Kedikilwe. To this list should be added top Permanent Secretaries within the Department of External Affairs and the Office of the President.

In Botswana, foreign affairs and defence information released to or shared with the media consists exclusively of emerging results, outcomes, decisions, or policies, *not* deliberations, debates, disagreements, or details of the decision-making structure or process itself.

It is little wonder that the Botswana foreign affairs establishment within the Public Service which emerged after independence in 1966 has remained tight-lipped and paternalistic in dealing with politicians and journalists, especially its own. Future rul-ing elites were trained amidst a British colonial administrative service ethic of tight information management and steeped in the sometimes stifling atmosphere of official British government attitudes and policies toward the press and broadcasting. This was no doubt exacerbated by the Cold War atmosphere of national security leaks and infor-mation-hoarding in these sensitive policy areas.

Government media elites have been socialized in the post-independence era amidst these same constricting norms and attitudes. It is not by coincidence, therefore, that *both* foreign affairs *and* mass media remain housed today, thirty years after independence, in the Office of the President, and that each is a subordinate department rather than a separate, independent ministry. Botswana did not even have a minister of foreign affairs until President Seretse Khama relinquished this portfolio eight years after independence.

Botswana foreign policy elites readily acknowledge that they rely on other sources in formulating policy, primarily international shortwave news and public affairs broadcasts of the BBC, and that foreign news items in the *Daily News* are of only marginal interest. News of Botswana in the world, however, especially items concerning national security or defence, are perceived as especially sensitive and important.

INTERNATIONAL NEWS IN BOTSWANA

Journalism in Botswana is poorly-paid, low-prestige work. A government media sector as small, overworked, and undertrained as this, typical of African states, has no choice but to depend for the vast bulk of its international news on foreign wire services, particularly AFP and Reuters. Also used are PANA, Gemini, BBC, VOA, SAPA, Associated Press, and UPI. The high costs of maintaining foreign correspondents, even on a regional or continental basis, negates this option for Botswana. Botswana Press Agency or *Daily News* reporters are sometimes asked, at government expense, to accompany officials and delegations on trips abroad. This allows for a brief period of international news items with a "Botswana slant" but duties connected with covering the president or top ministers leave little time or resources for other kinds of on-site foreign reporting.

Private press reporters are excluded and must depend upon BOPA to select news off the foreign wire services. *Mmegi* also runs editorial-style foreign news items, political cartoons, or sometimes uses its poorly trained, overstretched reporters to interview foreign visitors. Access to foreign policy and defense elites is difficult, if not impossible, for representatives of the private papers. There are very few press conferences or briefings called which center on international affairs.

Foreign policy elites have learned that they can gain greater exposure and public relations impact by speaking with foreign journalists than with their own. There have been times when South African papers broke important regional news stories before Batswana reporters got wind of them, a situation bitterly resented in Gaborone newsrooms.

The extent to which the *Daily News* is a major source of information on Botswana's foreign policy and international affairs in general for its elite readership remains an unanswered empirical question. International news fills roughly 30% of the eight-page daily paper. On average, roughly half of the one page of Setswana language news in the paper is devoted to translations of these same stories. Radio Botswana broadcasts the same items in its hourly newsbriefs as well. Botswana does not have a national television service. There are no other sources of locally produced foreign and defence news.

Stories concerning Botswana's own external relations and defence news appear almost daily in these same outlets. All of them have a Botswana Press Agency byline and are written exclusively by Department of Information news editors from External Affairs Department or Office of the President releases. Other sources include briefings, coverage of official speeches, texts of agreements, coverage of conferences or meetings in Gaborone, foreign visits, presidential or ministerial trips, and official announcements. These are normally placed within the "National News" section of the *Daily News*.

A significant development in recent—post-1990—media coverage, quite unlike anything possible in the vast majority of African states today, is the sudden appearance of news items detailing aspects of the structure, process, finance, and perceived internal problems with the External Affairs Department itself. Some of this critical coverage has been undertaken by the *Daily News*. Requests for full ministerial status for foreign affairs, criticism of understaffed overseas missions, the need to spend more on foreign diplomatic representation abroad, and detailed reporting of the budget debates on external affairs and defense.

Private papers run dramatically less foreign news content, averaging from 0-10% of available space. Content tends to center on the most controversial subjects, including levels of defence spending, construction of a jet airbase, and allegations of foreign—U.S.—influence, Army—BDF—participation in UN-sponsored peacekeeping missions, and relations with South Africa. Political cartoons are, without a doubt, the most potent form which "foreign affairs content" takes.

This is due, to a large extent, to the fact that these papers are catering to a much less sophisticated, less-interested—in foreign news—non-elite audience. The visual format also allows for a means of reaching non-literate "readers" and perhaps gives a bit more latitude in terms of charges of bias, subversion, or illegality under information and national security legislation. So long as the organization and politics of news in Botswana remain relatively unaltered, the media will continue to primarily offer foreign news from official sources passed through official channels. Post-Cold War change in news values or selection criteria have been and are likely to remain minimal.

For the media, covering Botswana foreign policy means covering the President. By convention, anything he says or does is news. The relative ease with which he and his senior cabinet colleagues can command coverage account for the frequency with which their words, comings and goings, too, dominate news content. As "news objects" as well as news sources, ministers, and the bureaucratic organizations which they represent, structure and define the commonly accepted parameters of newsworthiness. Foreign news is what these officials say it is; in the words of Sigal, "less a sampling of what is happening in the world than a selection of what officials think—or want the press to report—is happening" (Sigal, 1973, p. 188).

PROJECTING BOTSWANA

An important element of Botswana's new post-Cold War foreign policy involves formulating diplomatic, commercial, and security strategies for playing a more active, visible global role. Foreign affairs content in national media reflect this change in national self-perception, particularly in *Daily News* items built from foreign policy speeches by the President and Minister of External Affairs.

The most noteworthy manifestation of this change in foreign policy direction has been Botswana's involvement in United Nations peacekeeping, observer, and relief operations in Rwanda, Somalia, and Mozambique over the past few years. Private journalists have been almost universally supportive—or silent—on the merits of these operations. One mildly suggested that "the government seems unable to resist being drawn into all kinds of foreign adventures" (Dira, "BDP's Streak," 1994, p. 7). Botswana has also acted as a lead state in pushing for stronger mechanisms and commitments to conflict mediation in Africa. A prime example which received extensive press treatment, were mediation efforts undertaken by President Masire to resolve the 1994 political crisis in Lesotho. News reports, official and private, were uniformly supportive.

A central component of this expanded projection extends to media reporting abroad. Particularly desirable has been favorable attention to Botswana's international peacekeeping role by the BBC World Service and by the foreign press. Dozens of stories appeared in the *Daily News*. Most items were built around Presidential or ministerial statements of praise and support for the effort. When the exemplary performance of BDF troops in Somalia "made the news" on the BBC and the Johannesburg *Star* in 1993, the stories themselves became national news with "page-1 significance" and were not only reported by the *Daily News* and Radio Botswana but also got picked up by the private press.

CRITICAL REPORTING ON DEFENSE

By the mid-1990s, at least two instances of investigative reporting on national defence matters brought intensified government pressure to bear on the private press. One sustained media assault on an ongoing defence policy concerned Operation Eagle, a huge, costly, new jet airbase under construction for the BDF. Specifically, the press criticized the "unwarranted and excessive secrecy within the government" concerning the reasons for spending roughly 20% of the current annual GDP on a non-productive military project at a time when the security situation, in the wake of majority rule in South Africa, was better than it had ever been. Private press stories also criticized alleged U.S. involvement and strategic "hidden agendas" in connection with the base construction.

This case may also be viewed as part of a trend towards more direct press criticism of excessively high levels of defence spending in the wake of the end of a South African military threat and the end of superpower politics in southern Africa. Some of the criticism has included stories built around expressed concerns of members of the government itself.

A second example pitted the BDF and the private press directly against each other and was probably the most serious—in the eyes of the government—case of private media irresponsibility to date. In August 1994 *Mmegi* ran a story which alleged that factional splits within the ruling Botswana Democratic Party had become so serious that "the shock waves are beginning to rock the army… top brass are having to declare their loyalties"—to factional leaders. The article further alleged that BDF Commander Brigadier Ian Khama, son of the deceased former president and founder of the ruling party, "has expressed solidarity with Merafhe," one of the faction leaders. Implicit in the story was a further intimation of ethnic division: "it was a north-south—in Botswana—thing." It also alleged "regional bias" in Army promotions and implied a "secret agenda" within the Merafhe faction in senior officer promotions.

The next issue of *Mmegi* contained another provocative article under the headline "Military Rule Coming to Botswana", based on a press conference given by a senior opposition party leader. He warned that "Botswana risks being taken over by a military government if the ruling party government continues to ignore the requests of the opposition."

One week later, *Mmegi* editors ran an even more provocative two-page spread, complete with "classic" anti-BDF political cartoons and large-print excerpts from a press briefing for government journalists given by Brigadier Khama under the headline: "Army and the Press: When the Pen Crosses the Sword." The story was written from portions of his remarks which were especially critical of the private press. Ironically, a BOPA story on the press briefing was the main factual source of the *Mmegi* item.

The cumulative inflammatory effect of this series of articles was such that the Minister of Presidential Affairs, responsible for both media and defence, issued a scathing attack in National Assembly debate. He was joined by a prominent opposition MP, who cautioned the press against "compromising the good name of the BDF." Minister Merafhe warned the press against "undermining our stability" and accused the writer of [going out of his way] to promote dissention within the army."

Two weeks later, *Mmegi* turned the temperature down considerably, publishing a measured opinion piece under the headline: "The Army and the Press Need Each Other." Side by side with it, however, was another op-ed item criticizing the government and military of "too much secrecy… arrogan[ce] and insensitivi[ty]."

Some in government continue to push for greater press controls but the majority view seems to be to let it continue to develop. Self-censorship in Botswana national security and defense reporting remains high in the face of continuing government pressure for restraint. The Penal Code of Botswana contains a provision which gives the president the power to prohibit any publication which he considers to be contrary to the national interest, including defense reporting. Section 17 of the Botswana Constitution allows the government to declare a state of emergency and subsequently announce regulations giving it the power to censor newspapers. Finally, there is the Official Secrets Act, which forbids publication of information harmful to the security of the nation (White, 1983).

Clearly, government has the tools to severely restrict the press if it chooses. The fact that is has not is politically significant. State-run or free, the press cannot exist or function apart from the political-economic context within which it gathers, defines, transforms, selects, and disseminates political information—including foreign and defense policy information.

PARTISANSHIP IN FOREIGN NEWS

One month before the 1994 Botswana national elections, the leading opposition party, the Botswana National Front, issued its first party manifesto since the 1960s. The manifesto appeared in *Mmegi* as a two-page advertisement, strengthening the widely shared perception of the political leanings of the newspaper. It contains sections on defence and foreign policy which suggest that a BNF government would significantly alter policy priorities and objectives in defence (BNF, 1994, pp. 16–17). On October 15, 1994, the BNF captured 13 of 39 National Assembly seats, unprecedented opposition representation at the national level.

Out of power, the BNF can be expected to continue to use the private press, especially *Mmegi*, to convey opposition perspectives on foreign and defense policies of the BDP government into the future. How kindly it would take to such media criticism of foreign and security policy if it becomes the ruling party, however, remains open to speculation.

CONCLUSIONS

Botswana is not so much a "media-poor" polity as it is a media stratified one. The stratification is generational as well as locational and economic in nature. Key mechanisms dividing the generations are knowledge, access, and economic means. Young, university-educated Batswana elites share new attitudes toward information access, leadership, and governance. They are part of a generation that has never experienced colonialism and is more open to a global discourse in which events in Bosnia may have an immediate impact in Africa.

The Botswana press is nowhere near as important, in terms of influencing foreign policy-makers or informing interested elite publics, as new electronic mass media technologies, particularly "personalized" electronic ones, like satellite-microwave TV, fax, PCs, and the Internet. While still not true for the average person, Botswana diplomats, bureaucrats, politicians, and journalists are fast joining the ranks of an international information elite.

A newly-wired Gaborone is already enabling government and media elites with PCs and modems to bypass or dispense with Radio Botswana, BOPA, and the *Daily News*. Progressively, they will gain increased electronic access to foreign policy information, via data downloading, on-line libraries and archives, and on-line news services from around the world. The Office of the President and External Affairs will soon be able to communicate with embassies and missions over international electronic mail, radically transforming the roles of diplomatic and counsellor personnel at headquarters and abroad, and eventually, structures and processes of policy decision-making.

The same holds true for the Botswana media sector itself. Media dependence upon government for external affairs information will decrease. Technological innovations in news collection, processing, and dissemination are already transforming journalistic practice in Botswana. CNN, communications satellite feeds, fax, and internet connections in newsrooms at ever-lower costs have opened up a world of potential international news copy and background material for formerly marginalized newspapers in countries like Botswana. For example, the Media Institute of Southern Africa is moving ahead with a project to provide internet access to independent newspapers in the sub-region, freeing them from dependence on national or international wire services.

Traditional approaches and methods of formulating, implementing, reporting—and evaluating—foreign policies and international affairs are rapidly being challenged by overwhelming technological changes in transmission, storage and retrieval of information and interactive, instantaneous political communication. The press role, to the extent there ever was one, will be swept away. Why read the *Daily News* when there are CNN and the BBC? Why use fax when there is international electronic mail?

Botswana aspires to a regional, continental, and even global role in a transforming international system. A stronger, economically prosperous, politically stable and democratic Botswana offers a valuable example for the region and for Africa generally. Its successes, while trumpeted across the pages and airwaves of national mass media, have been almost totally invisible and unheard outside of its own borders. It remains to be seen just when and how this may change for the better in the years ahead.

REFERENCES

This chapter contains information and opinions gained by the author from interviews with Batswana journalists and diplomats in Gaborone, London, and Washington D.C. between 1985–93. Names and affiliations are withheld to protect the integrity and anonymity of individuals.

Ansah, P. (1981). In *Rural journalism in Africa*, (Paris: UNESCO).
Bennett, W. L. (1994). The Media and the foreign policy process. In D. A. Deese (Ed.), *The new politics of American foreign policy*, (pp.168–88). New York: St. Martin's Press.
Botswana National Front. (1994, September 9–15). Manifesto. In *Mmegi* (Gaborone), 16–17.
Cohen, B. C. (1963). *The press and foreign policy*, Princeton: Princeton University Press.
Dira, F. (1994, July 15–21). BDP's streak of conservatism. *Mmegi*, 7.
Gambari, I. A. (1989). *Theory and reality in foreign policy making: Nigeria after the second republic*. London: Humanities Press.
Graber, D. A. (1993). Foreign affairs coverage. In *Mass media and American politics* (4th ed.). (pp.360–402). Washington DC: Congressional Quarterly Press.
Harbison, J. W. & Rothchild, D. (Eds.), (1995). *Africa in world politics: Post-Cold War challenges*. Boulder, CO: Westview Press.
Herbst, J. (1993). *The politics of reform in Ghana*. Berkeley, CA: University of California Press.
Lamb, D. (1982). *The Africans*. (pp. 244–245). New York: Random House.
Merrill, J. C. (1991). *Global journalism* (2nd. ed.). (pp.161–64). New York: Longman.
Mytton, G. (1983). *Mass communication in Africa*. London: Edward Arnold.

Okere, L. C. (1992). The press and foreign policy in Nigeria. *The round table, (London), 321,* 61–71.

Sigal, L. V. (1973). *Reporters and officials.* Lexington, MA: D.C. Heath.

White, R. (1983, May 6). Censorship: The Botswana Reality. *The Examiner,* (Gaberone), 1.

Zaffiro, J. J. (1989). The press and political opposition in an African democracy. *Journal of Commonwealth and Comparative Politics, (London), 22(1),* 51-73.

Zaffiro, J. J. (1993). Foreign policy decision-making in an African democracy. In S. J. Stedman (Ed.), *Botswana: The political economy of democratic development* (pp.139–60). Boulder, CO: Lynne Reinner.

Zaffiro, J. J. (1995). Redesigning foreign policy for the 21st century: The new world order from a Botswana perspective. *Africa Insight, (Pretoria), 25(2),* 98–107.

chapter 13

New York Times' editorial position and U.S. foreign policy: the case of Iran revisited[*]

Abbas Malek
Howard University

I n our increasingly interconnected, interdependent and, some say, shrinking world, the media and their effectiveness in the international sphere has become heightened in importance. Indeed, the press as a dominant institution in American society has a particularly profound impact upon the foreign policy making process, by virtue of its role in informing citizens and decision-makers about the often less familiar, yet complex, issues of international relations.

With the thawing of the Cold War and the ending of its characteristic rigid bipolarity, an emerging configuration of multi-polarity has injected the increased potential for instability and conflict into the international system. It would appear that the U.S. focus on economic, political, and military concerns have become less defined and more complex, as more and more nations and regions, including the Middle East, have become important factors in international relations. The type of press coverage that the American public and policy-makers receive is, therefore, of critical importance, since it assists in shaping their perceptions and images of other regions and peoples of the world and defines the parameters of the global political environment.

In particular, an understanding of Iran, as a major state actor in the politics of the Middle East, is important in expanding Western conceptions of the region and its difficulties. The number of previous studies on U.S. press coverage of Iran is testimonial to the importance of Iran in Middle Eastern affairs, as well as the U.S.–Iranian relationship. Despite an array of scholarship on U.S. press coverage of Iran, these studies con-

[*] The author thanks Howard University for the summer research grant to complete this chapter. The author also would like to thank Tina Patterson for all her work on this chapter.

centrated exclusively on the decades leading up to the Iranian revolution and through the hostage crisis. After 1981, research and analysis concerning the media's treatment of Iran seems to have halted, even though Iran and the Middle East have since witnessed war and several crises.

This chapter, therefore, provides a unique exploration of the press and foreign policy relationship with respect to Iran in two ways. First, it will provide follow-up research to examine the question of the press's function in U.S. foreign policy, with Iran having been chosen as a case study to be analyzed as a continuation of previous studies and research. This study has been designed to relate particularly to previous research (Malek, 1984) and article (Malek, 1988) which focused on the press and foreign policy relationship from 1968 through 1981. Second, unlike most research that undertakes the study of foreign policy in abstract or isolation, this study investigates the similarity and dissimilarity between official government foreign policy and the *New York Times'* editorial content on international issues. The distinctiveness of such a project, therefore, rests on the intent to document and explore the interplay between an elite newspaper's foreign policy, as reflected in the editorial section, and official, foreign policy as represented by official government documents.

THE MEDIA & FOREIGN POLICY RELATIONSHIP: IN BRIEF

The press, as an independent actor in a democratic society, plays a mediating role, whereby it collects, monitors, and disseminates information between a government and its citizens. The filtering and informative function of the press has particular importance in the realm of international relations, as few citizens and even decision-makers have access through other sources to the types of general information needed to make informed decisions on issues of international concern (Cohen 1961, 1963; Entman 1989; O'Heffernan 1991). Indeed, due to the distinctive and exclusive nature of the foreign policy sphere and the existence of numerous barriers to the gathering of information in a foreign country, the press is much more likely, in international affairs than in other policy areas, to influence and shape the government response or approach to an international issue.

However, for the public to be well informed, it is simply not enough for the press to be free. One may argue that in a democratic society, such as the U.S., the press should assume the responsibility of disseminating information on issues from a broad range of sources in order to aid in the formation of a more enlightened and knowledgeable public. The importance of social responsibility on the part of the press is particularly great in international affairs coverage, since the public is further removed from the information needed to form opinions. It is, therefore, of the utmost importance that the press exercise the freedom it has been granted not only to gather accurate and thorough information on world affairs, but also to disseminate such information to the public. All too often, however, the press seems to be reluctant to question its government's interpretation of foreign affairs and, therefore, the public does not truly become better informed about international issues. Indeed, it might even be concluded that the interdependence of the news media-government relationship grants the government a degree of covert "control," or at least influence, over the media (Herman & Chomsky 1988; Bennett 1988; Malek & Leidig 1991).

In order to evaluate the success of the media in their job of reporting on international affairs, one may not even have to look past the headlines of the major, elite newspapers. If the press is fulfilling its obligations to society, tomorrow's headlines should never come as a shock to today's readers. Numerous studies of the press in its role in the international arena have, however, concluded "a failure" by the press, since the American public and policy-makers have been caught off guard by ensuing international events and issues (Kellner 1992; Parenti 1992; Mowlana 1992). One such example of this "failure" can be identified in the press treatment of Iran during the period leading up to and including the 1978–79 revolution and the 1979–81 hostage crisis (Dorman & Farhang 1987; Malek 1988). In addition, studies have demonstrated that there was a strong reliance by the press upon the official, stated U.S. policy toward Iran and a failure to analyze independently the social, economic, and political undercurrents surfacing during the "modernization" programs of the Shah. Thus, the failure of the press, despite its freedom and access, is evident in the coverage of Iran, where one day there were headlines heralding the stability and progress of Iran under the Shah and the next day there was the report of revolution.

METHODOLOGY

The overall objective of this study is to view the data that exists since 1981, in order to try to determine whether there have been any changes in the press's analysis of events and the political atmosphere in Iran since 1981, compared with the time period prior to the revolution, when a study concluded that it was inadequate. In this follow-up study, to previous research into the press treatment of Iran and U.S. governmental policy toward Iran, a content analysis was conducted on *New York Times'* editorials and policy statements documented in the *Department of State Bulletin* from 1981 through 1994. The uniqueness of such an undertaking is that it attempts to provide a means for the comparison of "the foreign policy" of the *New York Times*, as reflected through its editorial page, and actual U.S. foreign policy, as found in official policy statements. This task, therefore, required the collection, review, coding, and statistical analysis of two distinct data sets which could then ultimately be utilized to draw conclusions about the similarity and dissimilarity that has existed between U.S. foreign policy toward Iran and the press coverage of Iran since the conclusion of the American hostage crisis.

DATA COLLECTION

The actual research phase of this project began with the collection of editorial pieces and policy statements on Iran, however, it is important to first realize why the sources for the collection of this study's data were chosen. The *New York Times* was selected due to its role as a premier member of the elite press, which assigns to it an influential role in informing American leaders and interested members of the citizenry on international affairs. As one of the pioneers in the study of press and foreign policy put it: "The *Times* is uniformly regarded as the authoritative paper in foreign policy field" (Cohen, 1961, p. 220). Furthermore, the editorial section of the *New York Times*, rather than actual news, was isolated as representing the policy stances and leanings of the editorial staff and thus the newspaper as a whole. After all, the editorial section of an elite paper, like any other, represents a paper's stand and position on the issues discussed in the paper. As one of the *Times* chief editors once said: "Nobody should be left in doubt as to where the *Times* stands on any major subject." He implied that it is not only the opportunity, but the duty of the editorial page to enter and clarify the paper's position on any significant issue (Adams, 1966). For its part, the *Department of State Bulletin*[1] was chosen because it provides a uniform source, in which the official foreign policy statements of the President, Secretary of State, and other decision-makers are documented.

The actual collection of data started with several searches conducted through Lexis-Nexis, the *New York Times Index*, and various indices attached to the volumes of the *Department of State Bulletin* in order to determine the location of editorials and policy statements. This preliminary stage having been completed, the two data sets that emerged were a) all *New York Times* editorials in which, directly or indirectly, Iran was the subject of discussion between 1981 and 1994; and b) all policy statements and other documents relating to Iran, as published in the *Department of State Bulletin* for the period, 1981–1994.

REVIEW AND CODING

The coding stage began with the separate review of the editorials and policy statements in order to determine the major topics of discussion. The identification of these broad topic areas were then used to eliminate those editorials or policy statements which presented topics that did not appear in the other data set. For example, if *New York Times'* editorials contained a topic area, Iranian-Soviet Relations, and this topic did not appear in the *Department of State Bulletin* statements, then those editorials dealing with this topic would have been excluded from the data sets. This preliminary review assisted in condensing the amount of material involved and yielded the actual data sets which would then be used for the remainder of the study's analysis.

The remaining editorials and policy statements in the two data sets contained the mention and discussion of eight major topics: a) U.S.–Iran Relations; b) Terrorism; c) Internal Political Situation; d) Oil; e) Arms Sales; f) Regional Role; g) Iran-Iraq War;

---

[1] The official foreign policy data set is referred to throughout this study as the *Department of State Bulletin*, despite its being renamed as of 1989. In actuality the foreign policy statements on Iran were collected from the *Department of State Bulletin* (1981–1989) and its successor, the *Department of State Dispatch* (since 1989).

and h) Human Rights. The data sets were then reviewed again to reveal several subtopics within each major topic area, although the number of subtopics varied from topic to topic and from one source to the other.[2]

After identifying the topics and subtopics, they were evaluated through three different means: 1) a comparison in the distribution of editorials and policy documents by year and major subject area; 2) the general evaluation of an editorial or policy document as "favorable," "unfavorable," or "neutral;" and 3) for the evaluation of all of the topics and subtopics within a piece so that they adhered to the three coding categories—"favorable," "unfavorable," and "neutral." In other words, the content of each piece was first evaluated as one entity, based on its major topics and themes, and in the second stage each topic/ subtopic was evaluated independently.

FINDINGS

Analysis of Comparative Distribution

In viewing the data of this study it becomes immediately obvious that similarities exist in the annual distribution of editorial pieces and policy statements [see Table 13.1]. In fact, in studying the yearly distribution, three major trends appear to surface. First, after 1981 and the release of the American hostages in Iran, one may witness a trickling off effect in the attention paid to Iran in both the *New York Times* and *Department of State Bulletin*. With the exception of slight increases shown in 1983 and 1984, the time peri-

TABLE 13.1.
Yearly Distribution of Editorials and Policy Documents from *The New York Times* and
***Department of State Bulletin* (1981–1994)**

Year	NYT	DSB
1981	16	6
1982	4	5
1983	6	6
1984	6	5
1985	3	4
1986	4	3
1987	14	8
1988	16	11
1989	8	6
1990	2	0
1991	2	1
1992	4	5
1993	4	4
1994	1	0

---

[2] See APPENDIX ONE for a list of all major topics and their respective subtopics.

od from 1982 to 1986 represents a downward trend in the frequency of Iran content in editorials and policy statements. Second, 1987 and 1988 represent a rather significant upward swing in the frequency with which Iran was a subject for discussion in both data sources. During this period, the number of editorials—14 and 16—were higher than the frequency of policy statements—8 and 11. This slight inconsistency could possibly be seen as the press's response to increased public interest and heightened media cynicism in the government's relationships and policies toward Iran, given the aftermath of the Iran-Contra scandal. Third, 1989 through 1994 again signals a generally downward sloping trend in the frequency of editorials and policy statements. Only 1992 and 1993 provide a slight anomaly by showing a modest increase in the frequencies from both of the study's sources. This increase may be explained by an increased interest in the Middle Eastern region, given the events leading up to and through the Persian Gulf War and the U.S.'s involvement in the region through Operation Desert Storm. Despite the existence of these three general trends, it is interesting to note that, except for 1987 and 1988, the annual frequency of editorials in comparison to the frequency of policy statements differ by no more than two. Therefore, a high degree of similarity exists in the annual distribution of the two data sets in this study.

Table 13.2 illustrates the frequency distribution of editorials and policy statements based upon the eight major topic areas determined for this study. In viewing the percentages for the editorials and policy statements of each topic area, four topics—U.S.–Iran Relations, Terrorism, Internal Political Situation, and Human Rights—represent the widest margin of divergence between the two data sets. Whereas the other four major topics yielded a difference on average of 1.4%, these topics of greatest dissimilarity varied from a low of 8.1% to a high of 14.9%. A greater percentage of the *Department of State Bulletin*'s policy statements were devoted to U.S.–Iran Relations and Terrorism, while the *New York Times*' editorials showed a higher concentration in such topics as the Internal Political Situation and Human Rights.

In the case of these four topics, it is not always easy to provide an explanation for why such a divergence occurred between the distribution of editorials and policy doc-

TABLE 13.2.
Major Topic Distribution of Editorials and Policy Documents from the New York Times and Department of State Bulletin (1981–1994)

Topics	NYT		DSB	
U.S.-Iran Relations	16	(11.9%)	21	(20.0%)
Terrorism	11	(8.2%)	20	(19.0%)
Internal Political Situation	28	(20.9%)	12	(11.4%)
Oil	5	(3.7%)	4	(3.8%)
Arms Sale	2	(1.5%)	3	(2.8%)
Regional Role	16	(11.9%)	13	(12.3%)
Iran-Iraq War	31	(23.1%)	28	(26.7%)
Human Rights	25	(18.7%)	4	(3.8%)
TOTAL	134		105	

uments. As might be expected, the official government documents placed a higher degree of importance upon topics which had the greatest impact upon a state's right to control its security and relations with other states. While the press is also interested in presenting the topics of U.S.–Iran Relations and Terrorism to the public, the press would be far more likely to yield to the government's interpretation of these topics, because the U.S., as a state, is entrusted with the responsibility of providing security to its citizens and territorial integrity, while maintaining its legitimacy as a sovereign actor in international relations. An adequate explanation for why the *New York Times* referred to the topic of Iran's Internal Political Situation more frequently is more difficult to comprehend, although perhaps it does signal an effort by the press to remain more in tune with and aware of the intricacies of a state's—such as Iran—internal situation. Lastly, while a state may be concerned about human rights in the formulation of foreign policy, the press has recognized the role it can play in elevating human rights on the foreign policy agenda by keeping the images and issues of human rights' abuses in the minds of the public and decision-makers. Indeed, the *New York Times* may have been attempting to influence the U.S. government's response to human rights violations in Iran by maintaining a steady series of editorials detailing the dismal treatment of political opponents and members of the Baha'i' faith within Iran.

General Content Analysis

The next area of analysis in this chapter findings revolves around the overall comparison of the content analysis of the editorial pieces and policy documents for the time period of this study, 1981–1994. Table 13.3 provides a breakdown of *New York Times'* editorials and the Department of State Bulletin's statements, based upon the three evaluation categories, "negative," "neutral," and "positive." From this table, one quickly notices that the analysis of the content revealed that the majority of the data collected from both sources fell into the negative category, with 63.4% of the editorials and 52.4% of the policy statements containing content negative or unfavorable toward Iran. Furthermore, under 6% of either *New York Times'* editorials or *Department of State Bulletin's* statements presented a positive or favorable impression of Iran, its citizens, or major policies and activities. The remainder of the data, 35.2% of the editorials and 41.9% of the policy documents, represented or referred to Iran in a neutral light. This

TABLE 13.3.
Overall Evaluation of the Content Analysis from *The New York Times* and *Department of State Bulletin*, by Frequency and Percentage (1981–1994)

EVALUATION	NYT		DSB	
POSITIVE	2	(1.5%)	6	(5.7%)
NEUTRAL	47	(35.1%)	44	(41.9%)
NEGATIVE	85	(63.4%)	55	(52.4%)
TOTAL	134	(100.0%)	105	(100.0%)

overall evaluation, therefore, suggests that a high level of similarity existed between the *New York Times'* and the *Department of State Bulletin's* treatment of Iran from 1981 through 1994. One might even conclude that the press has remained dependent upon the government and official policy in establishing the focus and tone of their treatment and coverage of international affairs, specifically Iran.

Content Analysis by Topic and Subtopic

The final section necessary in the evaluation of this study's findings is a comparison of the content analysis of the two data sources by major topic areas and subtopics. A series of stacked bar graphs and pie charts, which provide a visual illustration of the positive, neutral, or negative treatment of each topic and subtopic for both the *New York Times* and the Department of State Bulletin have been integrated into the text of this study. The graphs and charts furnish an easy to detect means of observing the similarity and dissimilarity that has existed from 1981 until 1994 in editorial and official policy treatment of topics and subtopics specific to Iran. In addition, Table 13.4 has been included in the text to provide a statistical way to view the comparison of the two data sources' treatments of the eight major subject areas.

Figure 13.1 presents a stacked bar graph which illustrates an overall view of how editorials and policy documents treated the topic, U.S.-Iran Relations, while the series of pie charts (Figure 13.2) offer a means by which to compare the treatment of this topic's three subtopics. The bar graph shows that both the *New York Times* and the *Department of State Bulletin* devoted a similar amount of attention to U.S.–Iran Relations. Furthermore, these editorials and policy documents treated this topic with very little, if anything positive to say, since strong neutral and negative approaches were reflected in both the editorials and policy documents. Through the pie charts, one also notices that The *New York Times* appears to have mirrored official policy state-

TABLE 13.4.
Comparative Subject Evaluation of *The New York Times* and *Department of State Bulletin*
(1981–1994)

SUBJECT	POSITIVE		NEUTRAL		NEGATIVE	
	NYT	DSB	NYT	DSB	NYT	DSB
U.S.-IRAN RELATIONS	0.0%	4.8%	68.8%	76.2%	31.3%	19.0%
TERRORISM	0.0%	5.0%	27.3%	5.0%	72.7%	90.0%
INTERNAL POLITICAL SITUATION	3.6%	25.0%	17.9%	33.3%	78.6%	41.7%
OIL	20.0%	0.0%	20.0%	25.0%	60.0%	75.0%
ARMS SALE	0.0%	0.0%	50.0%	33.3%	50.0%	66.7%
REGIONAL ROLE	0.0%	0.0%	6.2%	30.8%	93.8%	69.2%
IRAN-IRAQ WAR	0.0%	3.6%	80.6%	60.7%	19.4%	35.7%
HUMAN RIGHTS	0.0%	0.0%	0.0%	0.0%	100.0%	100.0%

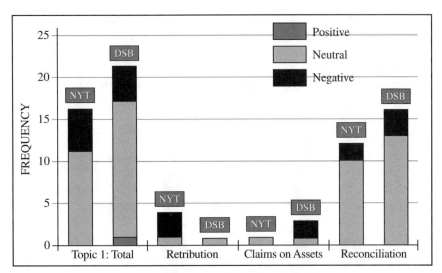

FIGURE 13.1. Topic 1: U.S.–Iran relations topic & subtopic distribution.

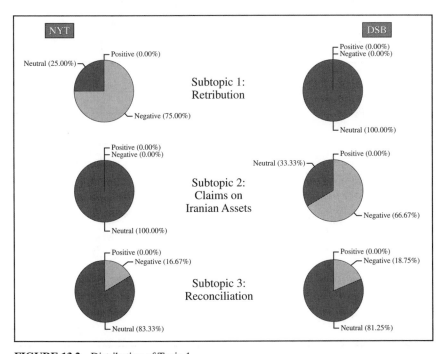

FIGURE 13.2. Distribution of Topic 1.

ments in that the treatment of retribution, claims on Iranian assets, and reconciliation were handled in an predominately neutral or negative manner.

On the topic of Terrorism [see Figure 13.3], the graphs and charts [see Figure 13.4] indicate a high level of similarity in the content of the editorials and policy statements from the two data sources. For example, in the case of terrorism, in general, both the

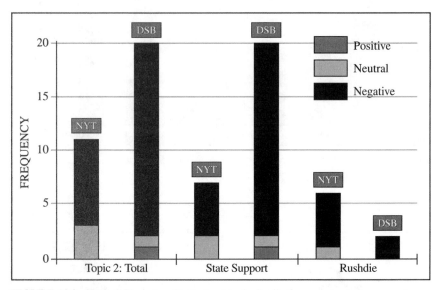

FIGURE 13.3. Topic 2: Terrorism. Topic & subtopic distribution.

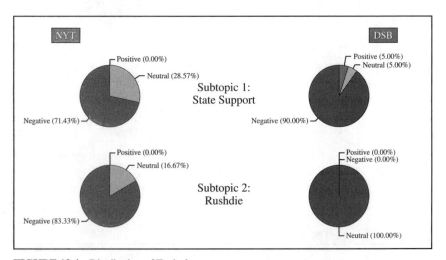

FIGURE 13.4. Distribution of Topic 2.

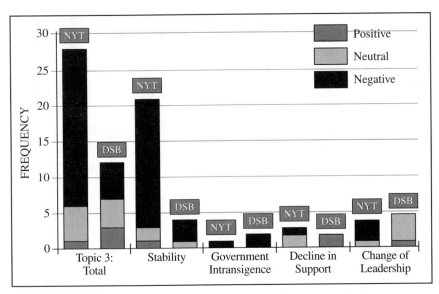

FIGURE 13.5. Topic 3: Internal political situation. Topic & subtopic distribution.

Department of State Bulletin and the *New York Times* presented content which was overwhelmingly unfavorable, as 90% of the policy documents and 72.7% of the editorial pieces were negative. This trend carried over into the treatment of the terrorism subtopics, state support of terrorism and Salmon Rushdie. The two subtopics were treated almost exclusively negatively by both data sets. Furthermore, *Times'* editorials seem to display an absence of analysis in trying to explain how or why Iran might have issued a death sentence against author, Salmon Rushdie. Instead, the unfavorable assessment of the editorials reflected the government's negative impressions and society's commitment to the freedom of expression. Indeed, it was not inherently anticipated that any positive statements would be observed in either source when discussing a subject like terrorism. The point is rather that the similarity existed between the two sources in almost all of the documented topics and subtopics, including terrorism.

In looking at the Internal Political Situation [see Figure 13.5], the *Times* presented a much more unfavorable treatment than that of the government's official policy documents. In fact, the *Department of State Bulletin* appears to have treated the general internal political situation in Iran with relative even handedness, from which one might conclude that U.S. government at some point was trying to express some inclination toward establishing a closer relationship with Iran. Both the editorials and policy documents presented a negative treatment of the stability and government intransigence of Iran's internal political situation [see Figure 13.6]. However, the treatment of the other two subtopics, a decline in political support and the changing of leadership, provide an example of where differences emerged. It would appear through the official policy documents that the prospects of changing leadership, brought about by a decline in political support for the Iranian government under the Ayatollah, were viewed as an entirely positive prospect. The media, through *New York Times'* editorials, however, seemed far more wary of such changes and even treated these subtopics unfavorably. This is perhaps a slight indication, in this case, that the press had recognized the need for more complex analysis of the social, economic, cultural, and political undercurrents in Iran, since changes in government and leadership usually reflect other trends and changes in the rest of society.

The topics of oil, arms sales, and Iran's regional role [see Figures 13.7, 13.9, and 13.11; and Figures 13.8, 13.10, and 13.12] may be looked at as illustrating the sim-

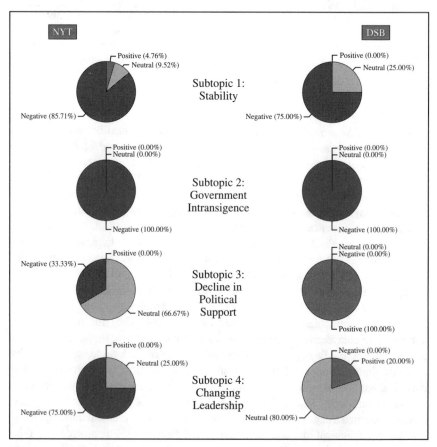

FIGURE 13.6. Distribution of Topic 3.

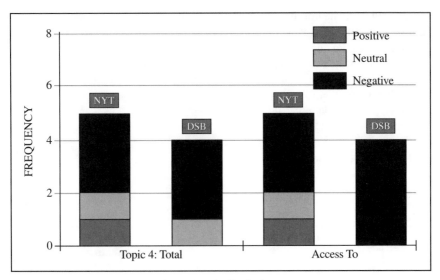

FIGURE 13.7. Topic 4: Oil. Topic & subtopic distribution.

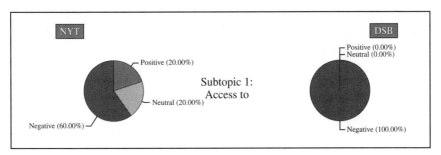

FIGURE 13.8. Distribution of Topic 4.

ilarities between the content contained in this study's editorials and policy documents. In these three topic areas, the editorial and policy treatment was overwhelmingly negative. Both the government and the press presented a united front in expressing distress over Iran's ability to adversely affect Western access to oil resources, the need to sever the supply of arms to Iran, and the fear that Iran's Islamic fundamentalism and expansionist aspirations could lead to the destabilization of the region. In fact, to the extent that Iran would be able to prevent access to valuable oil resources and continue to purchase weaponry, the U.S. government and the press would most likely have become increasingly concerned about Iran's impact upon the stability of the Middle Eastern region.

With regard to the Iran-Iraq War [see Figure 13.3], the *Times'* editorials reflected a relatively neutral stance, which was in accordance with that of the U.S. government's policy claim toward this war. In fact, of the eight topic areas, the Iran-Iraq War was the most neutrally treated subject area. When viewing the six subtopics of this subject [see Figure 13.14], however, some subtle differences seem to surface. For example, although the overall government approach to the Iran–Iraq War was one of neutrality, the press, through editorials, appeared to be encouraging the U.S.'s greater isolation

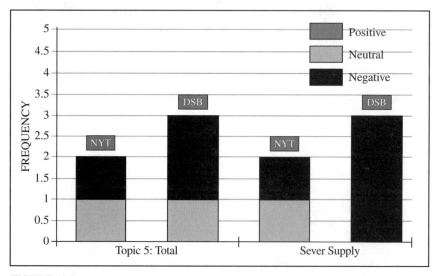

FIGURE 13.9. Topic 5: Arms sale. Topic & subtopic distribution.

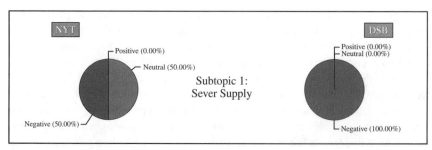

FIGURE 13.10. Distribution of Topic 5.

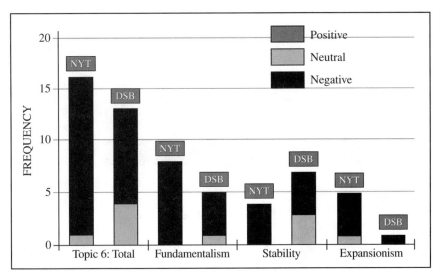

FIGURE 13.11. Topic 6: Regional role. Topic & subtopic distribution.

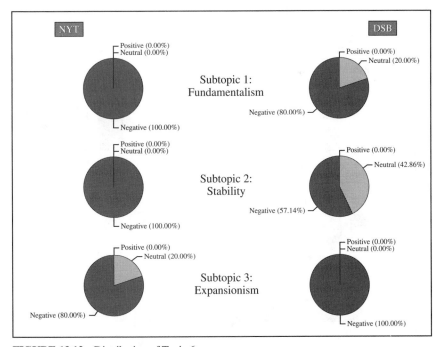

FIGURE 13.12. Distribution of Topic 6.

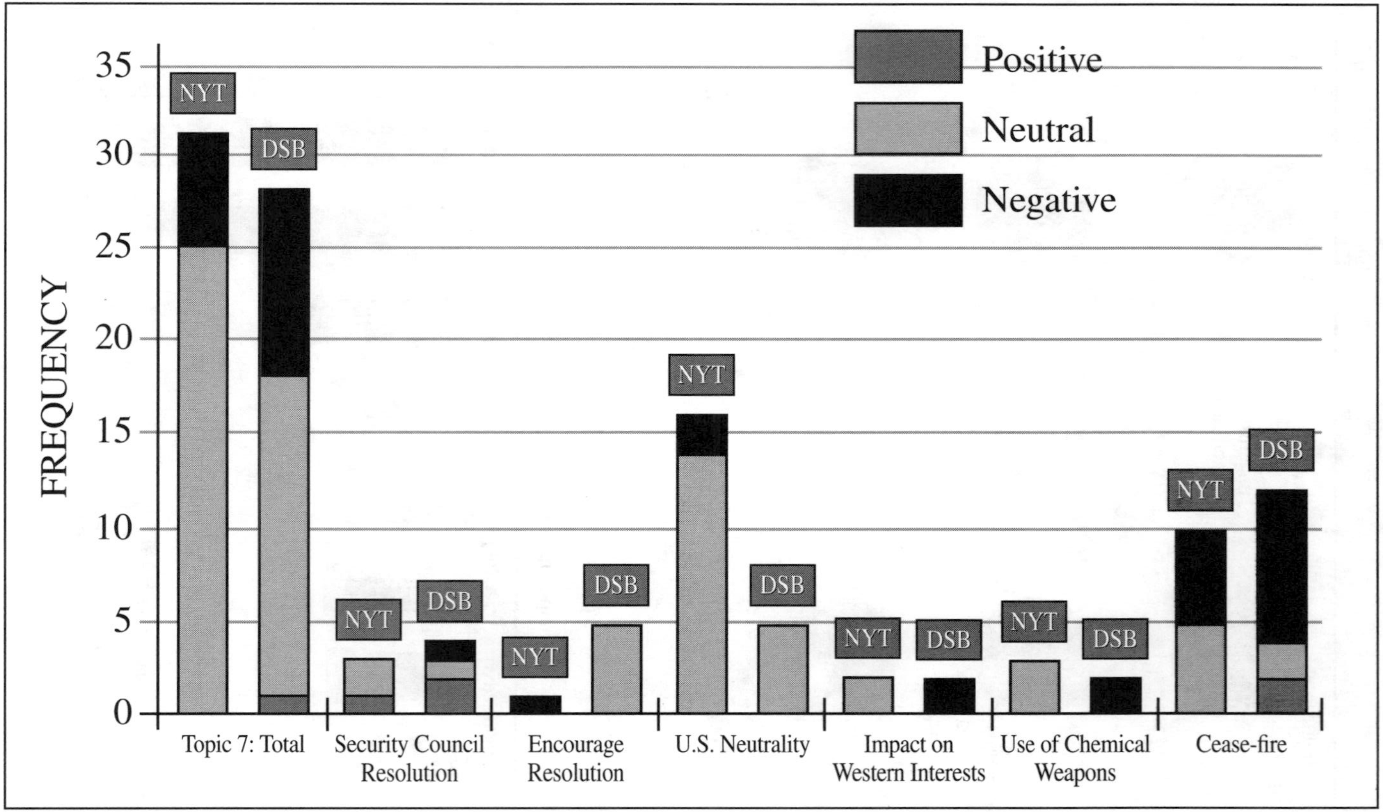

FIGURE 13.13. Topic 7: Iran–Iraq war. Topic & subtopic distribution.

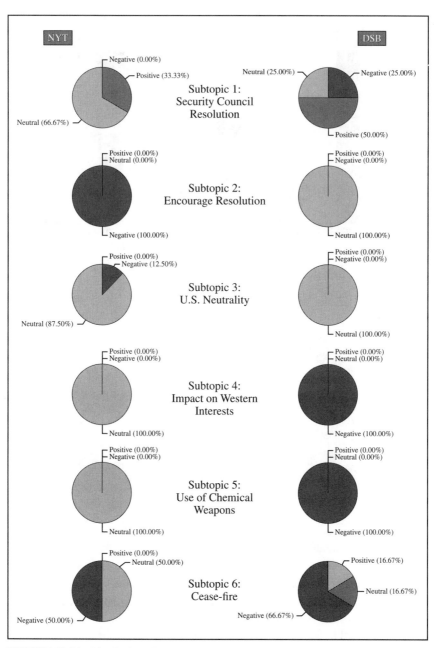

FIGURE 13.14. Distribution of Topic 7.

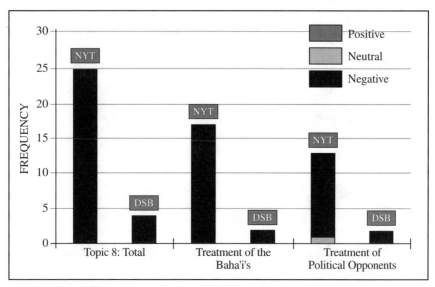

FIGURE 13.15. Topic 8: Human rights. Topic & subtopic distribution.

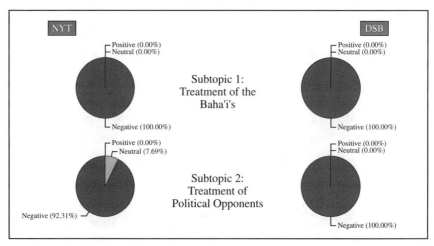

FIGURE 13.16. Distribution of Topic 8.

from this conflict. So whereas policy documents expressed some negative leanings toward the impact that the war was having on Western interests and the use of chemical weapons, the editorials communicated a higher commitment to neutrality. This is further illustrated in the *New York Times'* unfavorable view of the U.S. brokering or encouraging some sort of resolution, whereas the idea of a U.N. Security Council Resolution was more favorably received.

In the final topic category, Human Rights [see Figure 13.16], the press and government policy were almost entirely negative about Iran's experiences in this area. Indeed, both sources expressed nearly unanimous condemnation of Iran's treatment of political opponents to the government and the Baha'i's [see Figure 13.17]. Their coverage of the human rights issues of Iran was, however, not identical, since the *Times* ran approximately six times the number of policy statements published on the same issue. As alluded to previously, this discrepancy in the concentration on human rights issues between the press and the government is likely explained by the media's realization of the influence that it wields in the setting of foreign policy in the sphere of human rights. The media, through words and images, may consistently bombard the American public with examples of certain human rights abuses to the point that the government may feel pressured to act or respond to these abuses quicker or more forcefully than it would have otherwise.

A BRIEF COMPARATIVE ANALYSIS WITH
PREVIOUS FINDINGS

Since a major objective of this chapter was to provide the follow-up research necessary to update previous studies dealing with the news media and governmental policy toward Iran, it is only fitting to provide a comparison, albeit brief, of this new study and previous findings. Of particular assistance in this comparative exercise is this author's 1988 article, "*New York Times*' Editorial Position and the U.S. Foreign Policy: The Case of Iran," which used a similar methodology to this study, in order to examine the news media-foreign policy relationship with respect to Iran in the decade leading up to and through the 1979 Revolution and the end of the hostage crisis in 1981.

The 1988 article concluded that a similarity existed between the *Times*' editorial position and U.S. governmental policy towards Iran, during the time period between 1968 and 1981. By reviewing the charts, graphs, and tables generated from the data of this most recent research, results that are very similar to those found in the earlier study can be seen. Indeed, upon further exploring the data, it appears only reasonable to recognize that the media and government have an interdependent relationship whereby, given the nature of foreign affairs reporting, the press is highly influenced, directly and indirectly, by the government's policy or position toward an issue, conflict, or state.

Even though this study seems to show that the press continue to follow the governmental policy in reporting on international affairs, the press do appear to have made some minor changes in this case, since their failure in the decade leading up to the revolution in Iran. For example, on the attention given to Iran measured by the number of pieces published, on average, the number of *New York Times*' editorials per year devoted to issues related to Iran have nearly tripled since the previous study [see Table 13.5]. At the same time, it must be kept in mind that during the time period for this study, Iran was involved in a major eight years war with Iraq. However,

TABLE 13.5.
Comparative Distribution of Editorials and Documents Throughout Two Time Periods
(1968–1981; 1981–1995)

TIME PERIOD	FREQUENCY		PER YEAR	
	NYT	DSB	NYT	DSB
FIRST STUDY (1968–1981)	51	93	3.9	7.1
SECOND STUDY (1981–1995)	134	105	9.5	7.5

in comparing the number of policy documents per year between the time periods of the two studies, one will notice that number has barely changed. Therefore, whereas the average yearly attention to Iran given by policy documents has remained static, the annual average of editorials has increased considerably. While the sheer number of editorials about a particular topic is not an accurate indication as to whether the public or decision-makers are better informed on an issue, it does suggest that the press has given more thought and time to Iran, since the release of the hostages in 1981, than before.

As a further indication that the press has undergone change in its presentation of international affairs to the public, the beginning of some advances may be seen in this study's data on the editorial treatment of the topics of Iran's internal political situation, and human rights in Iran. First, in dealing with the issues of Iran's internal political situation, the *Times'* editorials appeared wary of merely mimicking the belief of official government's policy that change was good, as long as it challenged the political power of the Ayatollah and his government. This perhaps indicates an increased level of maturity, whereby the press has realized that they must provide better analysis of issues, rather than reporting them based on mere face value. Second, the number of editorials devoted to human rights displays that the press has recognized an area in which they can actually influence the foreign policy agenda, rather than merely report on it.

CONCLUSION

In summarizing this study's findings, the analysis insists that the conclusion should be drawn around three major points. First, a review of *New York Times'* editorials and *Department of State Bulletin's* policy documents dealing with Iran for the time period, 1981–1994, reveals that again similarity exists between their treatments toward Iran. In this case, this study reaffirms previous research and studies' conclusions that the press, to a great extent, merely reflects the U.S. government's policy toward a particular international issue or event. The existence of this ongoing similarity in the frequency and tone of editorials and policy documents is reflective of the continuing, interdependent relationship between the press and government.

Second, the press, as represented by *New York Time's* editorials, has made modest improvements in their presentation of international relations to citizens and decision-makers. Indeed, in comparing this study's results with those of previous research on the media-foreign policy relationship with respect to Iran, it has been noted that the frequency of editorials on Iran has increased. More attention to international relations will not necessarily ensure a more enlightened public or policymakers. The press, however, has advanced its cause in the foreign policy arena, through the exploitation of their ability to elevate certain issues, such as human rights, on the foreign policy agenda.

Third, this question remains: has the press learned from its "failure" to inform the public about the potential for turmoil and unrest in Iran that led to the 1979 Revolution? Despite some efforts at improvement, the likely answer continues to be *no*. An example of the press's lingering "failure" in presenting international affairs can be seen in the fact that the U.S. government's animosity toward Iran may have blinded the press from questioning the internal and foreign policies of Iraq, which ultimately resulted in U.S. involvement in the Persian Gulf War.

The conclusions of this study appear to be similar to those of previous studies on the media's relationship to the government in the process of foreign policy formulation. Coverage of international affairs involves a high degree of interdependency between the media and government, a relationship that does not always lend itself to the analysis necessary to produce a better-informed and enlightened public and foreign policy-making elite. However, to more adequately comprehend the news media-government relationship, further research should be conducted.

REFERENCES

Adams, F. S. (1966, Spring). In *The New York Times*. Editorial in the Masthead.

Bennett, W. L. (1988). *News: The politics of illusion* (2nd ed.). New York: Longman.

Cohen, B. C. (1961). Foreign policy makers and the press. In J. Rosenau (Ed.), *Public opinion and foreign policy: An operational formulation*. New York: Random House.

Cohen, B. C. (1963). *The press and foreign policy*. Princeton, NJ: The Princeton University Press.

Dorman, W. A. & Farhang, M. (1987). *The U.S. press and Iran: Foreign policy and the journalism of deference*. Berkeley, CA: University of California Press.

Entman, R. M. (1989). *Democracy without citizens: Media and the decay of American democracy*. New York: Oxford University Press.

Herman, E. S. & Chomsky, N. (1988). *Manufacturing consent: The political economy of the mass media*. New York: Pantheon Books.

Kellner, D. (1992). *The Persian Gulf TV war*. Boulder, CO: Westview Press.

Malek, A. & Leidig, L. (1991, October). US press coverage of the Gulf War. *Media Development*.

Malek, A. (1988). New York Times' Editorial Position and the US foreign policy: The case of Iran, *Gasette: International Journal for Mass Communication Studies, (4),* 104–119.

Malek, A. (1984). *Times, U.S. foreign policy and the Iranian revolution.* Doctoral Dessertation. School of International Service, The American University, Washington, DC.

Mowlana, H., Gerbner, G. & Schiller, H. I. (Eds.). (1992). *Triumph of the image: The media's war in the Persian Gulf—A global perspective,* Boulder, CO: Westview Press.

O'Heffernan, P. (1991). *Mass media and American foreign policy,* Norwood, NJ: Ablex.

Parenti, M. (1992). *Inventing reality: The politics of news media* (2nd ed.). New York: St. Martin's Press.

appendix a
topic and subtopic list

Topics	Subtopics
U.S.–Iran Relations	Retribution
	Claims on Iranian Assets
	Reconciliation
Terrorism	State Support
	Salmon Rushdie
Internal Political Situation	Stability
	Government Intransigence
	Decline in Political Support
	Changing Leadership
Oil	Access to
Arms Sales	Sever Supply
Regional Role	Fundamentalism
	Stability
	Expansionism
Iran–Iraq War	Security Council Resolution
	Encourage Resolution
	U.S. Neutrality
	Impact on Western Interests
	Use of Chemical Weapons
	Cease-fire
Human Rights	Treatment of the Baha'i's
	Treatment of Political Opponents

about the contributors

Richard Barton is a professor of communications in the College of Communications at Penn State University. His teaching and research interests center on the role of journalism in international relations, especially as they involve Canadian/American/British interests. He is a past Fellow of the European Media Institute and past President of the Middle Atlantic and New England Conference for Canadian Studies. He is the author of the book *Ties That Blind in Canadian/American Relations: Politics of News Discourse* (Erlbaum, 1990).

Dom Bonafede is an associate professor of communication at The American University and was previously a professional journalist for several prominent news organizations. He was a Nieman Fellow at Harvard University. During his journalism career, he served as Latin American correspondent for the *Miami Herald* and later *Newsweek* magazine, and White House correspondent for the *National Journal*. He has lectured abroad and written extensively on the presidency, U.S. politics, American foreign policy, and the news media for academic and professional publications. Books and journals to which he has contributed include: "The Presidency Reappraised," "The In-and-Outers: Presidential Appointees and Transient Government in Washington," "Studying the Presidency," "Guide to the Presidency," "Columbia Journalism Review," "Congress & the Presidency," and the University of Virginia's Miller Center Journal.

Rebecca Carrier, is an assistant professor of journalism at East Carolina University. Her primary research and teaching interests are in the social effects of mass communication, and her current focus is on international television news.

Catherine Cassara is an assistant professor in the Department of Journalism at Bowling Green State University. She has a doctorate in mass media and a master's in journalism from Michigan State University, and a bachelor's degree in Russian Studies from the University of Virginia. She has nine years experience working for American newspapers.

Bosah L. Ebo is an associate professor at the Department of Communications, Rider University. Among his most recent publications are: "Wars as Popular Culture: "The Gulf Conflict and the Technology of Illusionary Entertainment" *Journal of American Culture,* 1995.; "The Ethical Dilemma of African Journalists: A Nigerian Perspective" *Journal of Mass Media Ethics,* 1994.

Paul Grosswiler is an assistant professor in the department of communication and journalism at the University of Maine. He has conducted Q-methodology research on media worker attitudes in Tanzania and visited Cuba. His research interests include media systems in Third World socialist countries, as well as media and ideology.

Robert Hackett is an associate professor of communication at Simon Fraser University Canada. He is the author of *News and Dissent: The press and the politics of peace in Canada,* as well as various articles and chapters on politics, ideology and the news media. Currently he is co-director of Project Censored Canada, which researches Canada's national news agenda.

Hamid Mowlana is a professor and director of the International Communication Program at The American University, Washington, DC. He is president of International Association for Media and Communication Research. Among his most recent publications are: *Global Communication in Transition,* Sage Publications, 1996; *The Passing of Modernity,* Longman, 1990.

Nancy K. Rivenburgh is an assistant professor of international communication at the School of Communications, University of Washington, where her research and teaching focuses on the role of media in international and intercultural relations. Publications include: *Television in the Olympics* (John Libbey, 1995); "Images of Others: the presentation of nations in the 1992 Barcelona Olympics" *Journal of International Communication,* 1995; "National Image Richness in US-Televised Coverage of South Korea during the Seoul Olympics" *Asian Journal of Communication,* 1992; amoung others.

Shalini Venturelli is an assistant professor of international communication studies in the School of International Service at The American University in Washington, DC. Her research focuses on the supranational regulatory framework for the Global Information Infrastructure emerging in the WTO, the G7 and other multilateral settings, as well as information infrastructure and information society policy and law evolving in the European Union and North America. Her recent publications include "The Information Society in Europe," in Europe's Ambiguous Identity (Lynn Rienner, 1996), "The Competitive Order of the Information Society," in the European Journal of Communication (1996–97 volume), and "Freedom and Its Mystification: The Political Thought of Public Space," in Globalization, Communication, and the Transnational Public Sphere (Hampton, 1996).

Krista E. Wiegand is a graduate student at the International Communication Program, at The American University in Washington, DC. Among her most recent publications are: "The Lebanese Civil War: State-Centric vs New Realist Theory" *Swords and Ploughshares: A Journal of International Affairs* 1996; "Islam and the West: Cultural Encounter," in *The U.S. Media and the Middle East: Image and Perception,* 1995.

James J. Zaffiro is an associate professor of Political Science at Central College, Pella, Iowa. Author of *A Political History of Broadcasting in Botswana,* (1991), *Broadcasting, Political Change, and Regime Legitimacy in Zimbabwe,* (in press), and numerous articles on the politics of broadcasting and the press and on foreign policy-making in southern Africa.

author index

subject index